Quality Improvement and Audit in Dentistry

This book is an introduction to quality improvement methods for dentists and other oral health professionals. It includes audit, which will be familiar to many dental professionals, and sets it in the wider context of quality improvement theory and practice. The book provides sufficient information to allow dental practices to undertake clinical audit and quality improvement using current best practice.

The World Dental Federation has called for greater attention to quality in dentistry and has argued for the use of quality improvement methods. In the United Kingdom, the health services in Wales and Scotland have begun to produce materials to support dental quality improvement work. The Care Quality Commission in England has emphasised the requirement for audit in dental care. Dental practices in Scotland are now required to undertake QI projects. In the USA, the American Dental Association now encourages audit and QI training guidance has been issued by the California Department of Public Health Office of Oral Health.

This book provides dental teams with the information they need to meet these local, national and international requirements. It describes the components of quality and patient safety and sets dental quality improvement in the context of wider literature. Approaches to audit and quality improvement are discussed, with use of dental examples. It explains practical approaches that can be applied by any dental team. The methods described will support teams to improve the quality of their services and to meet the needs of their patients.

AF736462

Quality Improvement and Audit in Dentistry

Rhona Günhan
and Cameron Stark

Routledge
Taylor & Francis Group
A PRODUCTIVITY PRESS BOOK

Designed cover image: Shutterstock

First published 2026
by Routledge
605 Third Avenue, New York, NY 10158

and by Routledge
4 Park Square, Milton Park, Abingdon, Oxon, OX14 4RN

Routledge is an imprint of the Taylor & Francis Group, an informa business

© 2026 Rhona Günhan and Cameron Stark

The right of Rhona Günhan and Cameron Stark to be identified as authors of this work has been asserted by them in accordance with sections 77 and 78 of the Copyright, Designs and Patents Act 1988.

All rights reserved. No part of this book may be reprinted or reproduced or utilised in any form or by any electronic, mechanical, or other means, now known or hereafter invented, including photocopying and recording, or in any information storage or retrieval system, without permission in writing from the publishers.

Trademark notice: Product or corporate names may be trademarks or registered trademarks, and are used only for identification and explanation without intent to infringe.

ISBN: 9781032797243 (hbk)
ISBN: 9781032797236 (pbk)
ISBN: 9781003493532 (ebk)

DOI: 10.4324/9781003493532

Typeset in Garamond
by Deanta Global Publishing Services, Chennai, India

Rhona – Thank you to Mehmet for providing encouragement and support throughout my career and while writing this book.

Cameron – Thanks to Marilyn for her patience while I was working on this book. I hope you like it.

Contents

Acknowledgements

Dr Preeti Arora, owner and principal dentist of my practice, The Dental Centre, has given support and freedom to experiment with quality improvement ideas in her practice. Thanks to head dental nurse, Stacey-Ann Curran, who has become an invaluable colleague in running quality improvement work in the practice and contributing to the overall efforts. - Rhona Günhan

I am indebted to my colleagues from NHS Highland, NHS Scotland and the University of the Highlands and Islands (UHI) for sharing their wisdom and experience. Gavin Hookway collaborated with me on many improvement projects and taught me much about supporting teams to make changes. Dr Hugo van Woerden and Dr Tim Allison were generous in allowing me time to invest in quality improvement coaching. Students studying the Postgraduate Certificate in Healthcare Quality Improvement at the University of the Highlands and Islands, Scotland, have tested out ideas and taught me much from their experience in services across the world. I am grateful to them for sharing their insights. Dr Poonam Gupta and Kay Cordiner, Faculty at the Institute for Healthcare Improvement, and Jeff Rakover, Director, Institute for Healthcare Improvement, have shared ideas on quality improvement with me and I have benefited from their knowledge and experience. Thanks to Dr Michelle Beattie, Senior Lecturer, University of the Highlands and Islands (UHI), for her comments on some of the materials in this volume. Dr Rachel Erskine and Dr Megan Dickson have provided support and advice at UHI. I am grateful to Kristine Mednansky, Senior Editor at Taylor & Francis, for her advice and support with this and previous volumes. - Cameron Stark

About the Authors

Dr Rhona Günhan, Associate Dentist

Rhona is an associate dentist at The Dental Centre, a mixed NHS and private practice in Saltcoats, Scotland. She has worked in several settings including corporate and independent practices ranging from inner-city to rural locations. Rhona started her clinical career as a dental hygienist/therapist and then completed dental vocational training in Glasgow, Scotland. She graduated from the University of Dundee with a BDS and studied at the University of the Highlands and Islands for a postgraduate certificate in Quality Improvement in Healthcare, gaining a distinction. It was during this course that she developed a strong interest in quality improvement.

Dr Cameron Stark, Lecturer, University of the Highlands and Islands, Scotland

Cameron is a Module Leader at the University of the Highlands and Islands, Scotland, teaching on Patient Safety and healthcare quality improvement. He graduated in Medicine from the University of Glasgow and holds Master's degrees from the University of Glasgow and the University of Leicester, UK. Cameron worked as a Consultant in Public Health Medicine with NHS Scotland for over 20 years, and was Quality Improvement Science lead for NHS Highland. He has co-written or co-edited nine previous textbooks and has published over 60 papers in peer-reviewed journals.

Chapter 1

Introduction

Introduction

The need to deliver good quality is a universal desire across all oral health services. Dentists and dental teams work in hugely varying settings, from entirely private practices to state-funded clinics. Dentists may work in very specialised areas, undertake general dentistry or mix specialist and general practice. Treatment locations vary from hospitals to individual practices and include teams working largely alone with an individual owner, hospital and clinic services operating within a complex healthcare structure, or teams working as part of a corporate chain of dental services.

Despite these variations, teams have more similarities than differences. Dental treatment has a common denominator of clinicians or small teams working with individual patients, who in turn depend on the quality of the work provided by the dental team. This seems unlikely to change in the foreseeable future. Innovations in artificial intelligence (AI) may help to automate recording, risk scoring and even review, but the replacement of clinicians in direct care tasks remains unlikely (Dhingra, 2023). Where robots are already used in dentistry, they supplement and support the clinician rather than replacing them (Liu *et al.*, 2023, Bahrami *et al.*, 2024). The technologies available to dentists and to dental teams are set to widen rapidly (Wright, 2025), but the technologies will be integrated with dental care rather than replacing clinical skill.

This means that how dental teams function, and how they deliver services, will continue to be the arbiter of patient experience. New technologies will add new complexities to care delivery, and this will require more involvement from teams in making things work, rather than less. Maintaining quality will continue to be a core challenge for individual clinicians, practice owners, corporate managers and dental care leaders.

DOI: 10.4324/9781003493532-1

Quality

Quality is generally taken as something being fit for purpose and delivering the required outcomes (Juran, 1988, Deming, 1994). In healthcare, quality can be considered to have different aspects that contribute to the desired outcomes and to patient satisfaction. The Institute of Medicine (1990) and the World Health Organization (2006) suggest that dimensions of healthcare quality include care that is:

- Safe
- Effective
- Patient-centred
- Acceptable
- Timely
- Efficient
- Equitable

Looking specifically at dental care, Righolt and colleagues suggest a very similar list of seven domains of quality, identifying patient safety, effectiveness, efficiency, patient-centredness, equitability, timeliness and access to care (Righolt *et al.*, 2020). Their process to develop these domains included a literature review and a consultation event at the International Association for Dental Research annual conference (Righolt *et al.*, 2019). Their consultation supported the validity of the domains. Within each category, they identified key features that should be present to support quality in dental care. For example, in their patient-centredness category, the consultation concluded that dental teams should be 'respectful of and responsive to individual patient preferences, needs, values, fears, concerns, and/or cultures', and should follow a shared decision-making process. This work indicates that dental quality maps to internationally recognised dimensions of health care quality, and that these domains can be refined to fit with the concerns and needs of dental teams and their patients. Considering multiple dimensions of quality avoids the reductionism of seeking to identify single quality measures to encompass all dental practice (Campbell and Tickle, 2013a, Byrne and Tickle, 2019).

There can be trade-offs between dimensions of quality, particularly as there are invariably financial limits on what can be afforded. Most services take patient safety, discussed in more detail in Chapter 2, as a prerequisite of all dental care. Effectiveness is also an obvious requirement of dental care, accepting that there are occasions where there will be a choice between different treatment options where the best choice may be unclear.

Dental teams aim to meet patient needs, and this includes supporting patient choice, which also relates to how acceptable patients find different treatments. Patient-centred care, according to the Institute of Medicine, is care that (2001, p. 49):

> *r*esponds … to each patient's wants, needs, and preferences. It gives patients abundant opportunities to be informed and involved in medical decision making and guides and supports those providing care.… Patient-centered care is highly customized and incorporates cultural competence. Some patients wish to avoid risk; others may choose a risky intervention despite a relatively low likelihood of benefit. Patients' preferences are likely to change over time and to depend on the clinical problems in question; therefore, the enterprise of shared decision making is a dynamic one, changing as patients and circumstances change.

Mills *et al.* (2014) argue that patient-centred care remains a poorly understood concept in dental care. They emphasise the importance of communication, empathy and understanding and ideally of a long-term relationship between the dental team and patient. These concepts, of changing patient views over time and differences in perspective depending on risk, will be familiar to all dental teams.

Timely and efficient care speaks for itself. Timely care is respectful of patients' time, results in less distress, and reduces the likelihood of dissatisfied patients moving to other providers. Efficiency usually generates more timely care by increasing throughput and reducing delays. Equity in healthcare includes equal access to care that is not affected by non-clinical variables. As well as income, equity considers equal access by gender, ethnicity and geography. Some of these are structural issues in how health services are funded and delivered, but dental teams can do much within their own area of control by considering language and cultural barriers and requirements for people with disabilities.

Measurement of Quality

Funders, professional organisations and clinical teams all have good reasons to measure the quality of dental services. It is useful to distinguish between Quality Planning, Quality Control, Quality Assurance and Quality Improvement as there are different considerations for measurement. Definitions vary between authors, but definitions relevant to dental care are:

- **Quality Assurance:** This is 'all actions taken to establish, protect, promote, and improve the quality of healthcare' (Donabedian, 2003, p. xxiii). The sum of these actions together gives confidence that quality can be delivered.
- **Quality Planning:** The identification of the needs of patients and other customers, such as funders, and planning the service to meet those needs by creating a system that builds in quality (Juran, 1988).
- **Quality Control:** This is 'establishing performance standards, developing continuous information relay systems to track performance, identifying gaps between actual and desired performance, and applying standard work to close the gap' (Sampat *et al.*, 2021, p. 8).
- **Quality Improvement:** The process of improvement driven by the gaps identified in quality control activities.

It can be useful to think about quality planning, control and improvement as activities that together deliver quality assurance. In measuring quality, services need to be clear on what aspects of quality they want to measure. A wider quality assurance system would include ensuring that the design of services supports quality; that relevant policies are in place and being acted on; that staff have the requisite training; that there are processes in place to measure quality, and that a system exists to allow staff to improve identified quality defects.

Many of these issues will be of concern to accrediting bodies and funders who will want to measure evidence that systems are in place to create, deliver and maintain quality. When services talk about quality measurement, however, they are often referring to quality control activities, where performance is measured using agreed metrics. This does not in itself produce quality improvement, because services and teams then need a system to respond to any identified quality problem.

There are major challenges to the measurement of aspects of dental care (Box 1.1). A systematic review concluded that few measures have been developed with appropriate scientific rigour, but that some measures were beginning to appear, such as those from the Dental Quality Alliance (Righolt *et al.*, 2020, Byrne *et al.*, 2019). This offers scope for the further development of nested quality measures that practices, services, funders and accrediting bodies can use to overcome these common drawbacks of previous measures.

BOX 1.1 CHALLENGES IN THE MEASUREMENT OF QUALITY IN DENTAL CARE

- Current measures are not always valid, reliable and feasible. Lack of face validity is a particular challenge in acceptance by clinicians.
- Limited standardisation of measures, making comparison across and between services difficult.
- Lack of clarity in measures and on how they will be counted.
- Most measures with established clinimetrics were developed on European or American populations and may not be valid in other settings.
- Measurements rarely include patient satisfaction.
- Limited availability of measures on patient safety, organisational aspects of care and costs.
- Easier to count process measures than outcome measures.
- Limited measures that work in a layered fashion across multiple care delivery systems from individual practitioner to organisation to country level.

Sources: Campbell and Tickle (2013a, 2013b), Righolt *et al.* (2018), Dental Quality Alliance (2019), and Byrne (2021).

Increasing Attention to Quality in Dentistry

The value of quality improvement work in dental care, and the role of dentists and the dental team, has widespread support. The World Dental Federation identifies 'the imperative for quality in dentistry' and notes 'the importance of continuous quality improvement cycles to enhance outcomes for patients' (FDI, 2017). In the United States, the American Dental Association promotes quality measures through their Dental Quality Alliance (Ojha and Aravamudhan, 2016; American Dental Association, 2025) and there are regional initiatives, such as those by the Office of Oral Health in California (Byrne, 2020).

In Europe, the Royal College of Surgeons in Ireland's Faculty of Dentistry has partnered with the Institute of Healthcare Improvement to offer introductory training (Faculty of Dentistry, undated). The Department of Health in Wales offers a comprehensive suite of Quality Improvement support tools (Health Education and Information Wales undated), and the Care Quality Commission in England offers relevant information on audit.

The European Union funded Deliver programme aims to increase access to quality improvement knowledge in dental care (Deliver, 2025). The work will include development and testing of quality improvement interventions, including research on vulnerable patient groups and on building quality into commissioning arrangements. An early published output from this programme includes detailed interviews with oral health professionals working in the UK and Germany (Lin *et al.*, 2025). A significant finding from this research is that quality improvement work is not yet seen as a core part of the work of dental professionals, at least partly because of workload. The responsibility for quality improvement activity often falls on one person, such as a practice manager, and many of the clinicians interviewed were unconvinced that work on audit and quality improvement produced change.

Despite these worries, there is evidence of an increase in attention to quality improvement in dental care. Figure 1.1 shows the change in the use of the terms 'Dentistry' and 'Quality Improvement' and 'Dentistry' and 'Audit' over time in references included in PubMed, a database of published academic work. The use of a rate rather than absolute numbers helps to adjust for the increase in the volume of all types of publications over time. Both terms became more common in the 1990s, while Quality Improvement began to separate from Audit in the 2000s. This may reflect the broader nature of quality improvement compared to audit, and a wider increase in research and publications on quality improvement in healthcare from the early 2000s onwards. The relationship between quality improvement and audit is discussed later in the chapter.

A recent review found that published dental quality work referred to overall quality, or to one or more of patient satisfaction, service quality, internal processes improvement, or business outcomes (Crisan *et al.*, 2021). The largest number of identified papers referred to patient satisfaction and to internal processes. This contrasts with the work reported earlier on established measurement scales which had often omitted patient input. Patient satisfaction is of obvious interest to dental teams, so it is unsurprising that teams engaging in audit and quality improvement chose to prioritise it.

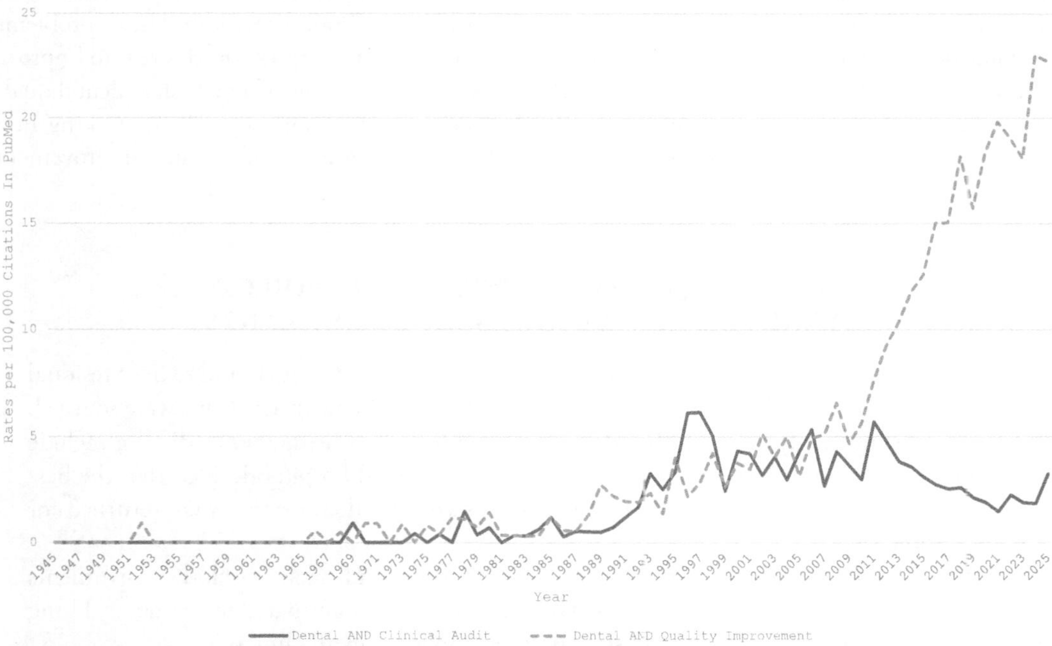

Figure 1.1 Use of the terms 'Clinical Audit' and 'Quality Improvement' with 'Dental' Results per 100,000 Citations in PubMed proportion for each search by year, 1961–2024. Source: Ed Sperr, PubMed by Year. https://esperr.github.io/pubmed-by-year/

Research, Audit and Quality Improvement

Dentists and the wider dental team are used to reading research articles with statistical analyses, research designs and Ethics Committee approval. This can produce concerns about the methods and permissions that are required for quality improvement work (Paxton *et al.*, 2006). It is useful to tease out the differences between research, audit, and quality improvement.

Research is intended to produce generalisable knowledge by applying rigorous, repeatable methods (Gould, 2008, Backhouse and Ogunlayi, 2020). Research usually has a hypothesis that is being tested and a protocol that sets out in advance all the steps and analyses to be taken. These steps are set out in a protocol which is agreed with a Research Ethics Committee before the work commences. The research design and its components are not revised after the research project has begun. There are some exceptions to this, but any scope to make alterations will be incorporated into the design and agreed by the Ethics Committee. The aim of the work is to be able to make a statement of new knowledge that can be applied in other settings.

By contrast, quality improvement is intended to produce a change in the way a service is delivered to produce a benefit in at least one of the dimensions of quality described above (Campbell and Tickle, 2013b). The quality improvement work may incorporate research evidence gained from previous work, for example on clinical effectiveness, but it is not itself intended as research. Structured methods, including those described in this book, and approaches such as Lean and Six Sigma, are used in the work (Davidoff *et al.*, 2015; Stark and Hookway, 2019; Arthur, 2016).

The precise approach will vary, but all quality improvement work incorporates the use of data and uses iterative cycles of improvement (see Chapter 6). Unlike most research, the focus of the work may shift in response to information gained in previous improvement cycles, as problems become better understood. There will often be no set endpoint to the work: the desire is to improve the service, and this is a continuous process. Box 1.2 shows an example of a published dental quality improvement project (Campbell *et al.*, 2016). It demonstrates the use of data, working in a team and using a series of improvement cycles which are all key features of a quality improvement approach.

BOX 1.2 QUALITY IMPROVEMENT PROJECT EXAMPLE: CLEANING DENTAL INSTRUMENTS

27% of instrument packs in Dundee Dental Hospital, Scotland, were found to have residual cement on at least one instrument. This created delays while new instruments were sourced.

A root cause analysis found that the contract with the sterilising service did not include manual inspection of instruments, so the team at the dental hospital decided that the best way to tackle it was to ensure that no instruments with residual cement were returned for sterilisation.

The team developed an information poster reminding students to check the instruments and a method of identifying which clinician had returned contaminated instruments. Using PDSA cycles, the team tested the poster and then applied it in all clinics.

By the end of the work, the proportion of packs found to have residual cement decreased to 7%.

Source: Campbell *et al.*, 2016.

Audit is a subset of Quality Improvement. In audit, there is an agreed standard to which current performance is compared (Care Quality Commission, 2024). This may be a standard from a clinical guideline, a required standard from a funder or regulator, or a locally agreed performance standard. The gap between current and expected performance is identified, the reasons for the difference analysed, and the information gained is used to develop cycles of change to bring the current performance closer to the desired performance. An example of a published audit project with a completed audit cycle is shown in Box 1.3 (Liew and Winston, 2022). The methods used to identify issues and to test out changes are the same as those used in quality improvement work other than that in generic quality improvement the standards are usually generated by the clinical team rather than driven by a pre-stated standard as in audit. Audit is discussed further in Chapter 3.

BOX 1.3 AUDIT PROJECT EXAMPLE: INTRAVENOUS SEDATION

- Conducted in a UK oral surgery service, where patients were referred by General Dental Practitioners for sedation.
- Randomly selected 22 records in each of two audit cycles.
- Compared the treatment records to five audit standards identified in two national guidelines.
- Data was extracted from the electronic patient record and entered into a spreadsheet.
- Most results in the first cycle met the expected standards, other than the recording of the patient American Society of Anaesthesiologists (ASA) rating, and a sedation score.
- Results from the first cycle were shared with all the practitioners, and the existing *pro forma* revised to include a sedation score prompt.
- A second cycle confirmed that the ASA category and the sedation scores were now being recorded.

Source: Liew and Winston (2022).

Unlike research, it is unusual for quality improvement or audit to require Research Ethics Committee approval. This does not mean that the work is free of constraints, and some services may require audit and quality improvement projects to be registered with the organisation. Appropriate ethical requirements from professional registering bodies apply, as do country-specific requirements on the use of data. Readers should review guidance from their own registering and funding bodies and organisation, and any relevant data protection guidance. The general finding is that, with the same approaches to patient confidentiality as are applied in clinical practice, quality improvement work fits well with regulatory requirements.

Quality Improvement Collaboratives are a variant approach (Institute for Healthcare Improvement, 2003, Wells *et al.*, 2018). In a Collaborative, work has already been undertaken, usually by a central body, to identify important aspects of quality in a particular type of service. In a Collaborative, many teams or services work on the same quality issue at once. The teams or services have group teaching sessions and share their experiences with one another. An example of a collaborative in dentistry was the Dental Primary Care collaborative in Scotland (Healthcare Improvement Scotland, 2023, Cassie *et al.*, 2021). The project ran between 2016 and 2018 (Box 1.4):

BOX 1.4 SCOTTISH PRIMARY CARE DENTAL COLLABORATIVE

- The Collaborative involved dental Vocational Trainees (VTs), who are dentists in their first year of practice after qualification from university, in three Health Board areas. Health Boards are administrative divisions of the National Health Service in Scotland.
- The VTs completed training on Quality Improvement using an online teaching system.
- A Periodontal Expert Reference Group developed aims, a driver diagram, care bundle and guidance on periodontal disease for use by the Collaborative participants.
- The trainees selected either the Periodontal option or chose to work on high-risk medicines such as warfarin.
- They completed a project using the information from the central group using the Quality Improvement tools and fed the results back to Healthcare Improvement Scotland.
- In a follow-up survey and interview, participants reported increased knowledge and skills.

Source: Cassie et al., 2021 and Healthcare Improvement Scotland, 2023.

Collaboratives are discussed further in Chapter 9, which deals with quality improvement at scale. Ideas from the collaborative approach have the potential to be applied in group practices, corporate groups and hospital settings.

Patient Views of Quality

The purpose of dentistry is to provide a service to patients. As the primary customers, patient views of quality are of great importance. In many healthcare systems, patients can take their custom elsewhere, so patient views of quality, and of how a dental service compares to their expectations, will also have a direct impact on practice and practitioner renumeration. Table 1.1 gives a brief selection of some of the research on patient views on what constitutes quality in dental practice.

Across many different settings, there is remarkable consistency in patient views of what constitutes quality in dental care. As would be expected, the technical competence of the dentist and dental team, and how the clinicians relate to patients including kindness and communication feature in most responses. The practice surroundings, waiting times, information giving and cleanliness are also cited. Access issues, such as distance and ease of booking, are seen as aspects of dental service quality by patients. It is unsurprising that these issues lead through to factors affecting patient satisfaction.

Patient Satisfaction

Patient satisfaction with treatment has several important impacts (Syngelakis *et al.* 2023). Satisfaction with treatment is one of the factors that influence compliance (Albrecht and Hoogstraten, 1998). Patient satisfaction is associated with higher rates of patient loyalty, as measured by retention and willingness to recommend a dentist to friends or family (El Dalatony *et al.*, 2023). A study in Saudi Arabia concluded that patients' ratings of the dentist had a higher association with their overall satisfaction, although this may have been influenced by good local access to services, making access less of a concern (Aldosaary *et al.*, 2023). The impact of some

Table 1.1 Selected literature on patient views of quality in dental care

Study	*Location and method*	*Items*
Davies and Ware (1981)	United States of America Development of a Dental Satisfaction Questionnaire.	Identified five broad areas – Access. Availability/ Convenience, Cost, Pain and Quality.
Kaldenberg *et al.* (1997)	United States of America Survey of American college students.	The items associated with higher quality scores included staff attitudes, such as reassurance, kindness and communication. Authors noted the importance of qualitative feedback from patients to better interpret the meaning of numerical scores.
Baldwin and Sohal (2003)	Australia Postal survey of 1485 patients with medical insurance that included dental care. 24.2% response rate.	Analysis identified four groups of factors associated with patient satisfaction: • The skill and ability of the clinician – the authors termed this 'craft skills'. • Punctuality – this included waiting times. • Personalised attention. • 'Tangibles' – décor, equipment, waiting room, uniforms etc. Other factors identified in qualitative responses included responsiveness, which included attention to the demands of the patient, instilling confidence and explaining rights and obligation, empathic assurance, which included treating patients as individuals and helping to reduce anxiety, and reliability, which included the patients' impression that the team was reliable.
Mazzei *et al.* (2009)	Italy Study conducted in private dentistry. Used individual interviews, focus groups and a survey.	Factors most associated with quality were, in order, the dentist's chair side manner, clarity of treatment information and the accessibility, comfort and cleanliness of the premises. The booking system, reception and respect for privacy were also cited, but were less important than the first three measures. In choosing a dentist, the most important factors were reported to be treatment effectiveness, service quality and the relationship with the dentist.

(Continued)

Table 1.1 Continued

Study	*Location and method*	*Items*
Ungureanu and Mocean (2015)	Romania Survey of 1,650 people who had visited a dentist in the previous year. 43.8% response rate. Asked what factors were important to them in choosing a dentist.	Competence (22.2%) Recommendation from someone known (20.6%) Overall quality of the service provided (19.7%) Dentists' patience (9.4%) Distance from home to dental office (8.6%) Dentists' respect for patients (6.4%)
Tickle *et al.* (2015)	England Survey of 534 people in randomly selected locations, with quota sampling for representativeness. Included a question asking what aspects of quality people used to judge dental services.	The most frequent responses to the question about judging quality were: Appointment availability (40%) Treatment quality (34.5%) Professionalism (30.6%) Hygiene/cleanliness (29.8%) Staff attitude (27.2%) Painless treatment (22.8%) Value for money (22.8%) Putting people at ease (20.9%) Quality of advice (19.3%)
Ali (2016)	Kuwait Self-completion survey of 550 dental patients (90% response rate)	Patients' perception of the performance of the dentist explained 42.6% of the overall satisfaction score, followed by their view of the quality of the clinical setting (31.5% of the variance).
Aldosari *et al.* (2017)	Brazil Interviews with 9,120 dental patients in public dental clinics.	Factors associated with higher levels of satisfaction included shorter waiting times, clinic facilities, the welcome to the clinic, being given information about their condition and feeling they were given enough time.
Luo *et al.* (2018)	China 30 dental hospital patients took part in one of four focus groups asking about their experience of care and views on dental care quality.	Components of quality mentioned included the availability of modern technology, equipment and facilities, the perceived skill of the dentists, infection control, staffing levels and clinical outcomes. Issues such as the attitude of the dentist and dental staff, pain control, accessibility and cost were also discussed as important issues.

factors varies by clinical context. Patients seeking treatment for an emergency are predictably more concerned with waiting times than patients seeking a routine appointment (Buss *et al.*, 2023). The use of communication tools, such as CAD models, enhances satisfaction, presumably by clarifying expectations (Touati *et al.*, 2022).

Patient satisfaction can be measured using standard forms or bespoke questions. Using standard forms with known psychometric properties offers consistency and comparability but sometimes requires licence fees and more complex analysis. In academic studies, consistency across sites is required to allow comparisons, meaning that standardised forms will be required (Finkelman *et al.*, 2020). Developing forms within a practice allows for individually tailored questions but loses the advantages of forms developed by academic departments.

Patient rated outcome measures (PROMs) and patient rated experience measures (PREMs) are structured instruments which usually have published evidence on their clinimetric properties. Their use is increasing in general healthcare (Nelson *et al.*, 2015, Bull, Teede and Watson, 2022). Interest in their use in dental care has also increased substantially (Reissmann, 2019, Leles *et al.*, 2022, Chanthavisouk *et al.*, 2022, Hua, 2025).

PROMs have been used in situations such as oral surgery (Grossman, Dungarwalla and Bailey, 2020) and with parents of children undergoing general anaesthesia for dental procedures (Patrick and Kandiah, 2020). The International Consortium on Health Outcomes Measurement (ICHOM) has developed a set of patient-centred outcome measures for adult oral health (Riordain *et al.*, 2021, International Consortium on Health Outcomes Measurement, no date). The PROM section of these measures has been translated into French and validated, which may be an indication that their use could become widespread (Nicolas-Boluda and Simon, 2023).

Forms can be administered in various ways, including using paper questionnaires, online surveys and apps on electronic tablets (Jain and Mohanty, 2023). The main challenge for the use of measures in routine practice is the time required to collect and analyse data. How patients and clinicians respond to the collection and potential display of data is also a consideration (Byrne, 2021, p. 119). Byrne raises the possibility that, at least for geographical areas, cloud-based automatic sentiment analysis could be used to gauge public opinion of dental services by automatic extraction and summarising of online reviews of dental practices. It seems likely that the use of PREMs and PROMs will increase, but given the ubiquity of cloud computing and services designed to analyse online data, other approaches such as sentiment analysis may also appear.

Change Management

The purpose of quality improvement work is to produce change. Change is often a challenge, and many dental teams will have experience of changes that have produced unhappiness, dissent, or where a change has been made, but the system has rapidly returned to the original state. There are many models of change management, and many of them relate to large-scale organisational change rather than to smaller changes. The models are helpful in looking at important features of the change process and in identifying issues that arise in many changes, no matter what their size or complexity.

One of the earliest change models to have proved useful over time is Lewin's model, which identified three phases (Lewin, 1951, Shirey, 2013):

- **Unfreeze:** This stage is where people identify a need for change and accept that it is required and agree what they want to achieve with the change. In organisational-level change, this may occur at senior level, but no matter who makes the decision, the wider team will inevitably become involved, and their understanding of the need for change is important to support the work.
- **Move:** In this phase, changes are made to shift the system from its original state to the desired future state. Methods to do this in quality improvement are reviewed in detail later in the book.
- **Refreeze:** Lewin recognised the need to stabilise the system after the change and to ensure that the change was embedded. While Lewin's model is often applied to policy change, the general structure is useful to consider in quality improvement.

This early model has much in common with a more recent model of change in complex services, the 3C model (Khalil and Kynoch, 2021). This model suggests three stages – consultation, collaboration and consolidation. It suggests that the consultation phase should include identification of areas of improvement, prioritisation and the production of a process map. The collaboration phase includes understanding organisational culture and creating clarity on who is doing what, while the consolidation phase is where sustainability of the change, a topic discussed in more detail in Chapter 8, is ensured. The 3C model was based on a review of recent literature. While the detail differs, its broad similarity to Lewin's model emphasises the widespread applicability of the concept of change, and the value of Lewin's categories over time.

Lewin also introduced the idea of 'force field analysis', which involves thinking about the factors in a service or team that push towards change in a topic, and the factors that are pushing towards things staying the same. Making this kind of explicit assessment is often a useful discipline, as it helps leaders to think through what they may need to tackle to make change more likely. Beckhard and Harris (1987) brought some of the influences on change together in an equation, suggesting that change is opposed unless the level of dissatisfaction with the status quo, the desire to reach the preferred end point, and the perceived plausibility of the change are felt to outweigh the effort and risk of making the change. This judgement will vary from person to person and team to team.

Any three-stage model will have some limitations, particularly for people who want to match their situation to the model in more detail. Kotter's change model, developed in the 1990s, has enjoyed considerable longevity, which is again testimony to its usefulness in different situations. Kotter's eight-stage model expanded on Lewin's three stages, although the same underlying shape is visible in Kotter's model (Kotter, 1996):

1. **Establish a Sense of Urgency:** The status quo may be unsatisfactory, but leaving things as they are often requires less effort than making a change. Some staff will fear that the new, currently unknown process may be worse than the current process, or that it may affect their job in ways that they may find uncongenial. Change also brings the possibility of failure, which most people find stressful, and they may be worried that they may be blamed. Even if the team or service can see a need for change, it may feel easier to put it off until there is a crisis. To overcome this inertia, Kotter argues, it is necessary to communicate the need for change and to persuade people that the current situation is unacceptable and that change needs to happen now.
2. **Form a Powerful Guiding Coalition:** The days when one person can analyse the problem, generate change options and produce the change are over, except in the smallest

organisations. In teams, particularly teams such as those in dentistry where people often work unobserved, multiple views on the situation are often required. Different professional groups may also be needed in a project team, and this is reviewed further in Chapter 3.

3. **Create a Vision:** Change is easy to agree on in the abstract, but any team that is going to succeed in producing meaningful change must agree on what they want to achieve. In quality improvement, this can be thought of as the future state – the new norm that the team wants to reach. This does not provide clarity at this stage on exactly how the change will be achieved. Rather, it acts as a true north against which the team can guide its progress. It is easy to become distracted with all the possibilities for improvement, and having a good understanding of what the team or service wants to achieve can help to reduce the risk of mission creep, where the team starts out working on one problem but then devotes much of its time to a different issue.
4. **Communicate the Vision:** In most change projects, the smaller team that has acted as Kotter's 'guiding coalition' will need to explain their work to others. People who are not involved are always liable to feel they could have done better and to question the work of others. This does not necessarily mean they could have done better, but much time can be lost if people oppose the project later. Taking time to communicate the problem, the analysis, and the idea for the future can save a lot of time in the long run. To the people who undertook the initial work, this can feel like time wasted, but this is rarely the case. Kotter's original work suggests that this phase always takes longer than people expect it to take, and experience supports this. These four stages are like Lewin's 'unfreeze' phase. Their use in quality improvement work is not identical to that needed in large-scale system change, but many of the same issues arise. The next three stages are similar to Lewin's 'Move' phase.
5. **Empower Others to Act on the Vision:** In most projects, the small team who originated it cannot do all the work. Micromanaging the changes is also problematic and can cause friction. Getting the balance right between giving staff the authority to make changes and influencing the direction of the change is always tricky. The work at the earlier stages, on producing a clear view of where the service wants to go, and communicating this vision, greatly helps things to go smoothly at this part of the change process.
6. **Plan for and Create Short-term Wins:** Any project needs successes. Successes become evidence for further change and energise teams (Breckenridge *et al.*, 2019). Deciding what to tackle first is important. It must be meaningful enough to be worth the effort, but selecting options that are likely to be successful is worthwhile. As the team gathers experience and energy, they can tackle the stickier problems later. A series of early failures can have a devastating effect on team morale and on the shared interest in quality improvement work.
7. **Consolidate Improvements and Produce More Change:** This differs from Lewin's model, which pays less attention to future change. In quality improvement in particular, there are always areas on which a team can work. This requires a team to embed the changes they have made so that they then form a base on which they can build future change. This is often done by developing agreed standard work. Kotter notes that the team should also feel that it has been rewarded for the previous work, even if only in recognition, thanks and improved work processes.
8. **Institutionalise New Approaches:** In Kotter's model this relates as much to the change model itself, as to the approach to change. In quality improvement the equivalent is the consistent application of the improvement methods discussed in later chapters, and the use of these methods in future work. This equates to Lewin's 'Refreeze' phase where processes are stabilised.

The Lewin and Kotter change management models are those most reported to be used in healthcare and are often used in quality improvement (Harrison *et al.*, 2021). There are other models of change management, some of which are well suited to large-scale organisational change, and to changes in complex organisations.

Organisational alignment is important. If most of the organisation is indifferent to the changes being made by a team or department, or worse, oppose the changes, then it is much more difficult to make the changes and to maintain them. This is less of an issue in smaller projects, and when the team has been actively involved, but most change models include a recognition that reversion to the previous state is easy and can occur unless active steps are taken to prevent it. Ways of reducing this risk in quality improvement are reviewed in Chapter 8. The general principles in Lewin and Kotter's models are useful to consider in quality improvement work. They can be thought of as a cycle, rather than a linear process with a static end point. The models are useful to revisit if a project runs into difficulty, as they may cast a useful light on the problems being experienced.

Other change management models can offer insights that are relevant to quality improvement. The McKinsey 7S model is also reported to be used in healthcare projects (Harrison *et al.*, 2021). This model looks at the characteristics of an organisation that support change. It includes the organisation's structure; approach to strategy; the systems used to make decisions; the degree to which there are shared values between the organisation and its employees; the skills in the organisation or team to make the changes, including capacity to undertake the work; the leadership style, and the staff (Kaplan, 2005). Leadership is discussed further in Chapter 3. The Diffusion of Innovation model, which looks at how ideas spread across a network, is also used and is discussed further in Chapter 9 (Rogers, 2003, Balas and Chapman, 2018).

Structure of the Book

Patient safety is accepted as an underpinning requirement of all dental treatment. Many factors can affect patient safety. Individual clinical performance is usually the end point when an error occurs, but many factors can affect the likelihood of an error happening. Chapter 2 explores patient safety in more detail and argues that it is important to consider the situation surrounding and supporting the clinician as well as thinking about individual clinical skills. Learning from error is also essential, and this is much more likely to happen in work situations where staff feel they will be treated fairly and with respect.

Dental teams want to assure themselves that their practice is appropriate. Funding, regulatory and governance bodies seek to know that structures are in place to support safety and to deliver good practice. Teams can decide to undertake audits themselves, but audits can also be required by some of these other organisations. Audits undertaken as a tick box exercise are unlikely to result in change, but the audit method can produce significant benefits for patients, staff and the organisation when completing audit cycles using the appropriate methods. Chapter 3 summarises the key features of audit and sets out the stages of an audit cycle that dental teams can apply in practice.

Making quality improvement work for services and their patients requires consideration of teamwork and leadership, as well as the quality improvement methods the dental team will use. Most dental care comes down to individual clinicians with individual patients, so staff engagement is essential to achieve meaningful quality improvement. Involving staff allows their combined knowledge of a service to be applied to a problem and increases the likelihood that change will be carried through. Quality improvement initiatives are sometimes driven by one interested staff member. Enthusiasm has great benefits, but it is difficult to sustain efforts over time. Chapter 4 discusses the benefits of spreading quality improvement work across the wider clinical team with benefits for knowledge, staff satisfaction and sustainment of the work.

For improvement work to be effective, the problem needs to be understood as far as possible. Chapter 5 describes how teams can seek to understand a problem, working as a team. The chapter describes methods of deciding which problem to prioritise, such as prioritisation matrices and Pareto charts, and methods that can be used to describe the issue in ways that can be shared.

Plan-Do-Study-Act (PDSA) cycles lie at the core of most quality improvement work. Chapter 6 describes the stages of a PDSA cycle and identifies the key issues for a team to consider at each stage. Being clear on what is being tested and why and agreeing how to measure any change are essential. While some quality improvement programmes may choose to undertake very large tests of change, dental teams new to the process can use a measured, structured approach which delivers new information with each test of change in a manageable way.

Measurement is essential in PDSA cycles because the information will be used to decide if the change has resulted in the anticipated improvement and will lead to further action. Chapter 7 reviews measurement. In some improvement projects, comparing percentages or absolute numbers before and after the intervention may deliver the information required, but in other situations, time series data, usually in the form of a Run Chart, will be required. Statistical Process Control charts can also be used to assess when a process is performing as expected.

Maintaining changes over time requires effort. Chapter 8 reviews methods of supporting change. Clarity on the change that has been made, helped by using standard work and visual controls, contributes to this. The wider literature of high reliability organisations and learning organisations also offers ideas for use in dental settings.

Some organisations will want to make changes across multiple sites. Many of the issues are like those encountered in one location, and similar solutions can assist, including staff engagement and management style. For some very large-scale pieces of work, creating an improvement collaborative should be considered, and these are explored in Chapter 9. Chapter 10 summarises core issues raised in the book and discusses potential developments in dental quality improvement.

Conclusions

Quality is multifaceted, and the different components are important to dental teams. Publications on audit and quality improvement in dental care have increased markedly in recent decades. This likely reflects both professional and public expectations of service quality. Public expectations of dental services, and factors affecting patient satisfaction, are topics that will be familiar to all dental professionals. Making changes is not easy, and models of change offer insights into the processes and what may need to be considered while making quality improvements in a dental service. The remainder of the book expands on quality, patient safety and the methods that can be used to improve services for staff and patients alike.

References

Albrecht G., Hoogstraten J. (1998) Satisfaction as a determinant of compliance. *Community Dentistry and Oral Epidemiology,* 26; (2): 139–146. Available at: https://doi.org/10.1111/j.1600-0528.1998.tb01940.x

Aldosari M. A., Tavares M. A., Matta-Machado A. T. G., Abreu M. H. N. G. (2017) Factors associated with patients' satisfaction in Brazilian dental primary health care. *PloS One*, 12; 11: e0187993. Available at: https://doi.org/10.1371/journal.pone.0187993

Aldossary M. S., Ismail E. H., Almutawaa M. M., Alhajri S. M., Almuaddi A. M., El Dalatony M. M. (2023) Exploring predictors of patient satisfaction in dental services: A secondary analysis study. *Patient Preference and Adherence*, 2023: 3259–3263. Available at: https://doi.org/10.2147/PPA.S433352

Ali D. A. (2016) Patient satisfaction in Dental Healthcare Centers. *European Journal of Dentistry*, 10; 3: 309–314.

American Dental Association (2025) *Dental Quality Alliance (DQA)*. Available at: https://www.ada.org/resources/research/dental-quality-alliance [Accessed 30 January 2025]

Arthur J. (2016) *Lean Six Sigma for Hospitals: Improving Patient Safety, Patient Flow and the Bottom Line*. 2nd Edition. New York: McGraw Hill.

Backhouse A., Ogunlayi F. (2020) Quality improvement into practice. *BMJ*, 368: m865. Available at: https://doi.org/10.1136/bmj.m865

Bahrami R., Pourhajibagher M., Nikparto N., Bahador A. (2024) Robot-assisted dental implant surgery procedure: A literature review. *Journal of Dental Sciences*, 19; 3: 1359–1368. Available at: https://doi.org/10.1016/j.jds.2024.03.011

Balas E. A., Chapman W. W. (2018) Road map for diffusion of innovation in health care. *Health Affairs*, 37; 2: 198–204. Available at: https://doi.org/10.1377/hlthaff.2017.1155

Baldwin A., Sohal A. (2003) Service quality factors and outcomes in dental care. *Managing Service Quality: An International Journal*, 13; 3: 207–216. Available at: https://doi.org/10.1108/09604520310476472

Beckhard R. F., Harris R. T. (1987) *Organizational Transitions: Managing Complex Change*. Reading, MA: Addison-Wesley.

Breckingridge J., Gray N., Toma M., Ashmore S., Glassborrow R., Stark C., Renfrew M. (2019) Motivating change: A grounded theory of how to achieve large scale, sustained change, co-created with improvement organisations across the UK. *BMJ Open Quality*, 8: e000553. Available at: https://doi.org/10.1136/bmjoq-2018-000553

Bull C., Teede H., Watson D., Callander E. J. (2022) Selecting and implementing patient-reported outcome and experience measures to assess health system performance. *JAMA Health Forum*, 3; 4: e220326. Available at: https://doi.org/10.1001/jamahealthforum.2022.0326

Buss K. D., Schindler D. K., Matis S. A., Lopez Mitnik G. V., Boroumand S., Dye B. A. (2023) Patient satisfaction in military dental clinics-findings from the department of defense dental patient satisfaction survey. *Military Medicine*, 188; 11–12: e3506–e13. Available at: https://doi.org/10.1093/milmed/usad329

Byrne J. (2020) *Quality Improvement in Dental Settings*. Sonoma County Department of Health Services' Dental Health Program / California Department of Public Health, Office of Oral Health.

Byrne M. (2021) *Defining and Measuring Quality in Primary Dental Care*. PhD Thesis, University of Manchester. Available at: https://pure.manchester.ac.uk/ws/portalfiles/portal/194688480/FULL_TEXT.PDF [Accessed 27 May 2025]

Byrne M., Tickle M. (2019) Conceptualising a framework for improving quality in primary dental care. *British Dental Journal*, 227: 865–868. Available at: https://doi.org/10.1038/s41415-019-0900-8

Byrne M. J., Tickle M., Glenny A. M., Campbell S., Goodwin T., O'Malley L. (2019) A systematic review of quality measures used in primary care dentistry. *International Dental Journal*, 69; 4: 252–264. Available at: https://doi.org/10.1111/idj.12453

Campbell L., Barton A., Boyle R., Tully V. (2016) Improving the inspection and manual cleaning of dental instruments in a dental hospital. *BMJ Quality Improvement Reports*, 5; 1, u205075.w2305. Available at: https:doi.org//10.1136/bmjquality.u205075.w2305

Campbell S., Tickle M. (2013a) What is quality primary dental care? *British Dental Journal*, 215; 3: 135–139. Available at: https://doi.org/10.1038/sj.bdj.2013.740

Campbell S., Tickle M. (2013b) How do we improve quality in primary dental care? *British Dental Journal*, 215: 239–243. Available at: https://doi.org/10.1038/sj.bdj.2013.831

Care Quality Commission (2024) *Dental Mythbuster 17: Audit and Improvement in Primary Dental Services*. London: Care Quality Commission. Available at: https://www.cqc.org.uk/guidance-providers/dentists/dental-mythbuster-17-audit-improvement-primary-dental-services [Accessed 5 February 2025]

Cassie H., Mistry V., Beaton L., Black I., Clarkson J. E., Young L. (2021) An evaluation of the implementation of quality improvement (QI) in primary care dentistry: A multi-method approach. *BMJ Open Quality*, 10: e000839. Available at: https://doi.org/10.1136/bmjoq-2019-000839

Chanthavisouk P., Pattanaik S., Warren C. E., Brickle C., Self K. (2022) Dental therapy and dental patient-reported outcomes (dPROs). *Journal of Evidence Based Dental Practice*, 22; 1S: 101660. Available at: https://doi.org/10.1016/j.jebdp.2021.101660

Crisan E. L., Covaliu B. F., Chis D. M. (2021) A systematic literature review of quality management initiatives in dental clinics. *International Journal of Environmental Research and Public Health*, 18; 21: 11084. Available at: https://doi.org/10.3390/ijerph182111084

Davies A. R., Ware Jr. J. E. (1981) Measuring patient satisfaction with dental care. *Social Science & Medicine. Part A: Medical Psychology & Medical Sociology*, 15; 6: 751–760.

Davidoff F., Dixon-Woods M., Leviton L. (2015) Demystifying theory and its use in improvement. *BMJ Quality & Safety* 24; 3: pp. 228-238. Available at: https://doi.org/10.1136/bmjqs-2014-003627

DELIVER (2025) *Deliver: Deliberative Improvement of Oral Care Quality*. [Online] Available at: https://deliverproject.eu/content-page/home [Accessed 28 August 2025]

Deming W. E. (1994) *The New Economics*. 2nd Edition. Baton Rouge: SPC Press.

Dental Quality Alliance (2019) Quality measurement in dentistry: A guidebook. American Dental Association. Available at: https://www.ada.org/-/media/project/ada-organization/ada/ada-org/files/resources/research/dqa/educational-resources/2019_guidebook.pdf?rev=ddef845838024bc7b72cf7312e8775b8&hash=CC40EC6E587CAC1778453826ADA15AB5 [Accessed 23 June 2025]

Dhingra K. (2023) Artificial intelligence in dentistry: Current state and future directions. *The Bulletin of the Royal College of Surgeons of England,* 105; 8 (online). Available at: https://doi.org/10.1308/rcsbull.2023.132

Donabedian A. (2003) *An Introduction to Quality Assurance in Health Care*. New York, NY: Oxford University Press.

El Dalatony M. M., Alshareef R. I., Alkahtani A. R., Shahad M. A., Alhumaidany T. M., AlQarni W. A., Almuaddi A. M., Aldossary M. S. (2023) Patient satisfaction as a determinant of patient loyalty to the dentist in dental clinics. *Journal of Patient Experience,* 10. Available at: https://doi.org/10.1177/23743735231166506

Faculty of Dentistry (Undated) *IHI Learning Management: How to Improve with the Model for Improvement*. Faculty of Dentistry, Royal College of Surgeons in Ireland. Available at: https://facultyofdentistry.ie/learning-ihi [Accessed 5 February 2025]

FDI World Dental Federation (2017) *Quality in Dentistry Policy Statement*. Geneva: FDI. Available online: https://www.fdiworlddental.org/quality-dentistry [Accessed 31 January 2025]

Finkleman S. A., Todoki L. S., Funkhouser E., Greenlee G. M., Choi K. W., Ko H., Wang H., Shapiro P. A., Khosravi R., Baltuck C., Allareddy V., Dolce C., Hao C., Shin K., de Jesus-Vinas J., Vermette M., Jolley C., Huang G. J. (2020) The national dental practice-based research network adult anterior open bite study: Patient satisfaction with treatment. *American Journal of Orthodontics and Dentofacial Orthopedics*, 58; 6: e121–e36. Available at: https://doi.org/10.1016/j.ajodo.2020.04.019

Gould, D. (2008) Audit and research: Similarities and differences. *Nursing Standard*, 22; 37: 51–58. Available at: https://doi.org/10.7748/ns2008.05.22.37.51.c6548

Grossman S., Dungarwalla M., Bailey E. (2020) Patient-reported experience and outcome measures in oral surgery: A dental hospital experience. *British Dental Journal*, 228; 2: 70–74. Available at: https://doi.org/10.1038/s41415-020-1198-2

Harrison R., Fischer S., Walpola R. L., Chauhan A., Babalola T., Mears S., Le-Dao H. (2021) Where do models for change management, improvement and implementation meet? A systematic review of the applications of change management models in healthcare. *Journal of Healthcare Leadership*, 13: 85–108. Available at: https://doi.org/10.2147/jhl.s289176

Health Education and Information Wales / Addysg a Gwella lechyd Cymru (Undated) Quality improvement. Health Education and Information Wales / Addysg a Gwella lechyd Cymru. Available at: https://heiw.nhs.wales/education-and-training/dental/quality-improvement/ [Accessed 5 February 2025]

Healthcare Improvement Scotland (2023) Dentistry in primary care collaborative. Edinburgh: Healthcare Improvement Scotland. Available at: https://ihub.scot/improvement-programmes/scottish-patient

-safety-programme-spsp/spsp-primary-care/quality-improvement-in-dental-practice/dentistry-in-primary-care-collaborative/ [Accessed 8 February 2025]

Hua F. (2025) Dental patient-reported outcomes update 2024. *Journal of Evidence Based Dental Practice*, 25; 1S: 102122. Available at: https://doi.org/10.1016/j.jebdp.2025.102122

Institute for Healthcare Improvement (2003) *The Breakthrough Series: IHI's Collaborative Model for Achieving Breakthrough Improvement. IHI Innovation Series White Paper.* Boston: Institute for Healthcare Improvement.

Institute of Medicine (2001) *Crossing the Quality Chasm: A New Health System for the 21st Century.* Washington, DC: National Academies Press.

Institute of Medicine, Committee to Design a Strategy for Quality Review and Assurance in Medicare (1990) *Medicare: A Strategy for Quality Assurance*, Volume 1, Lohr K. N. (Ed.). Washington, DC: National Academies Press.

International Consortium on Health Outcomes Measurement (no date) Patient-centered outcome measures adult oral health. [Online] Available at: https://www.ichom.org/patient-centered-outcome-measure/oral-health/ [Accessed 14 June 2025]

Jain S., Mohanty V. (2023) 'Assessing patient satisfaction toward mobile dental clinics using digital feedback form in Dehli, India' *Journal of Indian Association of Public Health Dentistry* 21 178 - 182. Https://10.4103/jiaphd.jiaphd_70_22

Juran J. M. (1988) *Juran on Planning for Quality.* New York: The Free Press.

Kaldenberg D., Becker B. W., Browne B. A., Browne W. G. (1997) Identifying service quality strengths and weaknesses using SERVQUAL: A study of dental services. *Health Marketing Quarterly,* 15; 2: 69–86.

Kaplan R. S. (2005) How the balanced scorecard complements the McKinsey 7-S model. *Strategy & Leadership*, 33; 3: 41–46. Available at: https://doi.org/10.1108/10878570510594442

Khalil H., Kynoch K. (2021) Implementation of sustainable complex interventions in health care services: The triple C model. *BMC Health Services Research*, 21: 1. Available at: http://dx.doi.org.uhi.idm.oclc.org/10.1186/s12913-021-06115-x

Kotter J. P. (1996) *Leading Change.* Boston, MA: Harvard Business School Press.

Leles C. R., Silva J. R., Curado T. F. F., Schimmel M., McKenna G. (2022) The potential role of dental patient-reported outcomes (dPROs) in evidence-based prosthodontics and clinical care: A narrative review. *Patient Related Outcome Measures*, 3; 13: 131–143. Available at: https://doi.org/10.2147/prom.s256724

Lewin K. (1951) *Field Theory in Social Science.* New York: Harper and Row.

Liew J., Winston M. (2022) Retrospective audit of midazolam dose and intravenous sedation record keeping in a primary care oral surgery service. *Primary Dental Journal,* 11; 1: 50–57. Available at: https://doi-org.uhi.idm.oclc.org/10.1177/20501684221085846

Lin C., Fehrer V., O'Malley L., Thompson W., Lorenz M., Byrne M. (2025) Quality improvement in general dental practice: Situational analysis for the United Kingdom and Germany. *JDR Clinical & Translational Research.* [Published online in advance of print, February 23, 2025]. Available at: https://doi-org.uhi.idm.oclc.org/10.1177/23800844241306734

Liu L., Watanabe M., Ichikawa T. (2023) Robotics in dentistry: A narrative review. *Dentistry Journal (Basel),* 11; 3: 62. Available at: https://doi.org/10.3390/dj11030062

Luo J. Y. N., Liu P. P., Wong M. C. M. (2018) Patients' satisfaction with dental care: A qualitative study to develop a satisfaction instrument. *BMC Oral Health*, 18: 15. Available at: https://doi.org/10.1186/s12903-018-0477-7

Mazzei A., Russo V., Crescentini A. (2009) Patient satisfaction and communication as competitive levers in dentistry. *The TQM Journal*, 21; 4: 365–381. Available at: https://doi.org/10.1108/17542730910965074

Mills I., Frost J., Cooper C., Moles D. R., Kay E. (2014) Patient-centred care in general dental practice – A systematic review of the literature. *BMC Oral Health,* 14: 64. Available at: https://doi.org/10.1186/1472-6831-14-64

Nelson E. C., Eftimovska E., Lind C., Hager A., Wasson J. H., Lindblad S. (2015) Patient reported outcome measures in practice. *BMJ*, 350: g7818. Available at: https://doi.org/10.1136/bmj.g7818

Nicolas-Boluda A., Simon S. (2023) Validation of the French version of the ICHOM adult oral health standard set. *Clinical and Experimental Dental Research*, 9; 1: 142–149. Available at: https://doi.org/10.1002/cre2.682

Ojha D., Aravamudhan K. (2016) Leading the dental quality movement: A dental quality alliance perspective. *Journal of the California Dental Association*, 44; 4: 239–244. Available at: https://doi.org/10.1080/19424396.2016.12221004

Patrick A., Kandiah T. (2020) How was that for you? PROMs and PREMs for paediatric dental treatment under general anaesthesia. *Faculty Dental Journal*, 11; 1: 16 - 21. Available at: https://doi.org/10.1308/rcsfdj.2020.16

Paxton R., Whitty P., Zaatar A., Fairbairn A., Lothian, J. (2006) Research, audit and quality improvement. *International Journal of Health Care Quality Assurance*, 19; 1: 105–111. Available at: https://doi.org/10.1108/09526860610642627

Reissmann D. R. (2019) Dental patient-reported outcome measures are essential for evidence-based prosthetic dentistry. *Journal of Evidence Based Dental Practice*, 19; 1: 1–6. Available at: https://doi.org/10.1016/j.jebdp.2019.01.003

Righolt A. J., Sidorenkov G., Faggion C. M. Jr, Listl S., Duijster D. (2019) Quality measures for dental care: A systematic review. *Community Dentistry and Oral Epidemiology*, 47; 1: 12–23.

Righolt A. J., Walji M. F., Feine J. S., Williams D. M., Kalenderian E., Listl S. (2020) An international working definition for quality of oral healthcare. *JDR Clinical and Translational Research*, 5: 102–106. Available at: https://doi.org/10.1177/2380084419875442

Riordain R. N., Glick M., Mashhadani S. S. A. A., Aravamudhan K., Barrow J., Cole D., Crall J. J., Gallagher J. E., Gibson J., Hegde S., Kaberry R., Kalenderian E., Karki A., Celeste R. K., Listl S., Myers S. N., Niederman R., Severin T., Smith M. W., Murray Thomson W., Tsakos G., Vujicic M., Watt R. G., Whittaker S., Williams D. M. (2021) Developing a standard set of patient-centred outcomes for adult oral health: An international, cross-disciplinary consensus. *International Dental Journal*, 71; 1: 40–52. Available at: https://doi.org/10.1111/idj.12604

Rogers E. M. (2003) *Diffusion of Innovations*. New York, NY: Simon and Schuster.

Sampat B., Rakover J., Baldoza K., Mate K., Lenoci-Edwards J., Barker P. (2021) *Whole System Quality: A Unified Approach To Building Responsive, Resilient Health Care Systems*. IHI White Paper. Boston, MA: Institute for Healthcare Improvement.

Shirey M. R. (2013) Lewin's theory of planned change as a strategic resource. *JONA: The Journal of Nursing Administration*, 43; 2: 69–72. Available at: https://doi.org/10.1097/nna.0b013e31827f20a9

Stark C., Hookway G. (2019) *Applying Lean in Health and Social Care Services*. New York: Productivity Press.

Syngelakis A., Kamariotou M. I., Madas M. A., Talias M. A., Kitsios F. C. (2023) Health service quality evaluation in dental care: Challenges and future research directions. In Nikolaos F., Matsatsinis N. F., Kitsios F. C., Madas M. A., Kamariotou M. I. (Eds.), *Operational Research in the Era of Digital Transformation and Business Analytics*. Cham: Springer Nature.

Tickle M., O' Malley L., Brocklehurst P., Glenny A., Walsh T., Campbell S. (2015) A national survey of the public's views on quality in dental care. *British Dental Journal*, 219; 3: E1. Available at: https://doi.org/10.1038/sj.bdj.2015.595

Touati R., Sailer I., Marchand L., Ducret M., Strasding M. (2022) Communication tools and patient satisfaction: A scoping review. *Journal of Esthetic and Restorative Dentistry*, 34; 1: 104–116. Available at: https://doi.org/10.1111/jerd.12854

Ungureanu M. I., Mocean F. (2015) What do patients take into account when they choose their dentist? Implications for quality improvement. *Patient Preference and Adherence*, 9: 1715–1720. Available at: https://doi-org.uhi.idm.oclc.org/10.2147/PPA.S94310

Wells S., Tamir O., Gray J., Naidoo D., Bekhit M., Goldmann D. (2018) Are quality improvement collaboratives effective? A systematic review. *BMJ Quality & Safety*, 27: 226–240. Available at: https://doi.org/10.1136/bmjqs-2017-006926

World Health Organisation (2006) *Quality of Care: A Process for Making Strategic Choices in Healthcare Systems*. Geneva: World Health Organisation.

Wright J. T. (2025) In the year 2025, dentistry is very much alive. *The Journal of the American Dental Association*, 156; 1: 1–2. Available at: https://doi.org/10.1016/j.adaj.2024.11.005

Chapter 2

Patient Safety

Introduction

Healthcare exists to aid and help people through difficult times; however, healthcare is a high-hazard sector and poses a significant risk of errors and adverse events (Sammer *et al.*, 2010). Patient safety is defined by the World Health Organization (2023) as 'the absence of preventable harm to a patient and reduction of risk of unnecessary harm associated with healthcare to an acceptable minimum'. The study of patient safety focuses on creating ways in which healthcare can be delivered with reduced risks, lowering the rate of avoidable harm (accidents, errors and complications), and minimising the impact of harm on patients when it does occur.

Dentistry differs from general medical care in that most interventions are surgical, which increases the possibility of immediate harm to patients (Bailey, Tickle and Campbell, 2014). Dental patient harm occurs in all countries (Renton and Sabbah, 2016, Ferlias *et al.*, 2024, Musa *et al.*, 2025). Incidents are underreported, particularly in primary care, so the true incidence of adverse events is unknown (Al-zain and Althumairi, 2021, Siriwatana and Pongpanich, 2025). The Patient Safety Network outlined the most common types of error or harm that occurred in dentistry in their retrospective case review as: delayed treatment, unnecessary treatment, or disease progression after misdiagnosis (Agency for Healthcare Research and Quality, 2020). They also reported that the commonest adverse impacts resulting from these errors were: pain, hard and soft tissue damage and nerve damage. Some of these adverse effects were permanent. Issues such as wrong site extraction remain important risks that can benefit from a patient safety approach (Cullingham, Saksena and Pemberton, 2017).

Patient safety and quality improvement are related issues. Quality imporvement methods can be used to systematically improve healthcare services by making changes that deliver better outcomes for patients. It uses a data-driven approach to identify what should change; how to make the improvement, and to establish whether the planned change was effective. When healthcare organisations make quality improvement a priority, it will help them to provide safe, timely, effective and patient-centred care, thus improving patient outcomes and increasing satisfaction.

DOI: 10.4324/9781003493532-2

Key Terms in Patient Safety

To discuss patient safety, it is helpful to be familiar with some commonly used terms. Table 2.1 gives definitions of some key terms.

Table 2.1 Key concepts in patient safety

Patient Safety	Patient safety refers to procedures and practices designed to minimise harm to individuals receiving healthcare. It involves reducing risks, preventing errors and improving the quality of care to maintain patient well-being and safety (Higgins and Herpy, 2021).
Adverse Event	An adverse event is an unplanned or harmful incident that takes place during the delivery of healthcare. These incidents, caused by medical errors, systemic issues, or both, can result in patient injury, disability, or death (Tokede *et al.*, 2017).
Medical Error	A medical error refers to an act of commission (performing an incorrect action) or omission (not performing the correct action) that leads to an unintended outcome for a patient. Such errors may occur at any stage in healthcare, including diagnosis, treatment, medication administration and communication (Hofer, Kerr and Hayward, 2000).
Near Miss	A near miss, often called a close call or near-incident, describes an event or circumstance that could cause harm to a patient but was averted or did not result in injury due to timely intervention, chance, or other mitigating factors. Near misses are important opportunities to recognise and reduce potential risks in healthcare processes (Hofer, Kerr and Hayward, 2000).
Root Cause Analysis	A systematic method employed to determine the root causes or contributing factors of errors and adverse events. This process includes analysing the occurrence, identifying relevant elements and developing strategies to mitigate similar incidents in the future Some practitioners dislike the term because they feel it encourages staff to identifiy one single cause rather than a series of potentially important factors. (Yamalik and Perea Pérez, 2012).
Safety Culture	Safety culture describes the collective values, beliefs, attitudes and behaviours regarding safety in an organisation or healthcare environment. It requires an emphasis on communication, learning from errors and continuous enhancement of patient safety (Pemberton, 2014).
Sentinel Events	A sentinel event is a serious, unexpected occurrence that results in death, permanent harm, or severe temporary harm. (Pemberton, 2014). These events are also referred to as 'never events'. Historically, sentinel events only included events that occurred to patients. The term is now usually expanded to include harm to staff members, visitors and other individuals in healthcare premises (Patra and Jesus, 2023).

Background and History

Patient safety in healthcare has rapidly improved by applying lessons from other high-risk industries such as aviation, and by learning from human factors engineering. The modern discipline of patient safety began in the 1990s. Healthcare professionals realised that although medicine had advanced dramatically, hospitals, clinics, dental surgeries and other healthcare environments were not always safe places for healing. Instead, they were settings where mistakes were made and harm to patients was common. The Institute of Medicine's report, 'To Err is Human: Building a Safer Health System' estimated that up to 98,000 people died because of healthcare errors in hospitals, and up to one million were injured, each year in the US alone (Kohn, Corrigan and Donaldson, 2000). This report and accompanying media reporting and commentary directed public and professional attention to patient safety. In the United States, there was an enormous increase in government grants directed towards patient safety, and a large increase in the publication of commentaries, guidelines and reviews (Stelfox *et al.,* 2006, St Pierre *et al.,* 2022).

There is now widespread acknowledgement of the importance of patient safety in healthcare with endorsement from the World Health Organization (2024). In dentistry, major organisations such as the British Dental Association, the American Dental Association and the FDI World Dental Federation have provided resources for dental teams to apply to patient safety. These are often focused on issues such as infection prevention and control, prescribing and radiation safety (FDI World Dental Federation, 2021, Benavides *et al.*, 2024, British Dental Association, 2025). In the United States, the Association for Dental Safety, previously the Organization for Safety, Asepsis and Prevention, now offers worldwide membership to oral health professionals interested in patient safety in dental care (Association for Dental Safety, 2025). Much work on dental care has focused on hospital care, with less attention to patient safety in primary care dentistry (Bailey, Tickle and Campbell, 2014). The development of patient safety work in dentistry is discussed in more detail later in the chapter.

Historically, when adverse events happened in healthcare that led to patient harm from errors, it was common for a 'single cause' to be identified and blame to be placed on an individual. With advancements in the field and the integration of systems thinking, there is a widespread acknowledgement that errors occur in an organisational context and that understanding and tackling all the factors that contribute to a patient safety problem is important (Niv and Tal, 2024, Bailey and Dungarwalla, 2025).

Principles and Frameworks

Several key principles and frameworks underpin patient safety in relation to healthcare organisations delivering safe care. One of the principles of care is 'do no harm', which means that patient safety should always be at the forefront in every aspect of care. The Swiss Cheese Model of adverse events, a concept developed by James Reason, illustrates that in healthcare settings there are often several problems that must coincide for an adverse event to occur (Reason, 1990, 2000). Reason's work argued that in adverse events there is often a combination of latent errors and active errors that come together to cause the failure. Latent errors are problems with the way a system is organised that make an adverse event more likely, often by making it easier for an individual error to occur. Examples of latent errors include poor equipment design; ineffective, incorrect or incomplete policy; ineffective training; inadequate supervision; ineffective communications; and uncertainties in roles and responsibilities (Health and Safety Executive, 1999, p. 11). Active errors are errors by staff, often made more likely by the latent conditions in the system. Figure 2.1 shows Reason's Swiss Cheese Model. A key insight is that changing any

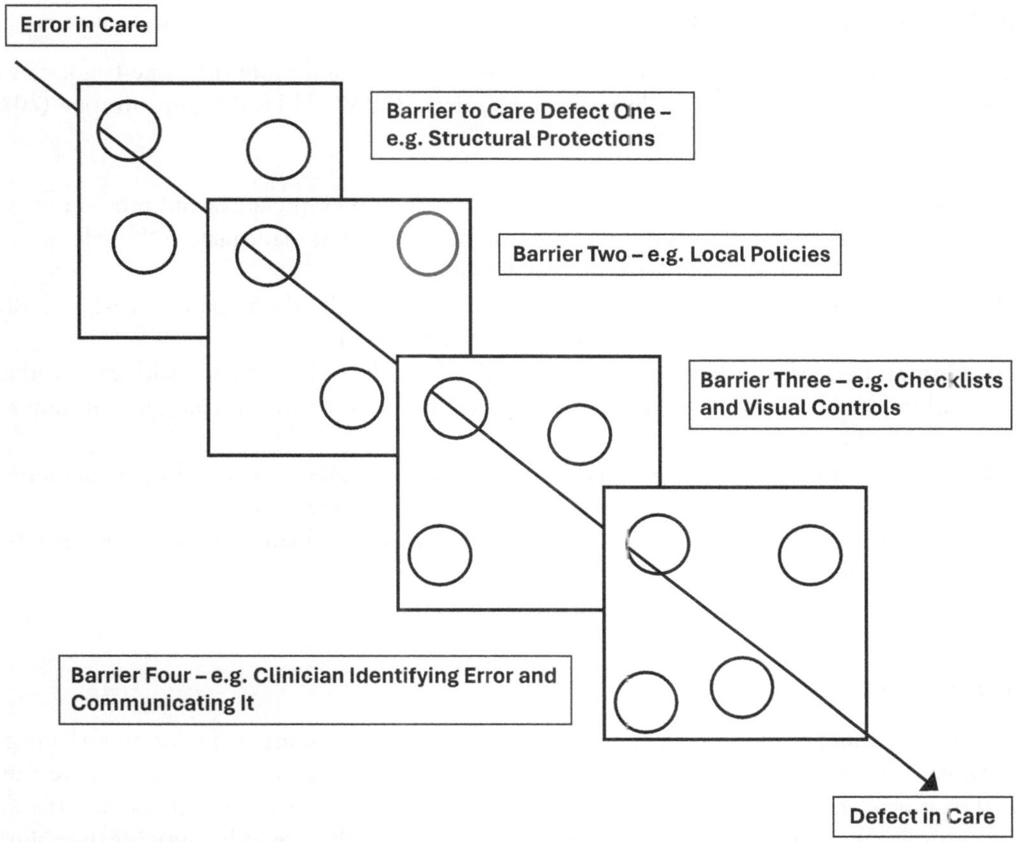

Figure 2.1 The Swiss cheese model. Source: Adapted from Reason, 1990, 2000.

of the conditions that make the adverse event more likely to occur will decrease the probability of it happening. The model accepts that staff play a key role in patient safety but acknowledges that other factors also affect safety, including issues such as policy and equipment design that may appear distant from the final event.

Many opportunities to learn from adverse events are lost because information is not shared. This can be because staff fear that they will be blamed. It can also occur because an organisation may be unwilling to acknowledge a failure in case it results in public criticism with a loss of confidence in the organisation, and potentially a loss in business. Reason argued for the need for a 'Just Culture', one in which staff feel able to report a problem, and do not fear that they will be unfairly blamed for it (Reason, 1997). While the initial impact of this approach was in industry, the concept is applicable to dental care (Pellegrino, 2019, Barkell and Snyder, 2021). This model moves a system away from automatic blame for an individual and produces opportunities to learn from mistakes (Marx, 2019). Assessment includes focusing on the error, rather than the harm that resulted from it, and taking time to understand all the factors that increased the likelihood of the error. Guidelines like the Patient Safety Curriculum Guide provided by the World Health Organisation (2011) have a systematic approach to embedding safety in healthcare systems, as illustrated by their emphasis on leadership, communication and patient involvement.

Factors Leading to Patient Harm

There are several factors that can contribute to patient harm, and more than one factor can be present in the case of an incident affecting patient safety. The World Health Organization (2023) describe five categories that can affect patient safety:

- **Systemic and Organisational Factors:** These include poor processes and procedures; systems that allow staff to be interrupted; resource constraints; inadequate staffing levels, and deficiencies in training and learning opportunities.
- **Technological Factors:** Issues such as problems with health information systems, including access to patient records and outdated or unreliable machines.
- **Human Factors and Behaviour:** Communication difficulties among health care workers, within teams, and with patients and families; challenges in teamwork; fatigue; burnout; and cognitive biases.
- **Patient Factors:** Concordance between the oral health professional and the patient on treatment options and limited or inconsistent engagement with treatment.
- **External Factors:** lack of policies, regulatory inconsistency, financial pressures and environmental challenges.

Types of Error

Errors can be thought of as being of two types (Figure 2.2): planning or performing (Perneger, 2005). An example of an error in planning in Dentistry would be planning a tooth to have a root canal treatment that was too complex for the practitioner to complete in general practice. If a root of a tooth has particularly curved roots or has lateral canals, this could be outwith the abilities

Performance Errors

Performance errors occur during a treatment.

A recent study reported that dental professionals are up to three times more likely to experience burnout than any other profession with 46% of those interviewed having experienced burnout (Garner, 2024).

With the increasing pressure on healthcare worldwide leading to staff shortages and a higher incidence of burnout, performance errors could increase.

System factors such as those discussed above can contribute to performance errors in other ways, for example by increasing workload, decreasing supervision, or giving inadequate access to training.

Planning Errors

Planning errors occur before a treatment is commenced.

Some planning errors are unavoidable, but most can be avoided when clinics are organised, well-stocked and properly staffed.

Having a dedicated member of staff look at the procedures booked in for the week ahead can be helpful to ensure all needed materials are ordered.

More experienced clinicians are better at judging which procedures are within their capability, and which need to be referred.

Some planning errors occur because of system issues. Chapter Five gives an example of clinic over runs that are affected by organisational issues as well as individual clinical practice.

Figure 2.2 Types of errors

of a general dentist. If the dentist then attempted the root canal treatment but had to stop due to the complexity, a planning error has occurred. The error was made before the procedure began and was preventable. Another example of a planning error could be if a material was not available that was needed to complete a procedure, for example, a cementing agent used to cement a dental crown. If the patient attended the appointment, and the crown was ready to be cemented but the required material was not available for use, this would be a planning error that again, could have been prevented. An example of a performing error could be if the wrong tooth was prepared for a restoration and a cavity was drilled. This was an error in performance as the planning was correct, but the clinician made a mistake when performing the plan.

Safety I and Safety II

Attention inevitably falls on adverse events and particularly on patient harm. Some harm occurs randomly because of known adverse effects of routine treatments. In many other harms, the clinician and organisation try to understand what went wrong. Teams can apply Root Cause Analysis, which is discussed further in Chapter 5, keeping in mind that there may be a number of contributory factors. On a large scale, organisations and even governments can analyse data and in some instances commission inquiries that seek to understand the underpinning causes of a problem in healthcare delivery. Many thousands of papers and reports tease out causal pathways to system failure. This has contributed to impressive gains in safety in some areas with enormous decreases in some adverse events (Carson-Stevens, Donaldson and Sheikh, 2018). Despite all this effort, many adverse events continue to occur in health care in general, and in dental care.

This problem has led some academics and safety practitioners to develop the idea of Safety I and Safety II. Safety I is the traditional model where teams work to learn from failures and to identify ways of reducing risk. Safety II asks why so few adverse events occur, considering the enormous number of patient contacts undertaken by any health care team (Hollnagel, Wears and Braithwaite, 2015). The solution to this question, some theorists argue, is that rather than following rigid guidelines, clinical staff adapt their work to the situation in which they and their patient find themselves. Clinical systems are complex and the myriads of interactions between patient problems and clinical circumstances are impossible to predict. Individual clinicians and clinical teams adapt continuously to differences in presenting conditions, patient mix, complexity, unexpected complications and available staffing. The focus, Safety II supporters argue, should be on understanding why staff manage to ensure that most patient contacts go well, rather than exclusively paying attention to why they sometimes fail.

There is nothing unreasonable about this argument. All clinical teams will recognise the work they do to adapt to changing clinical circumstances in the description above. Despite this, it is an oversimplification to assume that Safety I focuses solely on learning from failure. Much quality improvement and patient safety work takes active steps to design systems to be as safe as possible. Some procedures are linear, and guidelines and checklists can make a real difference to safety. There are several added advantages of taking the Safety II concept into account. Healthcare systems can be enormously complex, and taking every possible permutation of organisation, service, policy, guideline, available staff and equipment, and patient presentation into account is impossible. Staff will always have to respond to unforeseen circumstances. The advantage of considering the idea of what allows services to work despite numerous challenges is that it allows services to consider how they can support resilience and how they can understand and enable behaviours that make safety more likely in any circumstance (Verhagen *et al.*, 2022).

Challenges and Barriers in Patient Safety

Understanding and ensuring patient safety is an important part of providing high-quality dental care. Patient Safety aims to deliver safe, effective care and reduce risks or adverse events. However, achieving patient safety in healthcare comes with numerous challenges and barriers that healthcare providers must navigate. These challenges can hinder efforts to improve patient safety and lead to adverse patient outcomes.

One of the significant challenges in patient safety is communication breakdown. Clear communication keeps the team aligned on patient care. Communication breakdowns can occur between healthcare providers, leading to misunderstandings and errors and ultimately compromising patient safety (Tjia *et al.*, 2009). Critical information may be overlooked and when information is known, it may still be misinterpreted (O'Daniel and Rosenstein, 2008). Handoffs between professionals are a common time for information to be miscommunicated, misunderstood, or overlooked, potentially leading to adverse events (Birmingham *et al.*, 2015). To address this challenge, healthcare organisations must prioritise effective communication strategies, such as standardised handoff protocols and communication training for healthcare providers. In dentistry, keeping detailed and accurate patient notes is vital. Dentists primarily work independently, and an individual dentist could be the only oral health professional who knows about a patient's care and treatment. If the patient must see another clinician at the practice such as a hygienist or therapist, or be referred to a specialist, having organised and informative patient notes is essential to ensure high-quality care.

Medication errors illustrate further challenges. Medication errors are among the most common errors in healthcare and can have serious consequences for patients. These errors can happen at various stages of the medication process, from prescribing to administration. They can result from factors such as confusion between look-alike medications, improper dosing and lack of medication understanding (Benjamin, 2003). In dentistry, errors can occur while prescribing, such as authorising an incorrect dose of antibiotics or prescribing a drug that could interact with other medications the patient is taking (Teoh, McCullough and Moses, 2022). For example, the antibiotic metronidazole interacts with warfarin by increasing blood thinning, which could lead to complications for the patient (Howard-Thompson *et al.*, 2008). Errors can also occur because of incomplete knowledge about a patient, including drug allergies or other contraindications, or because of poor communication with the patient (Affifi *et al.*, 2025).

Workforce shortages in healthcare pose a significant barrier to patient safety. Healthcare facilities in many countries face a shortage of healthcare workers, including dentists, nurses, hygienists and technicians. This shortage can increase workloads, fatigue and burnout among healthcare providers, compromising patient safety (Lochmann, Deaconu and Czirfusz, 2024). To address this barrier, healthcare organisations must invest in strategies to recruit and retain healthcare professionals, such as offering competitive remuneration, providing professional development opportunities and creating a positive work environment (Dental Protection Society, 2024).

Enhancing Patient Safety

The overall culture of a team, practice or organisation is important and is referred to as Safety Culture. There is no one single definition of the term (Halligan and Zecevic, 2011). For the purposes of this chapter, it is useful to think of Safety Culture as the 'integrated pattern of individual and organisational behaviour, based upon shared beliefs and values that continuously seeks to minimise patient harm, which may result from the processes of care delivery' (Kristensen and Bartels, 2010, p. 4).

Safety Culture was initially thought of as something that is heavily influenced by managers and senior clinical staff and which cascades down the organisation (Glendon and Stanton, 2000). Others see it as a more complex phenomenon influenced by relationships within teams and organisations, and by external influences such as regulators as well as internal arrangements (Quenon *et al.*, 2020). In the context of dental care, practice owners and in larger organisations and hospitals, senior clinicians and managers will have a major impact on how a team thinks about, and whether it prioritises, patient safety. Dentists work with nurses, hygienists, therapists, specialists, administrators and receptionists; these interactions, as well as issues related to working conditions, will all affect patient safety (Choi *et al.*, 2019).

An organisation's safety culture is linked to its overall organisational culture (Antonsen, 2009). If the day-to-day culture of an organisation places trust in employees; prioritises quality; encourages the sharing of ideas; supports training and learning, and uses measured feedback, then the same concepts will support their safety culture. In organisations with rigid hierarchies and strict protocols with punitive enforcement, staff rarely report issues, suggest ideas, or highlight errors due to fear of repercussions. This would be a difficult situation in which to build a supportive patient safety culture as team members may reasonably feel that if they talk about a near miss or share an error, then the more usual disciplinary actions will take place. How much staff safety is prioritised will also influence how staff see patient safety. If their own welfare is not supported, then it will be more difficult to encourage staff to share issues. This relates to the Just Culture concept described above.

Human factors play a very large role in patient safety (Brennan, Jarvis and Oeppen, 2022). 'Human factors' refers to the interactions between people and between people and systems (Walshaw and Mannon, 2018). The World Health Organisation identifies three areas of human factors: physical, cognitive and organisational (World Health Organisation, 2016, p. 3). The physical domain refers to how people interact with physical objects, which covers an enormous area of activities in dentistry. The cognitive domain relates to factors such as memory, information processing and decision-making. The final domain, organisational, relates to how people and teams interact with systems and technologies. Other groups separate out additional domains, such as socio-technical and environmental domains. This thinking links to Reason's Swiss Cheese model discussed earlier in the chapter, where several factors can help or hinder safety. Surgical procedures, such as those used in dentistry, are particularly relevant for consideration of human factors because of the complex interaction of machines, surgical instruments, planned procedures and staff (Stahel and Mauffrey, 2014). The next section of this chapter summarises areas that deserve consideration in all dental teams.

1. **Leadership and Commitment**

Good leadership is important in establishing a culture of safety within healthcare settings (McFadden, Henagan and Gowen, 2009). Effective clinical leaders and managers commit to patient safety as a fundamental value and facilitate an environment where safety concerns can be openly discussed without fear of punishment. These leaders are responsible for setting clear expectations, allocating resources and implementing initiatives that prioritise patient safety at every level of the organisation. Although challenges may arise, this commitment is crucial because it shapes the overall safety culture as well as overall organisational culture. Genuine engagement from all levels of staff is necessary to sustain this culture.

2. **Effective Communication**

Communication is another important factor contributing to patient safety. Miscommunication or a lack of communication among healthcare providers can lead to serious errors that affect patient care. Involving patients in their care discussions is equally important because it fosters shared understanding and increases their confidence in their safety.

When sharing information with professionals, using standardised communication tools such as the SBAR (Situation-Background-Assessment-Recommendation) technique can enhance clarity and reduce misunderstandings (Müller *et al.*, 2018). Some practitioners prefer a variant, ISBAR, where the Introduction has a separate prompt, giving Introduction – Situation – Background – Assessment – Recommendation (Burgess *et al.*, 2020).

An example of using SBAR in dentistry is given below (Box 2.1). A general dentist sees a patient with severe facial swelling requiring drainage and a tooth extraction, but the severity of the facial swelling requires transfer to a hospital setting through a phone call referral.

BOX 2.1 EXAMPLE OF AN SBAR IN DENTAL CARE

Situation	I am Dr X, calling from Dental Clinic X. I am calling about patient X who has a severe spreading facial swelling due to an infected tooth.
Background	Patient X came to see me today for this infected tooth. They are an irregular dental attender with an overall poor dentition. They report several episodes of pain from this tooth in the past but as it went away they did not seek treatment.
Assessment	I have taken an x-ray and I believe the problem is that tooth 38 (lower left wisdom tooth) has unrestorable decay with an associated periapical infection. This infection has now spread to involve the facial tissues on that side of the face and is spreading inferiorly to the neck. The patient has difficulty opening the mouth (trismus) and reports pain and difficulty on swallowing.
Recommendation	I would like to refer this patient to you for assessment and treatment urgently, and I will send the x-ray I have taken. I believe they will require a surgical extraction and high dose antibiotics. Is there any other information you require from me?

The SBAR process works well for patient handovers. Communication with team members when side by side with them is of equal importance. In many dental settings, a single dentist and a single dental nurse are the only professionals who know the entire clinical situation. Being able to maximise the input of both professionals, and in hospital settings of an entire surgical team, is valuable.

Communication is not always easy, particularly in hierarchical situations. Crew Resource Management (CRM), an approach developed in aviation, is often used in training to improve communication in healthcare teams (Oriol, 2006). The aim of CRM is to help teams use technology, information and interpersonal factors such as problem-solving and decision-making to maintain safety and produce the desired outcomes (Helmreich and Foushee, 2019). In aviation, CRM is a widespread approach that covers more than interactions and processes in flight crew. There is much variation in which aspects of the method are taught in healthcare settings, and training often focuses on human factors (Gross *et al.*, 2019). Components relevant to dentistry include (Pinsky, Taichman and Sarment, 2010, Seager *et al.*, 2013):

- **Situational Awareness:** Keeping awareness of the whole clinical situation. It is easy to focus on one technical component of care. Working with other staff who are willing to draw other issues to attention can help to mitigate this, as can being aware of the risk of becoming lost in detail (Green *et al.*, 2017).
- **Threat and Error Management:** This involves the identification of potential risks and the active management of the clinical situation to reduce the chance of error and to mitigate the error if it occurs.
- **Peer Monitoring:** Some clinical errors happen in slow motion, with someone else in the room wondering if an error might be about to occur but not feeling able to raise the issue. This can be because the observer has less perceived seniority, fear of making a mistake, or even embarrassment. In peer monitoring, staff are encouraged to raise a concern in an appropriate manner, with an obligation for the treating clinician to consider the issue raised and to respond.
- **Briefings and Checklists:** Taking time to ensure that everyone knows what is planned at the start of a shift, clinic session or operation can help to increase situational awareness and to make it easier for other staff to know if they need to intervene. A surgical pause and the use of checklists have similar characteristics.
- **A Sterile Cockpit:** In aviation, at moments of high concentration and great mental work-load, only conversation directly related to the situation is permitted. Applied in dentistry, this still allows another staff member, such as a dental nurse, to tender a peer monitoring intervention, but it reduces other demands on the operator.

For these approaches to work in practice, staff must feel that they are allowed to raise an issue without fear of criticism. Senior or operative staff must be able to accept that there is a combined effort to deliver safety and to consider any query carefully.

3. **Education and Training**

Ongoing education and training for healthcare staff is crucial for sustaining high safety standards. Training should include clinical skills, but it must also cover non-technical competencies like effective teamwork and communication. Simulation-based training is often particularly effective in equipping healthcare professionals to respond to emergencies and unforeseen circumstances; this approach can help reduce potential harm to patients (Todd and Schaefer, 2018, Kishimoto *et al.*, 2023). Despite challenges, comprehensive training offers significant benefits.

4. **Incident Reporting and Analysis**

A strong incident reporting system allows healthcare organisations to learn from adverse events and near misses; however, this only works if staff feel they can report incidents without fear (Chance, Florence and Abdoul, 2024). This promotes a culture of safety and shows the organisation's commitment to improvement. Analysing reported incidents allows organisations to take corrective actions that can prevent recurrence.

5. **Patient Engagement**

Involving patients in their care is essential for ensuring their safety. Evidence on the most effective ways of doing this is limited (Pang *et al.*, 2025). By educating patients about their treatment plans, including the potential risks and benefits, they can be supported to take an active role in decision-making (Ho *et al.*, 2025). Encouraging patients to express their concerns fosters a collaborative environment between healthcare providers and patients, ultimately enhancing safety and trust. The degree of engagement in individual patients will vary, so the dental team needs to adapt to individual patient requirements (Duhn and Medves, 2018, Obadan-Udoh *et al.*, 2024). Artificial intelligence (AI) will offer greater ability to tailor solutions to individual patients, although work is needed to assess effectiveness (Thorat *et al.*, 2024).

6. **Use of Technology**

Integrating technology into healthcare practices can greatly improve patient safety. Electronic health records enhance information sharing and coordination among providers (Fricton *et al.*, 2011). Clinical decision support systems offer real-time guidance for safer prescribing and treatment choices. Systems can be tailored to the needs of different members of the clinical team (Russell *et al.*, 2015) and for specific patient groups (Thanathornwong, Suebnukarn and Ouivirach, 2023). Technology must be used carefully to avoid new risks like alarm fatigue from excessive alerts, but even faster change is likely. The increase in access to machine learning that can be incorporated into artificial intelligence (AI) is likely to bring a rapid change in the availability, comprehensiveness and accuracy of decision support systems (Al Turkestani *et al.*, 2021).

Patient Safety in Practice

This overview of patient safety in healthcare and in dental care identifies some key issues that practices and teams can consider for action:

- **Accepting that Adverse Events Occur:** All clinicians, teams and practices will experience adverse clinical events. Some events are random, while some are understood complications or risks of routine procedures. Other events, such as wrong site extraction, are preventable. Making an error is not a shameful event: no one can be perfect. The main issue is in seeking to understand what happened and undertaking mitigating actions to reduce the risk of future repetition. Near-miss events, where an adverse event almost occurred but was narrowly avoided, also provide learning.
- **Promoting a Just Culture:** Staff need to feel that they will be treated fairly if they make an error. If the automatic reaction is blame, they have a reason to avoid reporting or to minimise the error. This loses the opportunity to learn from what went wrong. Very few incidents are due to clinical negligence. Starting from the assumption that staff strive to deliver the best care they can, and then working to understand what happened is the best way to begin.
- **Taking a Wide View of Problems:** Clinical errors almost always involve an individual clinician or a small team who make the mistake. This does not mean that there are no other

factors at play. Crowded clinics; additional demands such as questions from receptionists; fatigue; poorly conveyed information; patients who are unclear on their previous dental and medical history; working with new colleagues; information system glitches; equipment problems, and technical problems only constitute a partial list of what can contribute. Look beyond the immediate error to understand the context.

- **Building Safer Systems:** Clinicians adapt to problems all the time. They juggle patient treatment slots, respond to emergencies, work around problems with machines and modify laboratory supplied items that do not quite fit. This will always happen, but teams, practices and hospital units can reduce issues that occur regularly. If time pressures dealing with emergency presentations result in staff rushing other work and making an error, then scheduling may need review, for example. If a referral was unclear and a mistake is made, then consider improving handover procedures and building in checks such as surgical pauses.
- **Investing in People:** Staff are not born knowing how to communicate risk. The risk of tunnel vision and the need for situational awareness will make sense to all dental staff, but recognising it and knowing how to mitigate risk are skills that can be learnt. Investing effort to teach and reinforce interpersonal skills and structured ways of addressing problems is time and money well spent.
- **Creating a Safety Culture:** Many of these approaches work best when there is a supportive work environment that is aligned with improvement ideas. Staff will hesitate to report errors or question a risk if this is not encouraged in the practice or team environment. Senior staff prompting and modelling the behaviour they want to encourage, linked to relevant training, can make a big difference in staff engagement and confidence.
- **Using a Quality Improvement Approach:** Problem scoping is reviewed in Chapter 5, and Plan – Do – Study – Act (PDSA) cycles are discussed in detail in Chapter 6. These approaches, together with measurement methods reviewed in Chapter 7, can be incorporated into patient safety work and provide helpful methods of considering a problem.

Conclusion

Patient safety feels like something that should be second nature to all clinicians. This overlooks the complexity of some problems and the wide-ranging factors that can influence them. Like most things in dental care, there is knowledge that can be acquired and skills that can be learnt to increase safety. Patient safety is not something that is achieved once and for all, but rather an aim towards which teams work. Learning from error and building safer systems that make it easier for staff to deliver the work they want takes time and perseverance but is rewarding and engaging for staff.

Further Reading and Resources

Association for Dental Safety. https://www.myads.org/
Useful resources, some of which can be accessed by non-members
Institute for Healthcare Improvement. https://www.ihi.org/
Incudes excellent free resources relevant to patient safety.
Leape L. L. (2021) *Making Healthcare Safe: The Story of the Patient Safety Movement.* Cham, Switzerland: Springer Nature.

An introduction to the history of patient safety in healthcare.

Sanchez J. A., Higgins R. S. D., Kent P. S. (Eds.). (2024) *Handbook of Perioperative and Procedural Patient Safety*. Elsevier Inc.

A useful discussion of surgical safety, with much material that is relevant to dental surgeons.

Vincent C., Amalberti R. (2016) *Safer Healthcare: Strategies for the Real World*. Cham, Switzerland: Springer.

A wide-ranging review of patient safety in healthcare.

References

Afifi H., Dheaa S., Albanna, F., Alqaderi F. (2025) Common prescription errors among dentists in the Middle East: A comprehensive literature review. *Journal of University Medical & Dental College*, 16; 2: 1082–1087. Available at: https://doi.org/10.37723/jumdc.v16i2.1051

Agency for Healthcare Research and Quality (2020) *Adverse Events in Dentistry*. Available at: https://psnet.ahrq.gov/perspective/adverse-events-dentistry [Accessed 29 July 2024]

Al Turkestani N., Bianchi J., Deleat-Besson R., Le C., Tengfei L., Prieto J. C., Gurgel M., Ruellas A. C. O., Massaro C., Aliaga Del Castillo A., Evangelista K., Yatabe M., Benavides E., Soki F., Zhang W., Najarian K., Gryak J., Styner M., Fillion-Robin J., Cevidanes L. H. S. (2021) Clinical decision support systems in orthodontics: A narrative review of data science approaches. *Orthodontics & Craniofacial Research*, 24; S2: 26–36. Available at: https://doi.org/10.1111/ocr.12492

Al-zain Z., Althumairi A. (2021) Awareness, attitudes, practices, and perceived barriers to medical error incident reporting among faculty and health care practitioners (HCPs) in a dental clinic. *Journal of Multidisciplinary Healthcare*, 14: 735–741. Available at: https://doi.org/10.2147/JMDH.S297965

Antonsen S. (2009) *Safety Culture Theory, Method and Improvement*. Farnham, Surrey: Ashgate Publishing Ltd.

Association for Dental Safety (2025) Global membership. [Online] Available at: https://www.myads.org/global-membership [Accessed 7 August 2025]

Bailey E., Dungarwalla M. (2021) Developing a patient safety culture in primary dental care. *Primary Dental Journal*, 10; 1: 89–95. https://doi.org/10.1177/2050168420980990

Bailey E., Dungarwalla M. (2025) Patient safety in dentistry – a decade in the making. *British Dental Journal*, 238; 10: 814–821. Available at: https://doi.org/10.1038/s41415-025-8384-1

Bailey E., Tickle M., Campbell S. (2014) Patient safety in primary care dentistry: where are we now? *British Dental Journal*, 217; 7: 339–344. Available at: https://doi.org/10.1038/sj.bdj.2014.857

Barkell N. P., Snyder S. S. (2021) Just culture in healthcare: An integrative review. *Nursing Forum*, 56; 1: 103–111. Available at: https://doi.org/10.1111/nuf.12525

Benavides E., Joseph R., Krecioch J. R., Connolly R. T., Allareddy T., Buchanan A., Spelic D., O'Brien K. K., Keels M. A., Mascarenhas A. K., Duong M., Aerne-Bowe M. J., Ziegler K. M., Lipman R. D. (2024) Optimizing radiation safety in dentistry. *The Journal of the American Dental Association*, 155; 4: 280–293.e4. Available at: http://dx.doi.org/10.1016/j.adaj.2024.04.003

Benjamin, D. M. (2003) Reducing medication errors and increasing patient safety: Case studies in clinical pharmacology. *The Journal of Clinical Pharmacology*, 43; 7: 768–783. Available at: https://doi.org/10.1177/0091270003254794

Birmingham P., Buffum M. D., Blegen M. A., Lyndon A. (2015) Handoffs and patient safety: Grasping the story and painting a full picture. *Western Journal of Nursing Research*, 37; 11: 1458–1478. Available at: https://doi.org/10.1177/0193945914539052

Brennan P. A., Jarvis S., Oeppen R. S. (2022) European Association of oral medicine 2021 conference – Crispian Scully lecture: Applying human factors to improve patient safety and performance. *Journal of Oral Pathology & Medicine*, 51; 1: 13–17. Available at: https://doi.org/10.1111/jop.13254

British Dental Association (2025) Patient care and safety. Available at: https://www.bda.org/advice/patient-care-and-safety/ [Accessed 7 August 2025]

Burgess A., van Diggele C., Roberts C., Mellis C. (2020) Teaching clinical handover with ISBAR. *BMC Medical Education*, 20; Suppl 2: 459. Available at: https://doi.org/10.1186/s12909-020-02285-0

Carson-Stevens A., Donaldson L., Sheikh A. (2018) The rise of patient safety-II: Should we give up hope on safety-I and extracting value from patient safety incidents? Comment on "False Dawns and New Horizons in Patient Safety Research and Practice."' *International Journal of Health Policy and Management*, 7; 7: 667–670. Available at: https://doi.org/10.15171/ijhpm.2018.23

Chance E. A., Florence D. and Abdoul I. S. (2024) The effectiveness of checklists and error reporting systems in enhancing patient safety and reducing medical errors in hospital settings-a narrative review. *International Journal of Nursing Sciences* 11; 3: 387–398. Available at: https://doi.org/10.1016/j.ijnss.2024.06.003

Choi E.-M., Mu, S.-J., Chung W.-G., Noh H.-J. (2019) Relationships between dental hygienists' work environment and patient safety culture. *BMC Health Services Research*, 19; 1: Article 299. Available at: https://doi.org/10.1186/s12913-019-4136-8

Cullingham P., Saksena A., Pemberton M. N. (2017) Patient safety: Reducing the risk of wrong tooth extraction. *British Dental Journal*, 222; 10: 759–763. Available at: https://doi.org/10.1038/sj.bdj.2017.448

Dental Protection Society (2024) *Combatting Workforce Shortages*. [Online] London: Dental Protection Society. Available at: https://www.dentalprotection.org/uk/articles/combatting-workforce-shortages [Accessed 5 August 2025]

Duhn L., Medves J. (2018) A 5-facet framework to describe patient engagement in patient safety. *Health Expectations : An International Journal of Public Participation in Health Care and Health Policy*, 21; 6: 1122–1133. Available at: https://doi.org/10.1111/hex.12815

FDI World Dental Federation (2021) Infection prevention and control in dental practice. [Online] Available at: https://www.fdiworlddental.org/infection-prevention-and-control-dental-practice [Accessed 7 August 2025]

Ferlias N., Nielsen H., Andersen E., Stoustrup P. (2024) Lessons learnt on patient safety in dentistry through a 5-year nationwide database study on iatrogenic harm. *Scientific Reports*, 14; 1: Article 11436. Available at: https://doi.org/10.1038/s41598-024-62107-x

Fricton J., Rindal D. B., Rush W., Flottemesch, T., Vazquez G., Thoele M. J., Durand E., Enstad C., Rhodus N. (2011) The effect of electronic health records on the use of clinical care guidelines for patients with medically complex conditions. *The Journal of the American Dental Association*, 142; 10: 1133–1142. Available at: https://doi.org/10.14219/jada.archive.2011.0082

Glendon A. I., Stanton N. A. (2000) Perspectives on safety culture. *Safety Science*, 34; 1–3: 193–214. Available at: https://doi.org/10.1016/S0925-7535(00)00013-8

Green B., Parry D., Oeppen R., Plint S., Dale T., Brennan P. (2017) Situational awareness – what it means for clinicians, its recognition and importance in patient safety. *Oral Diseases*, 23; 6: 721–725. Available at: https://doi.org/10.1111/odi.12547

Gross B., Rusin L., Kiesewetter J., Zottmann J. M., Fischer M. R., Prückner S., Zech A. (2019) Crew resource management training in healthcare: a systematic review of intervention design, training conditions and evaluation. *BMJ Open* 9: e025247. Available at: https://doi.org/10.1136/bmjopen-2018-025247

Halligan M., Zecevic A. (2011) Safety culture in healthcare: a review of concepts, dimensions, measures and progress. *BMJ Quality & Safety*, 20; 4: 338–343. Available at: https://doi.org/10.1136/bmjqs.2010.040964

Health and Safety Executive (1999) *Reducing Error and Influencing Behaviour*. Norwich: The Stationery Office.

Helmreich R. L., Foushee H. C. (2019) Why CRM? Empirical and theoretical bases of human factors training. In Kanki B. G., Anca J. M., Chidester T. R. (Eds.), *Crew Resource Management*, pp. 3–52. Third edition. London: Academic Press.

Higgins M. C., Herpy J. P. (2021) Medical error, adverse events, and complications in interventional radiology: Liability or opportunity? *Radiology*, 298; 2: 275–283. Available at: https://doi.org/10.1148/radiol.2020202341

Ho J. C. Y., Chai H. H., Luo B. W., Lo E. C. M., Huang M. Z., Chu C. H. (2025) An overview of dentist–patient communication in quality dental care. *Dentistry Journal*, 13; 1: 31. Available at: https://doi.org/10.3390/dj13010031

Hofer T. P., Kerr E. A., Hayward R. A. (2000) What is an error?. *Effective Clinical Practice* 3; 6: 261–269. Available at: https://pubmed.ncbi.nlm.nih.gov/11151522/

Hollnagel E., Wears R. L., Braithwaite J. (2015) *From Safety-I to Safety-II: A White Paper. The Resilient Health Care Net.* University of Southern Denmark, University of Florida, USA, and Macquarie University, Australia. Available at: https://www.england.nhs.uk/signuptosafety/wp-content/uploads/sites/16/2015/10/safety-1-safety-2-whte-papr.pdf [Accessed 8 August 2025]

Howard-Thompson A., Hurdle A. C., Arnold L. B., Finch C. K., Sands C., Self T. H. (2008) Intracerebral haemorrhage secondary to a warfarin-metronidazole interaction. *The American Journal of Geriatric Pharmacotherapy,* 6; 1: 33–36. Available at: https://doi.org/10.1016/j.amjopharm.2008.03.003

Kishimoto N., Sanuki T., Liu Y., Tran S. D., Seo K. (2023) Simulation training for medical emergencies of dental patients: A review of the dental literature. *The Japanese Dental Science Review,* 59: 104–113. Available at: https://doi.org/10.1016/j.jdsr.2023.02.004

Kohn L. T., Corrigan J. M., Donaldson M. S. (Eds.). (2000) *To Err is Human: Building a Safer Health System.* Washington: National Academies Press. Available at: https://doi.org/10.17226/9728

Kristensen S., Bartels P. (2010) *Use of Patient Safety Culture Instruments and Recommendations.* Denmark: European Society for Quality in Healthcare – Office for Quality Indicators. Available at: https://seguridaddelpaciente.sanidad.gob.es/proyectos/participacionInternacional/docs/WP1-REPORT__Use_of__PSCI_and_recommandations_-_March__2010.pdf [Accessed 23 July 2025]

Larouzee J., Le Coze J. (2020) Good and bad reasons: The Swiss cheese model and its critics. *Safety Science,* 126: 104660. Available at: https://doi.org/10.1016/j.ssci.2020.104660

Lee J., Wickens C., Liu Y., Boyle L. (2017) *Designing for People: An Introduction to Human Factors Engineering.* North Charleston, SC: Createspace.

Lochmann J., Deaconu D., Czirfusz A. (2024) Stress in dental practices: A literature review of potential effects on patient care. *Clinical Social Work Journal / CWS,* 15; 3: 34–41. Available at: https://doi.org/10.22359/cswhi_15_3_05

McFadden K. L., Henagan S. C., Gowen C. R. (2009) The patient safety chain: Transformational leadership's effect on patient safety culture, initiatives, and outcomes. *Journal of Operations Management,* 27; 5: 390–404. Available at: https://doi.org/10.1016/j.jom.2009.01.001

Marx D. (2019) Patient safety and the just culture. *Obstetrics and Gynecology Clinics of North America,* 46; 2: 239–245. Available at: https://doi.org/10.1016/j.ogc.2019.01.003

Müller M., Jürgens J., Redaèlli M., Klingberg K., Hautz W. E., Stock S. (2018) Impact of the communication and patient hand-off tool SBAR on patient safety: A systematic review. *BMJ Open,* 8; 8: e 022202. Available at: https://doi.org/10.1136/bmjopen-2018-022202

Musa A., Witton R., Ali K., McColl E. (2025) A five-year retrospective analysis (2017–2022) of reported incidents from a primary care-based education provider. *British Dental Journal.* Available at: https://doi.org/10.1038/s41415-024-7952-0

Niv Y., Tal Y. (2024) *Patient Safety and Risk Management in Medicine: From Theory to Practice.* Cham, Switzerland: Springer.

O'Daniel M., Rosenstein A. H. (2008) Professional communication and team collaboration. In Hughes R. G. (Ed.), Patient *Safety and Quality: An Evidence-Based Handbook for Nurses*. Rockville, MD: Agency for Healthcare Research and Quality; Chapter 33. Available at: https://www.ncbi.nlm.nih.gov/books/NBK2637/

Obadan-Udoh E., Sundararajan V., Sanchez G. A., Howard R., Chandrupatla S., Worley D. (2024) Dental patients as partners in promoting quality and safety: A qualitative exploratory study. *BMC Oral Health,* 24; 1: Article 438. Available at: https://doi.org/10.1186/s12903-024-04030-1

Oriol M. D. (2006) Crew resource management: Applications in healthcare organizations. *The Journal of Nursing Administration* 36; 9: 402–406. Available at: https://www.jstor.org/stable/26818811

Pang Y., Szuecs A., Ricci-Cabello I., Gangannagaripalli J., Goh L. H., Leong F. L., Zhou L. F., Valderas J. (2025) Patient and family engagement interventions in primary care patient safety: Systematic review and meta-analysis of randomised controlled trials. *British Journal of General Practice.* E-print in advance of publication. Available at: https://doi.org/10.3399/bjgp.2024.0369

Pellegrino F. (2019) *The Just Culture Principles in Aviation Law: Towards a Safety-Oriented Approach.* Cham, Switzerland: Springer.

Pemberton M. N. (2014) Developing patient safety in dentistry. *British Dental Journal,* 217; 7: 335–337. Available at: https://doi.org/10.1038/sj.bdj.2014.856

Pinsky H. M., Taichman R. S., Sarment D. P. (2010) Adaptation of airline crew resource management principles to dentistry. *The Journal of the American Dental Association,* 141; 8: 1010–1018. Available at: https://doi.org/10.14219/jada.archive.2010.0316

Patra K. P., Jesus O. D. (2023) Sentinel event. [Updated 2023 Mar 29]. In: *StatPearls* [Online]. Treasure Island, FL: StatPearls Publishing. Available at: https://www.ncbi.nlm.nih.gov/sites/books/NBK564388/

Perneger T. V. (2005) The Swiss cheese model of safety incidents: Are there holes in the metaphor? *BMC Health Services Research* 5; 71. Available at: https://doi.org/10.1186/1472-6963-5-71

Quenon J.-L., Vacher A., Faget M., Levif-Lecourt M., Roberts T., Fucks I., Promé-Visinoni M., Cadot C., Bousigue J.-Y., Quintard B., Parneix P., Pourin C. (2020) Exploring the role of managers in the development of a safety culture in seven French healthcare facilities: A qualitative study. *BMC Health Services Research,* 20; 1: 517. Available at: https://doi.org/10.1186/s12913-020-05331-1

Reason J. (1990) *Human Error.* Cambridge: Cambridge University Press.

Reason J. (1997) *Managing the Risks of Organizational Accidents.* Aldershot: Ashgate.

Reason J. (2000) Human error: Models and management. *BMJ,* 320: 768-. Available at: https://doi.org/10.1136/bmj.320.7237.768

Renton T., Sabbah W. (2016) Review of never and serious events related to dentistry 2005–2014. *British Dental Journal,* 221; 2: 71–79. Available at: https://doi.org/10.1038/sj.bdj.2016.526

Russell S. L., Greenblatt A. P., Gomes D., Birenz S., Golembeski C. A., Shelley D., McGuirk M., Eisenberg E., Northridge M. E. (2015) Toward implementing primary care at chairside: Developing a clinical decision support system for dental hygienists. *The Journal of Evidence-Based Dental Practice,* 15; 4: 145–151. Available at: https://doi.org/10.1016/j.jebdp.2015.08.003

Sammer C. E., Lykens K., Singh K. P., Mains D. A., Lackan N. A. (2010) What is patient safety culture? A review of the literature. *Journal of Nursing Scholarship,* 42: 156–165. Available at: https://pubmed.ncbi.nlm.nih.gov/20618600/

Seager L., Smith D. W., Patel A., Brunt H., Brennan P. A. (2013) Applying aviation factors to oral and maxillofacial surgery – the human element. *British Journal of Oral & Maxillofacial Surgery,* 51; 1: 8–13. Available at: https://doi.org/10.1016/j.bjoms.2011.11.024

Siriwatana K., Pongpanich S. (2025) Developing and evaluating a dental incident reporting system: A user-centered approach to risk management. *BMC Oral Health,* 25; 1: Article 339. Available at: https://doi.org/10.1186/s12903-025-05729-5

Stahel P. F., Mauffrey C. (2014) *Patient Safety in Surgery.* London: Springer-Verlag.

Stelfox H. T., Palmisani S., Scurlock C., Orav E. J., Bates W. W. (2006) The "To Err is Human" report and the patient safety literature. *BMJ Quality & Safety,* 15: 174–178. Available at: https://doi.org/10.1136/qshc.2006.017947

St. Pierre M., Grawe P., Bergstrom J., Neuhaus C. (2022) 20 years after To Err Is Human: A bibliometric analysis of 'the IOM report's' impact on research on patient safety. *Safety Science,* 147: 105593. Available at: https://doi.org/10.1016/j.ssci.2021.105593

Teoh L., McCullough M., Moses G. (2022) Preventing medication errors in dental practice: An Australian perspective. *Journal of Dentistry,* 119: 104086. Available at: https://doi.org/10.1016/j.jdent.2022.104086

Thanathornwong B., Suebnukarn S., Ouivirach K. (2023) Clinical decision support system for geriatric dental treatment using a Bayesian network and a convolutional neural network. *Healthcare Informatics Research,* 29; 1: 23–30. Available at: https://doi.org/10.4258/hir.2023.29.1.23

Thorat V., Rao P., Joshi N., Talreja P., Shetty A. R. (2024) Role of Artificial Intelligence (AI) in patient education and communication in dentistry. *Curēus,* 16; 5: e59799. Available at: https://doi.org/10.7759/cureus.59799

Tjia J., Mazor K. M., Field T., Meterko V., Spenard A., Gurwitz J. H. (2009) Nurse-physician communication in the long-term care setting. *Journal of Patient Safety* 5; 3: 145–152. Available at: https://doi.org/10.1097/pts.0b013e3181b53f9b

Todd D. W., Schaefer J. J. (2018) The American Association of Oral and Maxillofacial Surgeons simulation program. *Oral and Maxillofacial Surgery Clinics of North America*, 30; 2: 195–206. Available at: https://doi.org/10.1016/j.coms.2018.01.007

Tokede O., Walji M., Ramoni R., Rindal D. B., Worley D., Hebballi N., Kumar K., van Strien C., Chen, M., Navat-Pelli S., Liu H., Etolue J., Yansane A., Obadan-Udoh E., Easterday, C., Enstad, C., Kane, S., Rush, W., Kalenderian E. (2017) Quantifying dental office–originating adverse events: The dental practice study methods. *Journal of Patient Safety*, 17; 8: 1080–1087. Available at: https://doi.org/10.1097/pts.0000000000000444

Verhagen M. J., de Vos M. S., Sujan M., Hamming, J. F. (2022) The problem with making Safety-II work in healthcare. *BMJ Quality & Safety*, 31; 5: 402–408. Available at: https://doi.org/10.1136/bmjqs-2021-014396

Walshaw E., Mannion C. J. (2018) Dentists are humans too – education in human factors within dental care. *British Dental Journal*, 224; 11: 901–904. Available at: https://doi.org/10.1038/sj.bdj.2018.438

World Health Organization (2011) *Patient Safety Curriculum Guide: Multi-Professional Edition*. Geneva: World Health Organization. Available at: https://www.who.int/publications/i/item/9789241501958 [Accessed 12 July 2024]

World Health Organisation (2016) *Human Factors: Technical Series on Safer Primary Care*. Geneva: World Health Organization. Available at: https://iris.who.int/bitstream/handle/10665/252273/9789241511612-eng.pdf;sequence=1

World Health Organisation (2023) *Patient Safety Fact Sheet*. Geneva, Switzerland: World Health Organisation. [Online] Available at: https://www.who.int/news-room/fact-sheets/detail/patient-safety [Accessed 14/06/2025]

World Health Organisation (2024) *Global Patient Safety Report 2024*. Geneva: World Health Organization.

Yamalik N., Perea Pérez B. (2012) Patient safety and dentistry: What do we need to know? Fundamentals of patient safety, the safety culture and implementation of patient safety measures in dental practice. *International Dental Journal*, 62; 4: 189–196. Available at: https://doi.org/10.1111/j.1875-595x.2012.00119.x

Chapter 3

Audit

Introduction

Clinical Audit is a structured approach to improving the quality of care and has been used for many years (Butler, 1958). It applies to both clinical care and to associated processes such as the management of records and call and recall processes. Audit is part of the clinical governance process of any clinical service (MacCarrick, 2014, Patel and Jenkyn, 2021). In an audit a team:

- Considers what standard it wants to reach in a particular area of work.
- Compares its current performance to this standard.
- If the standard is not met, the team considers what may be preventing them from reaching the desired standard.
- Take steps to adjust their work to address the identified issues.
- Measures their performance again to complete the audit cycle, and to see what further work may be required.

Audit is used to assess and improve the quality of care, to comply with regulatory standards, and to increase efficiency. Audit can be conducted as a single process, or as part of a wider approach to quality improvement (Iver *et al.*, 2012). An audit reviews clinical, administrative, or financial practices to find strengths and areas for improvement and can link into other governance arrangements (Cannell, 2005). Audits help healthcare providers uphold care standards, lower risks and ensure accountability by reviewing data, policies and procedures. They promote transparency, efficient resource use and improved patient outcomes. Taking part in audit also allows practices to demonstrate the attention they pay to delivering safe, high-quality services (Hook, 2020).

Audit has become increasingly recognised in dentistry. In the United Kingdom (UK), all countries have requirements for dentists to complete audit activities, although arrangements differ depending on the country. The UK-based Dental Defence Union highlights the importance of audit in dentistry (Dental Defence Union, 2022) and states that 'Clinical audits and peer reviews

DOI: 10.4324/9781003493532-3

are central to effective quality assurance. They help make sure best practice is being followed and highlight any improvements in providing care'.

Experience of Audit in Dental Care

Audit has been widely used by dental services. Hospitals and dental schools were early adopters of audit, probably because of their existing structures and availability of academic staff. Many audits have used the work of dental students and practices in dental hospitals as subjects. Some examples of audits conducted in dental education settings are shown in Table 3.1. All involve aspects of patient safety. Some other university department work described as audits included only establishing baseline measurement, so do not complete the audit cycle discussed in more detail later in the chapter.

Examples of audits in other dental settings are shown in Table 3.2. This table presents a small but typical selection of published dental audits. Patient safety is again the major area of work. Topics published are on well-known issues that will be familiar in all countries. In both Table 3.1 and Table 3.2, the standards used are in the main from national and international guidelines, often modified to produce a checklist that can be used to gather data. When no guidelines are available, services have created their own checklist based on published literature and the most relevant guidelines.

Most dental audit cycles, particularly those conducted outside dental academic settings, are not published. This limits the wider impact of audits and the sharing of experience, although this

Table 3.1 Examples of audits conducted in dental education settings

Reference	*Setting*	*Issue*	*Standard*	*Notes*
Chong *et al.*, 2015	International Medical University, Kuala Lumpur, Malaysia.	Record keeping by students.	Record keeping standards developed by students and adapted so record keeping could be rated.	The work included creating an agreed standard, which then provided a baseline for audit.
Fong *et al.*, 2018	International Medical University, Kuala Lumpur, Malaysia.	Root canal treatment and record keeping.	Standards adapted from guidelines by the European Society of Endodontology and turned into a checklist.	Linked to training in audit and conducted in a series of audits over four years.
Stevenson, Waterhouse and Rogers, 2025	Newcastle Dental Hospital, England.	Airway protection during Hall procedure.	Two objective measures derived from Hall technique user guide.	Observations by trainers. Improvement from cycle 1 to cycle 2, 3rd cycle planned.

Table 3.2 Examples of audits in dental practice

Reference	*Setting*	*Issue*	*Standard*	*Notes*
Chate *et al.*, 2006.	General Dental Practice, Eastern England, UK.	Antibiotic prescribing.	UK Faculty of General Dental Practitioners and Royal College of Surgeons antibiotic prescribing guidelines.	43% reduction in prescriptions following feedback and an educational intervention. Another audit cycle was planned.
Shafie *et al.*, 2012	Oral and Maxillofacial Department, Homerton Hospital and referring General Dental Practices, UK.	Referral letters to an Oral and Maxillofacial Department from General Dental Practitioners.	No set standard available. Team created a standard based on published reports and relevant guidelines. Created a checklist from the standard.	General Dental Practitioners were not involved in the design. A restructured referral form resulted in improvements in the data provided.
Simons and Williams, 2013.	Community Dental Service, London, UK.	Root canal treatment.	Self-developed audit tool using European Society of Endodontology Guidelines.	The re-audit to complete the cycle was seven years after the initial audit and intervention.
Yesudian *et al.*, 2015.	Three hospital paediatric dental departments in Liverpool, Manchester and Sheffield, UK.	Antibiotic prescribing.	Standards based on three national and international guidelines.	Prescription appropriateness increased from 28% in the first cycle, to 71% in the third audit cycle.
Anwar and Waring, 2017	University Dental Hospital of Manchester, UK.	Wrong tooth extraction.	Based on British Orthodontic Society and Dental Defence Union recommendations.	Five audit cycles with a worsening of performance before improvements in cycles 3–5.

(*Continued*)

Table 3.2 Continued

Reference	*Setting*	*Issue*	*Standard*	*Notes*
Heggie, 2019.	General Dental Practice, Manchester, UK.	Appropriate triaging of emergency appointments, and timing of appointments.	National standard, modified to account for patient refusal of first available appointment. Standard 1: 90% of patients with urgent conditions should be seen within the 24-hour period defined Standard 2: 80% of patients allocated urgent appointments should attend with urgent or emergency conditions.	Created a flowchart to guide receptionists.
Goff *et al.*, 2022.	Private practice dentists, United States.	Antibiotic stewardship.	No definitive statement available so based on information from the dental literature, and information from systematic reviews.	Included individual feedback to dentists as well as group feedback. Statistically significant improvements after an educational intervention.
Dhamdhere *et al.*, 2023.	Sharad Pawar Dental College, Wardha, India.	Handwashing and glove donning before minor dental surgical procedures.	Used WHO handwashing and glove donning guidelines, modified into a checklist.	Percentage of clinicians performing adequate hand hygiene increased by 40%.
Tadin *et al.*, 2024	Hospital and private practice sites, Split, Croatia.	Oral hygiene in orthodontic patients.	Developed yes/no criteria based on an evidence review.	Interventions delivered by dentists at chair side. Significant improvements in the follow-up audit.

does not diminish their value to individual teams and practices (Simons and Williams, 2013). Larger organisations can develop an organisational resilience that allows audit to continue over time. The University of Manchester and the University Dental Hospital of Manchester described a long-term use of audit as part of their clinical governance process (Ashley *et al.,* 2014). The University created an audit committee which reports into their clinical effectiveness structure. Their arrangements, a good example of a well-developed audit programme integrated with clinical governance, are shown in Box 3.1.

BOX 3.1 UNIVERSITY DENTAL HOSPITAL OF MANCHESTER/ UNIVERSITY OF MANCHESTER AUDIT STRUCTURE

- A central Dental Clinical Audit Committee that reports to a service-wide audit committee that in turn reports to a service clinical effectiveness committee.
- Each staff group and dental speciality is represented on the Dental Clinical Audit Committee.
- Audit projects from each area are agreed with the committee.
- Projects align with the organisations' clinical effectiveness priorities and are of interest to staff.
- Committee produces a biannual newsletter.
- Days four times a year when there is no clinical work, and projects are presented to the whole organisation as part of an audit and clinical effectiveness day.

Source: Ashley *et al.,* 2014

Some dental schools have increased undergraduate exposure to audit. At the University of Cardiff, a group audit project for final-year students was introduced in 2002 (Lynch *et al.*, 2011) and there are similar arrangements at the University of Manchester (Ashley *et al.*, 2014). The International Medical University, Kuala Lumpur, Malaysia, introduced training in audit for fourth- and fifth-year students (Chong *et al.*, 2014),

In the UK new dentists complete an audit as part of their foundation or vocational training year, the first year after graduation. Dentists may undertake a cycle of an ongoing audit or audit a new topic with the agreement of the practice. Off the shelf audits are often regarded as dull, but auditing a new topic involves the new dentist in more decision-making on standards, data collection and analysis (Thornley et al., 2015, 2017). Recent surveys suggest that dentists working in England find the audit process manageable, although survey response rates are low (Jayawardena *et al.*, 2024, Mordi, 2024).

Integrating audit into practice in individual practices has the advantage that there are fewer staff to involve and decision-making power is often held by the practice owner and senior staff. The more difficult aspects are that there is unlikely to be any staff member with dedicated time for audit, except perhaps a practice manager. It is also more difficult to access technical advice on standards, data analysis and audit methods than is often the case in a larger organisation, particularly in a university setting.

Important Considerations in Audit

This section summarises issues around conducting a baseline audit and discusses the value of an audit team. Further practical information on both these topics is included later in the chapter. Information in Chapters 5 and 6 is also relevant to the topic.

Definition and Purpose of a Baseline

As noted above, many publications report a 'baseline audit'. This is not a complete audit but forms the foundation for later work. The concept of baseline data is used extensively in all quality improvement work and is discussed further in Chapters 5 and 6. Many published studies do not progress beyond a descriptive baseline audit, so they are distinct from the idea of an audit cycle where changes are made and the work is re-audited.

In healthcare audits, a baseline is the starting position used to compare to the standard and to future performance. A baseline is essential as it serves as a reference for an organisation's current practices, processes and outcomes. This benchmark allows healthcare providers to identify areas of strength and those needing improvement, facilitating a more targeted and effective audit process. In some organisations, this may be done by using a benchmarking process by which organisational performance is systematically compared to norms, often set by external agencies (Willmington *et al.*, 2022). By understanding where they currently stand, healthcare organisations can better assess the impact of changes and interventions over time.

Methods for Establishing a Baseline

Healthcare audits often start by reviewing routinely collected historical data. This has the advantage that it is readily available or at least accessible. Information can often be obtained through electronic databases or existing spreadsheets. Depending on the topic of interest, the information used could include waiting times; patient numbers in a session; antibiotic prescriptions; use of treatment types; test results; patient outcomes; compliance rates, or in some types of audit work, financial metrics which may also be used as a balancing measure (Stark *et al.*, 2026). If the data are collected but not routinely presented, help may be needed to output it from an electronic system. Once this is available, however, the ongoing collection of the data usually means that future comparisons will be straightforward.

In some cases, the information does not exist and must be obtained from scratch. Information on processes and current practice can be obtained by talking to staff and stakeholders and by conducting surveys, interviews, or focus groups. Focus groups and one-to-one interviews are more likely to be used by specialist quality improvement staff who have the time, training and experience, but surveys are now straightforward to conduct using apps.

Some new data collection may be required to identify current performance. This can be conducted using paper records, spreadsheets or databases, or in more complex audits, for example in a corporate group or hospital, using bespoke software. An example of a single practice audit using a shared spreadsheet is presented later in this chapter. Whether the method of collection is paper-based or electronic it is important to have clear definitions of what is being counted, and agreement on how it will be collected, and by whom. If using electronic data, the team needs to take some time to be sure that the data being accessed is showing what they want it to show.

Impact of Baseline on Audit Outcomes

A strong baseline is essential for audits, as it allows practices to track progress and assess the impact of changes. Without a reliable baseline, it is difficult to determine if there is an improvement to performance as the team may not agree on the original performance. Taking the time to agree on what is being measured and involving the team in the review of the data helps to avoid any later controversy about the nature of the starting position. The length of the baseline needed depends on the issue and on the circumstances of the audit. No team wants to expend more effort than required on a baseline audit, but it is worth taking the time to ensure that the data feels representative to the team, and that there is confidence in it. For example, a one-week period of data collection when a key staff member is on annual leave can leave uncertainty about whether the period was appropriately representative. On the other hand, letting a baseline audit drag on can sap staff enthusiasm and reduce interest, so compromises may be required to agree on a period that feels reasonable to the team.

In complex situations, for example in a corporate dental practice covering many sites or a hospital with multiple dental clinics or even multiple locations across a hospital chain, creating a longer agreed baseline can be very helpful. For example, there may be systematic differences between sites, or issues affecting some locations but not others that will need to be considered when agreeing the interpretation of the information and the required actions. In other situations, there may be existing trends that a service wants to consider. In these less common situations, it makes sense to take advice from an audit specialist or improvement adviser.

Establishing the Team in Healthcare Audits

The audit process in healthcare necessarily involves a clinical team, each member playing a vital role in ensuring the success of the work (Ullman *et al.*, 2018). The mixture of stakeholders will be different depending on the setting. Large hospitals will have different processes and aims compared to smaller dental settings. Independent dental practices, corporate-owned practice groups and community or hospital dental settings all operate differently. Key stakeholders may include:

1. **Healthcare Providers:** Clinicians, dental nurses, dental therapists and hygienists participate in clinical audits to assess care quality and highlight areas for improvement. They will have a good understanding of clinical guidelines and patient needs.
2. **Administrative Staff:** Administrators, receptionists and managers can have important insights into problems and play an essential role in improving processes. They help to implement audit recommendations, ensure policy compliance and support the audit process.
3. **Quality Improvement Staff and Teams:** Larger organisations such as hospitals and corporate groups may have specialist quality improvement staff. These staff, sometimes working in multidisciplinary teams, are responsible for evaluating and improving patient care, safety and service quality. They commonly conduct clinical audits, analyse the resulting findings and help the service to create and implement improvement plans.
4. **Regulatory Bodies:** Organisations like the Quality Care Commission (QCC) and National Institute for Health and Clinical Excellence (NICE) in the UK set standards and guidelines for healthcare providers, ensuring compliance through audits. Most countries have similar organisations which often require evidence that dental services meet the requisite standards. In some very large organisations, regulatory bodies may be directly involved in

commissioning or even participating in audit processes, but for most services their role is in recommending or requiring topics and, in some cases, receiving results.

5. **Patients:** Patients are central to audits in healthcare and should benefit from the outcomes of audit activities. Their feedback and experience contribute to the audit process and help identify areas for potential improvement when appropriate.

Stages of an Audit Cycle

Audit is a cycle of activities that combine to produce change (Hook, 2020). The important point is that a baseline audit is not done for its own sake, but rather to contribute to an improvement process. Figure 3.1 shows the stages of an audit cycle.

1. Identify a Topic

Choosing an audit topic should be considered carefully. Any audit takes time and effort, so the topic should be of sufficient potential benefit in the environment it is being conducted to ensure resources are being spent wisely and that teams will be sufficiently engaged. If an audit topic feels esoteric or focused only on a management concern unrelated to direct clinical care, staff are less likely to invest in the project. Looking at areas of high volume, high risk or high cost and at issues which staff feel are important helps both management support and staff engagement (Benjamin, 2008). In a dental setting, most audits will have a direct impact on patient outcomes by improving safety and results. Many audits are set against national service frameworks, published guidelines, or regulatory requirements.

In the UK, for example, there are various bodies that affect the funding or licensing of dental practices. In England, the independent regulator is the Care Quality Commission (Care Quality

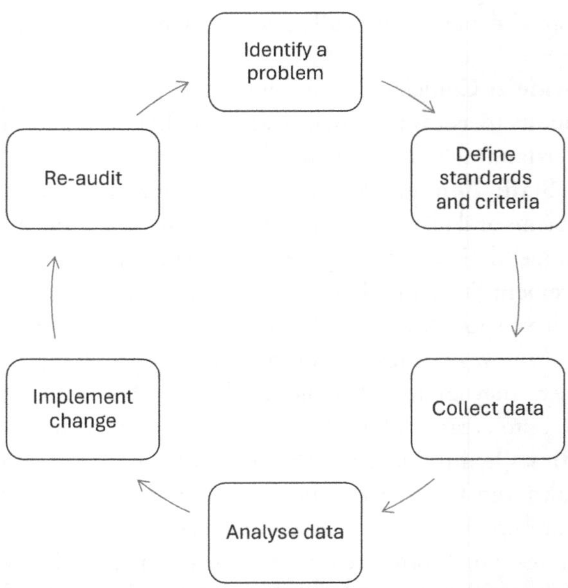

Figure 3.1 Stages of an audit cycle

Commission, 2022). The Care Quality Commission's compulsory audit topics for dental services that it regulates are (Care Quality Commission, 2024):

- Infection prevention (decontamination) and control.
- X-ray taking and reporting.
- Accessibility to the practice.

There are also topics that are recommended and classed as 'desirable' by the Care Quality Commission, which include:

- Antimicrobial prescribing.
- Clinical record keeping.
- Other audit topics suitable for the practice.

These are likely to be familiar topics to dental services in all countries and working within all funding arrangements. Precise requirements will vary by setting, but the main issues identified above will resonate in other countries. The important last point on the list, that there may be other topics which are of interest and importance to practices, should be kept in mind. Practices can audit their own topics rather than always working off a preset list. Early work in audit will be most effective when there is wide local interest in the topic, even if it is not part of a national or local requirement. Whatever the topic chosen, both team interest and results are likely to be greatest when there is a persuasive evidence base for benefit from improving performance in that area (National Institute for Clinical Excellence, 2002).

This is a good stage at which to establish the team described earlier that will lead the audit. In an individual dental practice, this might be made up of only a few people; for example, the practice owner, a clinician with an interest in patient safety and quality improvement, and the practice manager or head nurse. In larger practices, hospitals or corporate settings, a larger team may be required. In very large audit projects, for example covering multiple sites, there may need to be a central coordinating team and a small local group at each participating site.

In a single dental practice, although clinicians or managers are likely to take responsibility for running the audit cycle, if other members of the team are likely to be affected by the results, it is important to involve them. If appropriate, it can also be helpful to include a patient's input, depending on the topic chosen (Kelson, 1998).

2. Define Standards and Criteria

Clinical audits require comparison to an explicit standard (National Institute for Clinical Excellence, 2002). This means that the dental team need to identify a performance standard to which they can compare their practice, and which they can measure objectively. Box 3.2 gives factors to consider when selecting a performance standard. In the UK, there are national guidelines for infection control in dental surgeries; guidance on radiographs and radiation exposure; antibiotic prescribing guidelines; requirements for control of hazardous substances, and so on. Similar requirements and guidance are often country-specific but tend to cover very similar ground because they are based on the same evidence.

For technical dental issues, there are often guidelines from national professional organisations that can be accessed relating to topics such as endodontics, aesthetics, etc. There may also be requirements from funding or regulatory bodies that can be applied, such as requirements in record keeping and billing. In some instances, the topic will not have a guideline. One can often be constructed by reviewing published literature, but other topics may require the service to agree its own standard, such as waiting times, if not covered by other guidance. Once a standard is agreed, it can be split into smaller, more manageable objectives which improve a process with the aim of gradually shifting an outcome, if that is required.

BOX 3.2 SELECTING CRITERIA FOR AN AUDIT

- The audit can use process or outcome measures. Select what fits best with the project.
- Explicit criteria – something that can be measured.
- Practical and easy to review.
- Relate to an issue that feels important to staff.
- Make use of evidence-based materials such as published papers, guidelines and standards.
- If no standard is available, for example waiting times for non-urgent private appointments, consider conducting a baseline audit and then deciding on a practice standard.
- Apply SMART principles – Specific, Measurable, Achievable, Relevant, Timely.
- Consider exclusion and inclusion criteria. Are some people to be excluded from the audit, for example, children? Is it only to apply to people with a specific condition?

Source: Adapted from Hearnshaw *et al., 2001,* Hearnshaw *et al.,* 2002, National Institute for Clinical Excellence, 2002, HSE National Centre for Clinical Audit, 2025.

3. Collect Data

Data collection needs to be as straightforward as possible. It may be possible to extract information from routinely collected data, for example via an electronic patient record system. If this is the case, the team still requires explicit agreement on how this will be done, what will be extracted, for what period and by whom. If routine data can be used, then baseline data can be produced from historical data which speeds up the process.

Patient confidentiality needs to be protected using the organisation's usual policies. Patient identifiable data should not be collected unless there is an agreed and unavoidable need. If, exceptionally, patient identifiable data is required, it should be kept carefully and destroyed as soon as possible. Organisations and countries will have specific data protection requirements that should be consulted.

In a clinical audit, staff confidentiality also becomes an issue. It is usually best to collect data that can be linked to individual clinicians so that they can access their individual data for their personal review and if it is needed in revalidation processes. This does not mean that individually identifiable information must be shared in every case. Some teams may be comfortable with this, but when starting out in audit it can be helpful to present combined group data and to provide each individual clinician with their own data until they have confidence in the process.

As discussed above, if collecting the data specifically for the audit, this can be done electronically, using a database or spreadsheet, or on paper. There is no need to overcomplicate an audit. If a sheet at the reception desk allows collection of the data, adding electronic data collection may bring no benefit other than saving on later data entry. If using paper, a sheet can be drawn up and used.

The parameters of the audit need to be set before data can be collected. A set time-frame that the data will be collected should be agreed. This can be based on the expected number of patients/cases/incidents that will occur and that the team agree is sufficient to allow them to make decisions. The time agreed needs to be long enough for an adequate amount of information to be collected. The recording period should not be so long that it interferes with making required improvements.

Other methods of collecting data include conducting interviews, observing clinical or administrative work, or reviewing documents, depending on the topic. These methods are more likely to be used in other types of quality improvement projects, although case note and record review can be a good way of conducting some audits, with staff knowledge and agreement.

The more clarity on data collection in advance, the less the confusion that is likely to occur when the audit is underway. Piloting a data collection form or other method with one staff member, revising it and then checking it with one or two others, often reveals unidentified problems. These are usually resolved by minor changes to a form and by amending instructions on data collection. A well-designed and straightforward data collection tool or sheet can ensure consistency among all dental professionals involved, simplifying the process of gathering, organising and comparing data.

Being clear on who will collect the data, and when, is essential. The team also needs to know where completed forms should be taken, or who will collect them. The time required for data collection must feel proportionate to the importance of the topic. If staff know the data collection period is for a particular length of time, it is generally straightforward to obtain cooperation, particularly when the team has been involved in agreeing the topic and setting the standard.

4. Analyse the Data

The method of analysis can be agreed in advance. Knowing how the data will be used helps to clarify what needs to be collected and avoids recording information that is not required for the audit. Measurement is discussed in more detail in Chapter 7. Most audits involve a comparison against the pre-defined standards and criteria. This means the result is often a percentage or series of percentages that can be compared to the standard. Bar charts are often suitable.

All members of staff who participated in the audit should be included in the review of the audit results. Any other relevant stakeholders, such as a practice manager and owner, can also be involved. A practice meeting can be organised to review the audit findings, discuss potential solutions and brainstorm ideas for improvement. The team can agree on what changes to implement, apply them, and then re-audit to see if there has been an improvement. Educational measures are often applied. It is also common to find system issues that affect the results, such as issues with data systems, booking arrangements, and case mix. The team should take time to consider what may be influencing the results and to consider countermeasures.

5. Implement change

Audit improvement plans are essential for translating findings into actionable steps that enhance patient care and operational efficiency. Once the audit analysis stage identifies gaps or areas for improvement, a structured plan is developed to address these issues. The primary focus of changes made is to improve the process to bring the results closer to the agreed standard. This plan typically includes specific, measurable goals, timelines for implementation and assigned responsibilities to ensure accountability. Strategies may involve staff training, redesigning processes, policy updates, or introducing new technologies. Regular monitoring and evaluation help to track progress and ensure effective changes. By fostering a culture of continuous improvement, dental practices can meet regulatory standards and deliver higher-quality care, improve patient outcomes and optimise resource utilisation.

6. Re-Audit

Clinical audit is a cyclical process, making the final step of the audit cycle essential. The re-audit phase is required to demonstrate that improvements in clinical practice and the quality of patient care have been achieved and maintained.

In some cases, the changes implemented may not be sufficient to meet the standards or guidelines. When this occurs, the audit cycle should be repeated: data should be re-analysed, further changes should be introduced and another re-audit should be conducted. If the standards were significantly unmet or patient safety concerns were identified, the time interval between audits should be shortened to ensure a quick resolution. This process is often called an audit spiral as it is a series of cycles leading to improvement rather than a single iteration.

Audit is an ongoing process fundamental to the continuous improvement of patient care. Changes implemented in the audit process can be regularly reviewed to ensure they are still in place and that the desired standards are sustained long-term. This continual monitoring helps maintain high-quality care and supports the long-term success of the improvements made.

Example of an Audit in General Dental Practice

This section describes an audit in general dental practice. At the time of the audit, the practice had three regular dentists, all of whom worked in the practice at least three days a week. There was one dental therapist and one hygienist, both of whom worked five days a week. A specialist dentist visited the practice once a fortnight to place implants. The dentists and the dental therapist always occupied the same treatment rooms. The hygienist sometimes used different rooms depending on availability. Where possible, each dentist or therapist worked with a single dental nurse.

As described earlier, audits can be conducted for many reasons ranging from mandatory audits required by regulators to issues identified in individual practices. In practice, these often overlap as many of the issues of concern to regulators are equally important to individual clinicians. Some of the methods discussed in Chapter 5, 'Scoping a Problem', can be applied in audit, for example, when deciding what matters to prioritise.

Using the steps in the audit process described above:

1. **Identification of a Problem**

The team met to discuss possible topics for audit in a session arranged by a dentist with an interest in audit and quality improvement. Staff members, including dentists, nurses, hygienists, therapists and the practice manager and administrator, were encouraged to think about any areas of clinical care that caused them concern and to be ready to describe them at the meeting. The visiting implant specialist was not included in this meeting.

Seven ideas for audits were identified. After discussion, the team focused on the proportions of diagnostically acceptable and unacceptable x-ray exposures. Several team members had the same concern that unacceptable radiographs were sometimes processed. This resulted in unneeded radiation exposure to patients when an x-ray had to be repeated and required additional clinical time. As the topic impacted all clinical staff, the team agreed that all clinicians and dental nurses would participate in the work.

2. **Define Standards and Criteria**

As noted above, conducting an audit requires the service to decide what standard it is going to use as its benchmark. Following the points that a standard, where possible, should be widely accepted and evidence-based, the team decided to use the UK Faculty of General Dental Practice standard. The faculty recommends that 90% of film radiographs taken should be diagnostically acceptable (Horner and Eaton, 2018). Their definitions and recommended targets are (Horner and Eaton, 2018, p. 111):

- Excellent – no errors of exposure, positioning or processing. Target, not less than 70%.
- Diagnostically acceptable – some errors of exposure, positioning or processing, but no impact on the diagnostic utility of the radiograph. Target, not greater than 20%.
- Unacceptable – errors of exposure, positioning, or processing that make the radiograph diagnostically unacceptable. Target, not greater than 10%.

These standards are set to limit the number of re-exposures taken by clinicians while also taking into consideration that not all radiographs will be acceptable on the first attempt due to issues such as machine faults, poor cooperation from patients or miscommunication. The aim is to ensure the radiation dose to patients is 'as low as reasonably possible', or 'ALARP' (Stabin, 2007). Radiographs can be imperfect while still being considered diagnostically acceptable, if all required information is gained through the exposure. For example, if the collimator cuts off a small segment of the film when exposed but this section was not the area being investigated then the film is still able to contribute to an accurate and informed diagnosis.

The team agreed to focus their work on the standard that unacceptable x-rays constitute no more than 10% of all radiographs taken. Once this standard was met, the team felt they could move on to work to improve overall quality. The focus on unacceptable radiographs was because of the resulting increased radiation dose for patients and time for clinicians.

3. **Collect Data**

A holiday period was upcoming, which would decrease data collection. To obtain useful data, the team decided to run the baseline audit for two months. The surgeries of four clinicians would be included: that of the three regular dentists and the dental therapist. The team elected not to include the implant dentist in this round of the audit, as their work constituted a small proportion of the day-to-day work of the practice.

A simple, easy-to-navigate spreadsheet was created (Figure 3.2). All clinical staff at the practice had access to the spreadsheet through the practice computer network. Four tabs were set up in the spreadsheet, one for each surgery contributing. Dental nurses were shown how to complete the spreadsheet and asked to record information for every radiograph exposure the clinician made:

- The date.
- Patient ID number to allow further review if required.
- The type of radiograph taken.

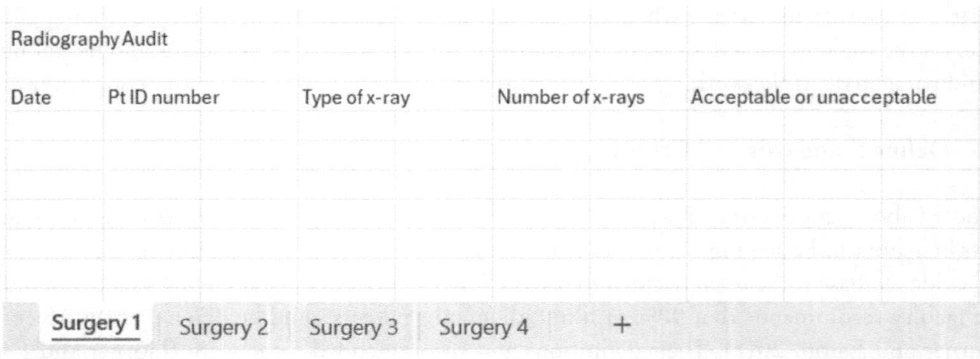

Figure 3.2 Spreadsheet used for data collection

- How many radiographs were taken.
- Whether the clinicians decided the radiograph was acceptable or diagnostically unacceptable after they reviewed the film.

The team discussed whether peer review of each dentist's decisions on acceptability was required. The team were used to working with one another and often talked over clinical problems and reviewed incidents. They decided that for the first round of the audit, each dentist's decision on acceptability would be satisfactory. When the team progressed to look at the more nuanced decision of which radiographs were graded as excellent in a later audit phase, then a peer review process might be required.

4. **Analyse the Data**

After two months, the dentist with a particular interest in quality improvement collated the results. The data collected in the spreadsheet was formatted into a bar chart to show the results (Figure 3.3). The chart was split into four columns showing the results from each surgery/clinician. The data was divided into three types of radiographs taken – bitewings, anterior periapical and posterior periapical. The results showed that surgeries 1 and 3 achieved the 90% standard for all three categories of radiographs taken.

Surgery 2 fell short of the standard with anterior periapical radiographs by 5%. Surgery 4 fell short on both anterior and posterior periapical radiographs by 7% and 5%, respectively. There is more variation in smaller numbers. It would have been possible to calculate confidence intervals for the proportions, but the dentist felt that, because of the team's unfamiliarity with the technique, it would probably make interpretation more rather than less difficult. They decided to leave it as unadjusted percentages and to share it with the team.

A practice meeting was held with all clinical staff, the practice manager and practice principal dentist in attendance. The clinicians and dental nurses discussed any difficulties in taking radiographs and were encouraged to be transparent in a non-judgemental setting.

Surgery two was occupied by the Vocational Trainee dentist who had recently graduated. The trainee explained that they struggled to take anterior periapical radiographs and felt that they had not been taught an adequate technique at dental school. As a newly qualified dentist, they

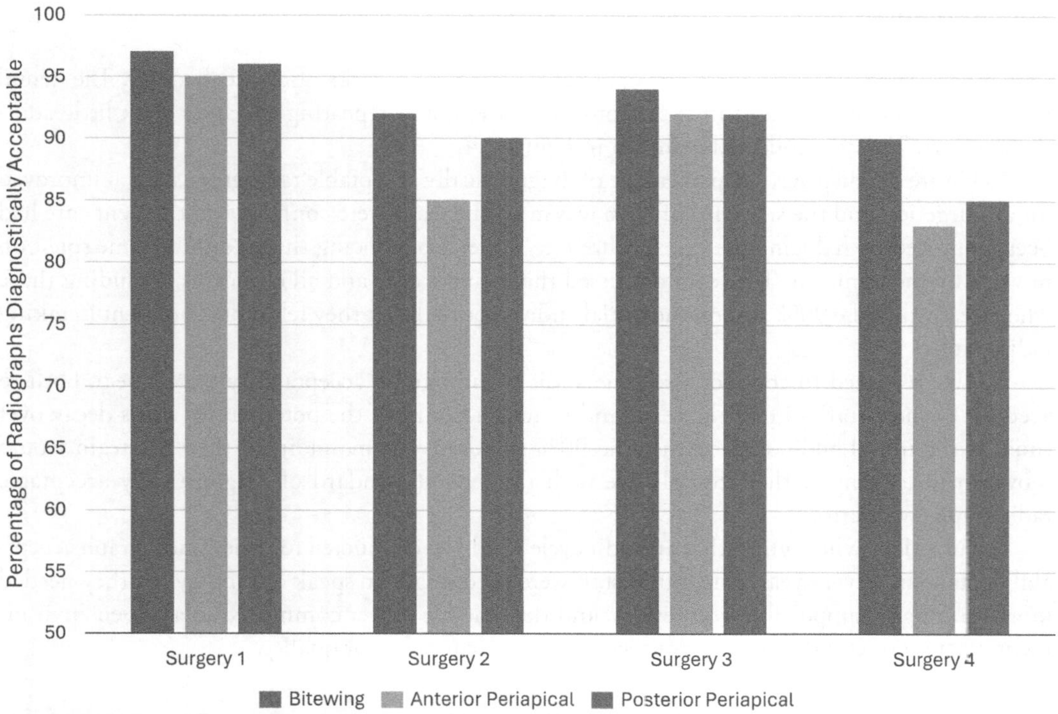

Figure 3.3 Diagnostically acceptable radiographs by surgery baseline audit

had not raised this spontaneously for fear that they would be judged and that it would harm their reputation with the rest of the clinical team. The clinician who worked in surgery four was the dental therapist. They explained that they regularly took bitewing radiographs but did not take many periapical radiographs. They felt that this contributed to the higher rate of repetition of these x-rays. The group discussed the findings and felt that while the highest results met the standard, there was scope to improve in all the groups. The team agreed that they would prioritise further education in radiograph techniques, combined with encouraging less experienced staff to ask for help when required.

5. Implement Change

The practice owner arranged for all the clinicians to attend a radiography refresher session that was being held in the nearest city the following month. This was paid for by the practice principal. The training included hands-on training by a dental radiographer to improve technique in all types of intra-oral radiographs. The clinicians were encouraged to take photos, videos and notes of the techniques used and asked the radiographer questions on how to overcome difficult situations. Once the training session had concluded, the team talked over what they had learned and agreed what changes they would put into practice.

The dentist with an interest in quality improvement produced a report that summarised the initial audit findings, described the training that had been undertaken and developed an action plan. The team reviewed and agreed the action plan at their next meeting and agreed to apply what they had learnt from the following week, and to re-audit.

6. **Re-audit**

One month later, a second audit was conducted, using four weeks of data collection. The dental nurses were now experienced in the recording method, and repeating the audit took little additional effort. The data collected is shown in Figure 3.4.

As Figure 3.4 displays, the percentage of diagnostically acceptable radiographs taken improved for all surgeries, and the standard of 90% was met. The team were confident that patient care had been improved by reducing the re-exposure rate while also reducing the amount of time spent on re-work by the clinician. The team discussed the re-audit data and all clinicians, including those who already met the 90% aim on the initial audit, reported that they felt more confident in taking radiographs.

The team agreed to conduct a routine audit of radiograph acceptability once a year, both to account for new staff joining the team and to take account of the potential for skills decay over time. If the initial audit showed that the 90% standard was maintained, then the team would move on to looking at their compliance with the second standard of diagnostically acceptable radiographs with errors.

The practice owner agreed that an audit cycle would be conducted to review radiograph acceptability standards every year. All clinical staff were encouraged to speak out if they felt they needed more training or support between cycles, and the practice owner committed to an open environment where staff could voice any concerns about patient safety or quality.

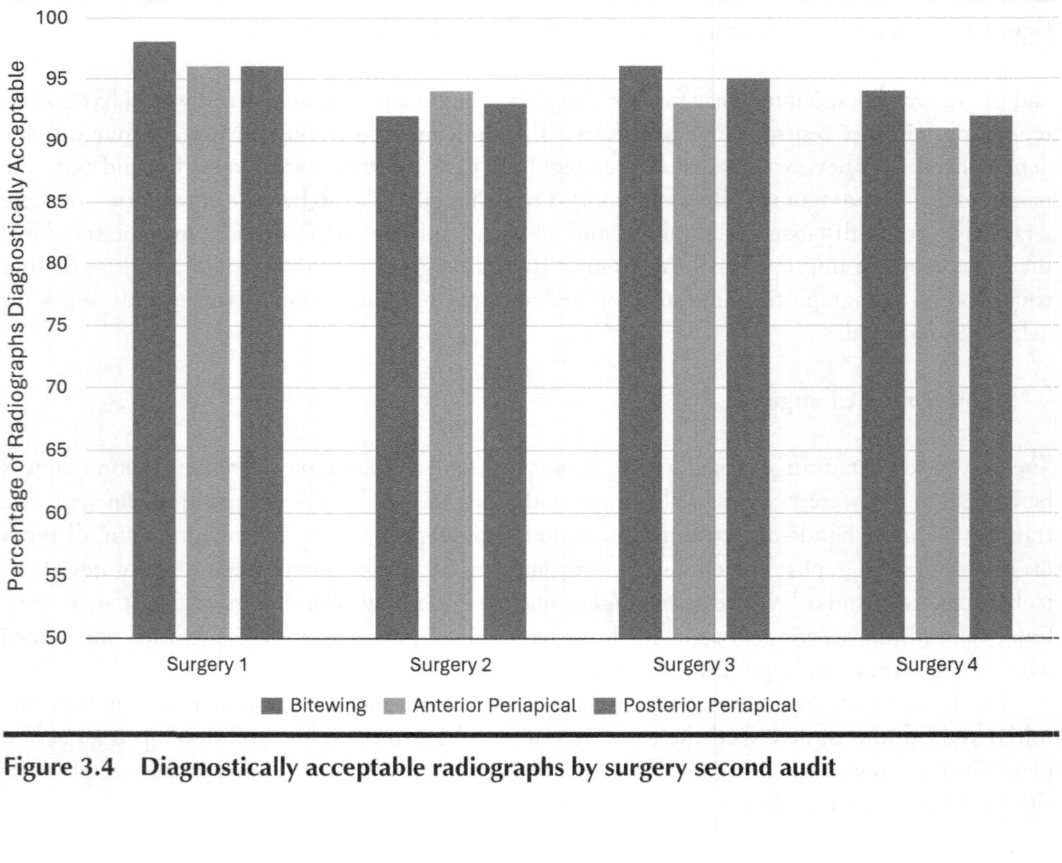

Figure 3.4 Diagnostically acceptable radiographs by surgery second audit

Conclusions

Clinical audit is a structured process to improve patient care and care quality by comparison to an agreed standard. The method has been used extensively in dental care and oral health services. To be a complete clinical audit, it is necessary to make changes and re-audit to establish the impact of any changes made. Audits can be repeated year by year to check that standards are being maintained. If the desired results are not obtained, then audit cycles can be linked together in an audit spiral to gradually improve performance over time.

References

Anwar H., Waring D. (2017) Improving patient safety through a clinical audit spiral: Prevention of wrong tooth extraction in orthodontics. *British Dental Journal*, 223; 1: 48–52. Available at: https://doi.org/10.1038/sj.bdj.2017.586

Ashley M. P., Pemberton M. N., Saksena A., Shaw A., Dickson S. (2014) Improving patient safety in a UK dental hospital: Long-term use of clinical audit. *British Dental Journal*, 217; 7: 369–373. Available at: https://doi.org/10.1038/sj.bdj.2014.861

Benjamin A. (2008) Audit: How to do it in practice. *British Medical Journal*, 336; 7655: 1241–1245. Available at: https://doi.org/10.1136/bmj.39527.628322.AD

Butler J. J., Quinlan, J. W. (1958) Internal audit in the department of medicine of a community hospital: Two years' experience. *Journal of the American Medical Association*, 167; 5: 567–572. Available at: https://doi.org/10.1001/jama.1958.02990220037011

Cannell P. (2005) Linking clinical audit in General Dental Services to Primary Care Trust clinical governance: Progress report of an approach used in Southend. *Primary Dental Care*, os12; 1: 23–26. Available at: https://doi.org/10.1308/1355761052894266

Care Quality Commission (2022) *About Us: What We Do and How We Do It*. Newcastle Upon Tyne: Care Quality Commission. Available at: https://www.cqc.org.uk/sites/default/files/20170504_CQC_About-us.pdf [Accessed 14 August 2025]

Care Quality Commission (2024) *Dental Mythbuster 17: Audit and Improvement in Primary Dental Service*. Newcastle Upon Tyne: Care Quality Commission. Available at: https://www.cqc.org.uk/guidance-providers/dentists/dental-mythbuster-17-audit-improvement-primary-dental-services [Accessed 14 August 2025]

Chate R. A. C., White S., Hale L. R. O., Howat A. P., Bottomley J., Barnet-Lamb J., Lindsay J., Davies T. I., Heath J. M. (2006) The impact of clinical audit on antibiotic prescribing in general dental practice. *British Dental Journal*, 201; 10: 635–641. Available at: https://doi.org/10.1038/sj.bdj.4814261

Chong J. A., Chew J. K. Y., Ravindranath S., Pau A. (2014) Clinical audit teaching in record–keeping for dental undergraduates at International Medical University, Kuala Lumpur, Malaysia. *Journal of Dental Education*, 78; 2: 206–212. Available at: https://doi.org/10.1002/j.0022-0337.2014.78.2.tb05671.x

Dental Defence Union (2022) *Clinical Audit, Peer Review and CPD*. Available at: https://www.theddu.com/guidance-and-advice/guides/clinical-audit-peer-review-and-cpd [Accessed 12 August 2025]

Fong J. Y. M., Tan V. J. H., Lee J. R., Tong Z. G. M., Foong Y. K., Tan J. M. E., Parolia A., Pau A. (2018) Clinical audit training improves undergraduates' performance in root canal therapy. *European Journal of Dental Education*, 22; 3: 160–166. Available at: https://doi.org/10.1111/eje.12297

Goff D. A., Mangino J. E., Trolli E., Scheetz R., Goff D. (2022) Private practice dentists improve antibiotic use after dental antibiotic stewardship education from infectious diseases experts. *Open Forum Infectious Diseases*, 9; 8: ofac361. Available at: https://doi.org/10.1093/ofid/ofac361

Hearnshaw H. M., Harker R. M., Cheater F. M., Baker R. H., Grimshaw G. M. (2001) Expert consensus on the desirable characteristics of review criteria for improvement of health care quality. *Quality in Health Care*, 10; 3: 173–178. Available at: https://doi.org/10.1136/qhc.0100173

Hearnshaw H., Harker R., Cheater F., Baker R., Grimshaw G. (2002) A study of the methods used to select review criteria for clinical audit: Executive summary. *Health Technology Assessment,* 6; 1.

Heggie C. (2019) Triaging of non-scheduled appointments in general dental practice: A clinical audit. *British Dental Journal*, 226; 3: 203–206. Available at: https://doi.org/10.1038/sj.bdj.2019.97

Hook H. (2020) A guide to clinical audit for the dental team. *BDJ Team,* 7: 34–37. Available at: https://doi.org/10.1038/s41407-020-0437-3

Horner K., Eaton K. A. (2018) *Selection Criteria for Dental Radiography.* 3rd Edition. London: Faculty of General Dental Practice (UK). Available at: https://cgdent.uk/wp-content/uploads/securepdfs/FGDP-SCDR-ALL-Web.pdf

HSE National Centre for Clinical Audit (2025) *Clinical Audit – A Practical Guide.* Dublin: HSE National Centre for Clinical Audit, Health Service Executive. Available at: https://assets.hse.ie/media/documents/HSE_National_Centre_for_Clinical_Audit_-_A_Practical_Guide_booklet_2025.pdf

Ivers N., Jamtvedt G., Flottorp S., Young J., Odgaard-Jensen J., French S., O'Brien M., Johansen M., Grimshaw J., Oxman A. (2012) Audit and feedback: Effects on professional practice and healthcare outcomes. *Cochrane Database of Systematic Reviews* Issue 6: Article Number CD000259. Available at: https://doi.org/10.1002/14651858.cd000259.pub3

Jayawardena D. S., Richardson R., Kellett F., Heidari E. (2024) A survey of foundation dentists' experiences of clinical audit: A survey of foundation dentists' experiences of clinical audit. *British Dental Journal,* 237; 12: 929–933. Available at: https://doi.org/10.1038/s41415-024-8155-4

Kelson M. (1998) *Promoting Patient Involvement in Clinical Audit: Practical Guidance on Achieving Effective Involvement.* London: College of Health.

Lynch C., Llewelyn J., Ash P., Chadwick B. L. (2011) Preparing dental students for careers as independent dental professionals: Clinical audit and community-based clinical teaching. *British Dental Journal,* 210: 475–478. Available at: https://doi.org/10.1038/sj.bdj.2011.383

MacCarrick G. (2014) *Medical Leadership and Management: A Case-based Approach.* London: Springer Verlag.

Mordi V. (2024) A survey of foundation dentists' experiences of clinical audit. *British Dental Journal,* 237: 929–933. Available at: https://doi.org/10.1038/s41415-024-8155-4

National Institute for Clinical Excellence (2002) *Principles for Best Practice in Clinical Audit.* Oxford: Radical Medical Press.

Patel K., Jenkyn I. (2021) An introduction to clinical governance in dentistry. *British Dental Journal*, 230; 8: 539–543. Available at: https://doi.org/10.1038/s41415-021-2839-9

Shaffie N., Cheng L. (2012) Improving the quality of oral surgery referrals. *British Dental Journal*, 213; 8: 411–413. Available at: https://doi.org/10.1038/sj.bdj.2012.929

Simons D., Williams D. (2013) Can audit improve patient care and treatment outcomes in endodontics? *British Dental Journal*, 214; 9: E25. Available at: https://doi.org/10.1038/sj.bdj.2013.434

Sperr E. (2016) PubMed by Year [Internet]. [cited 17 August 2025]. Available at: http://esperr.github.io/pubmed-by-year/

Stabin M. G. (2007) *Radiation Protection and Dosimetry: An Introduction to Health Physics.* New York, NY: Springer-Verlag.

Stark C., Cordiner K., Gupta P., Rakover J. (2026) *Continuous Value Management in Healthcare: Elevating Safety, Cost and Efficiency with a Staff-led Approach.* New York, NY: Routledge.

Stevenson D., Waterhouse P., Rogers H. J. (2025) Safety first! An audit to improve airway protection during student placement of preformed metal crowns. *British Dental Journal*, 239; 3: 204–208. Available at: https://doi.org/10.1038/s41415-025-8493-x

Tadin A., Badrov M., Vitasovic B. M., Pericic T. P. (2024) Oral hygiene practices and oral health knowledge among adult orthodontic patients: A best practice implementation project. *Hygiene*, 4; 2: 221–230. Available at: https://doi.org/10.3390/hygiene4020018

Thornley P., Quinn A. (2017) A qualitative evaluation of clinical audit in UK dental foundation training. *Dentistry Journal*, 5; 4: 31. Available at: https://doi.org/10.3390/dj5040031

Thornley P., Quinn A., Elley K. (2015) A qualitative evaluation of foundation dentists' and training programme directors' perceptions of clinical audit in general dental practice. *British Dental Journal*, 219; 4: 177–181. Available at: https://doi.org/10.1038/sj.bdj.2015.647

Ullman A. J., Ray-Barruel G., Rickard C. M., Cooke M. (2018) Clinical audits to improve critical care: Part 1 Prepare and collect data. *Australian Critical Care*, 31; 2: 101–105. Available at: https://doi.org/10.1016/j.aucc.2017.04.003.

Willmington C., Belardi P., Murante A. M., Vainieri M. (2022) The contribution of benchmarking to quality improvement in healthcare. A systematic literature review. *BMC Health Services Research*, 22; 1: Article 139. Available at: https://doi.org/10.1186/s12913-022-07467-8

Yesudian G. T., Gilchrist F., Bebb K., Albadri S., Aspinall A., Swales K., Deery C. (2015) A multicentre, multicycle audit of the prescribing practices of three paediatric dental departments in the North of England. *British Dental Journal*, 218; 12: 681–685. Available at: https://doi.org/10.1038/sj.bdj.2015.440

Chapter 4

Quality Improvement

Introduction

This chapter looks at the differences between the structured situations usually encountered in audit projects and less well delineated problems that often occur in practice. Making progress with quality improvement needs consideration of the context, including the team or department's previous experience with quality improvement. This includes any previous audit or quality improvement efforts in the area; what training team members have had, if any; the degree of management support for improvement initiatives and how challenging it will be to make time for the work.

The stages of any quality improvement work include identifying problems, taking stock of possible reasons for the issue and generating countermeasures that can be tested out using Plan-Do-Study-Act (PDSA) cycles. When changes are successfully made, the team needs to embed the changes in their methods of working and use the new improved state as the base on which to build future change. In some cases, the work may need to be spread to teams and areas that were not involved in the original work, and this brings its own set of challenges.

Leadership styles are important in quality improvement. Some teams are used to following instructions, and having little personal influence on what they are to do. This is necessary in some situations, but when a problem needs to be understood and changes tested out by staff, active engagement is better. Making this possible is easier with a leadership style that seeks involvement and which recognises the experience and value of the team's staff. Making the switch from a more directive form of leadership can be tricky but is an effort worth making. It also allows leadership for parts of the project to be spread across the team, which increases ownership, spreads learning and experience and reduces pressure on team leaders and managers.

Team involvement is important in any quality improvement work and pursuing it from the start can have a major impact on how dental teams perceive the work. Team members have day to day experience of the processes and together with information from patients and from available data, can contribute information on problems and help to generate solutions. Their participation in the work also helps to spread skills and understanding and makes long-term gains more likely because staff feel ownership of the problem analysis, and the solutions that are implemented.

DOI: 10.4324/9781003493532-4

Quality Improvement

Chapter 3 describes audit, where there is an established standard to which a team wants to compare themselves, or are required to do so. Audit is a subset of a wider quality improvement approach and, as Chapter 1 discussed, methods overlap. In some instances, there may be an expectation of what standard should be achieved, even if there is no monitored requirement. Most patient safety issues fall into this category, where the aim is either to achieve no errors or to adhere to requirements 100% of the time. Examples include adherence to radiation protection guidelines, antibiotic prescribing guidelines and guidelines on intravenous sedation. The expected performance may not always be achieved, but the aim itself is clear, even in the absence of a norm.

In other instances, a dental team or dental service may want to work on an issue for which there is no established norm. Examples include:

- Disruptions to treatment sessions because of misplaced equipment.
- A reception being left unattended because of other demands in the service/practice.
- The proportion of patients who cancel too late for the appointment to be reallocated.
- Frequent breakdowns in a vital piece of equipment, resulting in inconvenience, delays or the rescheduling of patients.
- A deterioration in the performance of a key external supplier, such as a dental laboratory.
- Vital materials needed are out of stock from the supplying company.
- Frequent instances of patient emergencies resulting in overbooked clinic sessions, missed lunch times, late finishing times and stressed staff.
- Verbal abuse of staff in the service or practice.
- Difficulty accessing translation services.

In some of these examples, the aim should be to have no occurrences, such as abuse towards staff, even if that is unlikely to be achieved. The direction of travel – to have as few instances as possible, and to take seriously any that do occur – is clear. In other situations, the target may be less obvious. A private dental service may not have any external requirements for waiting times but may still want to reduce waits to increase patient satisfaction, and to avoid unnecessary delays in treatment. When deciding on a target waiting time, the practice is free to make its own decision, based on its understanding of the market, and of the wants of its patient group.

Other waiting times, such as telephone waiting times when calling the department or practice and waiting times after arrival in a practice or department before being seen, generally have no agreed standard against which they can be monitored. In many cases, the aim will be to reduce the issue as far as possible, and then to keep it under review.

A key difference from an audit is that there may be no clear guideline against which performance can be judged, and no previously agreed set of actions to undertake to attempt to improve the situation. Often, the problem will be poorly understood, and the reasons it occurs may be unclear.

Starting Positions in Quality Improvement

This textbook is intended to be useful to teams with little or no experience of quality improvement and to act as a reference for individuals with more experience. Most dental professionals have limited training in quality improvement methods. When some members of teams do have training, either from undergraduate education or from later stages of training, they may have no practical experience of applying the methods in practice. Some hospital dental staff may have had access to quality improvement support or have worked on large-scale improvement projects developed by others, but this experience does not always transfer across easily to independent practice.

Involvement of the wider team is essential in quality improvement. The roles of teams are discussed in greater detail later in the chapter. When teams or team leaders plan to work on a quality improvement project, perhaps for the first time, it is helpful to take stock of the previous experience of the team and of the context in which the work is to be conducted. The following factors should be considered:

Previous Quality Improvement Initiatives: There may have been previous work. This can bring its own challenges depending on how the work was conducted and the degree of success it enjoyed. If there has been no previous work, then the team will need to understand why quality improvement work is planned. It is always possible to improve the quality of any service, but staff may have worked in the same place, providing the same services using the same processes for many years. It is unlikely that they designed the process, but teams can find it difficult to separate themselves from the work they deliver. This means that a plan to work on service quality can feel like a criticism of their work and can be greeted with hostility. Some people see quality improvement as synonymous with attempts to increase efficiency or to streamline services and so may see it as a veiled threat of decreased hours, lower pay or even redundancy. Taking time to understand concerns and to discuss them is always worthwhile. Passive resistance to quality improvement work can be very difficult to overcome, and it usually stems from fear. If the source of the concerns is not understood, then it is very challenging to address them.

Where there has been previous work, it is valuable to take stock of what happened, or at least what any remaining staff believe happened, how the work was conducted, and what results, if any, it produced. Sometimes stories about previous quality improvement work have been passed down, often with varying degrees of accuracy. If work was conducted in the past, but there is no current quality improvement activity, then it suggests that the work lost momentum in some way. This can occur because of changes in managers and team leaders, movement away of a staff member with a particular interest in quality improvement, or because of a change in emphasis within the team or wider organisation. Quality improvement activities are sometimes regarded as something that can be cut when an organisation comes under financial pressure, and if this has happened, then it gives a clear message about the relative organisational priority accorded to quality improvement work.

If interest has fluctuated, then the obvious question for any staff member is how likely this is to happen again. If they see the work as a fad, based on previous experience, either personal or from a story transmitted in team folklore, then they may feel that any investment of effort is likely to be wasted. This can result in unwillingness to become involved, and in cynicism about the probable benefits. Staff may feel that if they keep their head down, feign interest and wait for the work to pass as it did previously, then this path is the best option for them. Team involvement is of central importance in quality improvement work, so understanding any issues that may affect participation is important.

If a team has had previous quality improvement experience, and the work was a success, then there are usually few issues. Staff are often enthusiastic to undertake more work to produce further benefits. If, however, any of the problems described above are present, then they need to be tackled head-on. Leadership styles, discussed further later in the chapter, have an important role in how this is done. Simply stating the importance of the work and requiring participation can work but is unlikely to produce wholehearted involvement. Anything less than engaged input is a waste of human talent, so taking time to address concerns will bring later dividends.

Talking through quality with the team, using the concepts presented in Chapter 1, often helps. Asking them about their own reflections on quality using the dimensions identified earlier in the book gives them an opportunity to share their experiences and frustrations. It also helps to separate the staff from the work, by helping people to see that there are many aspects of a service that can be improved, and that the system is not synonymous with the staff.

Dental teams almost always have more work than they have staff time available. Concerns about reduced hours and redundancies from improvements are therefore almost always unfounded as there is no shortage of work to be done. Assuming this is the case, then making this explicit from the beginning can make a big difference to staff engagement. It may not be possible to guarantee that jobs may not alter because of changes to processes, but it is usually possible to make an unequivocal statement that no post will be lost as a direct result of quality improvement work.

Taking time to explore the origins of existing processes can also be useful. Commonly, working methods have been passed down to new staff, who have followed the processes asked of them.

Training: It is common to find that no one in a team has had access to any previous training on quality improvement. In this situation, think about what information is needed at each stage of the project. Dental teams have many competing demands, and taking a half day to run through methods with the team may be impractical. Most quality improvement techniques are straightforward to explain and to put into practice. Giving a brief overview of the approach and then explaining each stage in more detail when the team reaches that part of the process may be all that is needed.

Dental professionals have a great deal of scientific training, and there are parts of the quality improvement approach that may cause them to pause. It is common for dental professionals to want to see evidence on the effectiveness of quality improvement methods. There are many published papers to which they can be directed to find academic evaluations of quality improvement work, so this does not usually prove too onerous a problem. A larger issue can be a feeling among some staff that quality improvement should use the same methods as research. They may want to see previous research to confirm that a proposed change has been effective elsewhere, and to use statistical techniques to analyse change.

The central challenge is that the context of dental work varies between teams, and most quality improvement work is not published. Finding a precise analogy to a proposed change may be next to impossible. It can help to note that process improvements very rarely stray into territory that would make a clinical change, and if they do, ethical approval may be required. Quality improvement work usually focuses on the way a process works, rather than on issues related to clinical decision-making. A team may agree standard work to apply to a situation, but there will always be clinical discretion to overrule the approach if there is reason why it cannot be applied in a particular patient.

Measurement is discussed in Chapter 7. The use of techniques such as Run Charts and Statistical Process Control charts can help to assuage worries, but for most quality improvement work, the decisions are reasonably straightforward. The question is whether one approach is better than another, in one of the dimensions of quality reviewed in Chapter 1. Identifying whether the average time taken for something decreases, whether interruptions to staff decrease, if staff members feel less stressed, or whether it is easier to pick up an error is usually clear-cut. The team is not trying to produce transferable knowledge, as in a research project, but rather to remove problems from their workflow, for the benefit of both the team and their patients. It can also be reassuring for concerned staff to realise that any changes they agree on after testing are not set in stone: if the team members have an idea for a further improvement, they can test it out and create a new process if it succeeds.

Where there are staff with previous training, it will often be possible to support them to take on a larger role in the project. Interest and enthusiasm are more important than position in the organisation. Having practical experience of change in practice is ideal, but if the staff member has previous academic training on quality improvement but no practical experience, then leading part of a project helps to reinforce the academic learning.

Time and Capacity: Every team is busy. Becoming involved in quality improvement can feel daunting, or even impossible. The problem is that at least some of the business in every team relates to time spent responding to problems, and delays related to issues in processes that do not flow as smoothly as the team would like. Other problems can create patient safety issues that carry high risk for the team, its reputation and for individual members. Stresses can feel unrelenting, with consequent impacts on staff, sometimes leading to illness or staff turnover. This means that some of the demands on the time of the team are related to the type of problems that quality improvement work can resolve. Finding time is difficult, but the team is already devoting time to quality issues. Without taking the time to make changes, there is little prospect that these problems will improve and little chance that they will spontaneously resolve.

While teams and managers can see the logic of this argument, that does not make it any easier to find time. It is helpful to keep in mind that quality improvement projects are straightforward to break into manageable sections, and not everyone needs to be involved at every stage. It is advantageous to conduct at least some stages of the project with a wider group, but this does not need to happen for every component of the work. Having a regular group meeting to keep everyone informed is valuable. This can be added to an existing team meeting if required, although having a brief weekly or monthly meeting focused on quality improvement alone can be a good way of demonstrating the interest and value the team or department places on the work. Meetings can be conducted as huddles, lasting no more than 15 minutes. Details on the potential use of huddles are given later in the book.

One way to structure the work is to have a team session to identify problems, and to decide what to prioritise. A smaller group can then take away the details and undertake the work. As described in Chapter 6, Plan-Do-Study-Act (PDSA) cycles usually start small, trying a change with one staff member and one patient, and then gradually scale up. This means that if the change is not as effective as hoped, little time has been devoted to it. It also gives an early opportunity to learn from any mistakes.

Organisational Commitment: One of the consistent findings from research is that explicit organisational commitment over time contributes to success (Alexander *et al.*, 2022). If the work is a first project and there is no track record of using the approach, then this needs to be demonstrated in other ways. Managers expressing interest, asking about the work and helping to overcome any barriers go a long way towards demonstrating commitment. Actions, as usual, have more impact than words, and active involvement and visible support have a larger impact than statements of memorandums. The role of leadership is reviewed in detail later in the chapter. This is not synonymous with management, but managers can display their support even if it is not practical for them to have daily involvement with the quality improvement work being conducted.

Stages of a Quality Improvement Project

Later chapters review the detail of a quality improvement project. It is helpful to set out a summary of the usual stages here, to put the rest of the book in context. There are many ways of tackling quality improvement, and some methods have different structures. The overall approach tends to be similar, however, and this book presents a generic model of quality improvement that can be applied in any setting.

1. **Identifying and Prioritising Problems:** This stage, best done with the wider team, if possible, gives staff an opportunity to share issues they have identified and which they would like to improve. This is generally a long list, so some prioritisation is usually required. A method of doing this is described in Chapter 5. Teams which are undertaking quality improvement work for the first time, or after a hiatus, are usually best gaining experience by tackling a manageable-sized problem that will be likely to bring immediate visible benefits.
2. **Identifying and Prioritising Potential Solutions:** Again, best done as a team, this stage identifies possible options to tackle problems, building on the understanding of the issue created in stage one. Letting teams generate as many options as they wish is beneficial as it lets team members gain a better understanding of how other team members understand the problem. Agreeing which possibility to test out first helps to increase ownership and engagement.
3. **Testing out Options:** This is done using Plan-Do-Study-Act cycles. These are small tests of change where ideas are tried out in practice. This cuts through the risk of lengthy arguments about what will or will not work by implementing an idea in practice. As noted above, cycles start small and gradually increase in size as evidence of effectiveness is gathered, and confidence grows in the change. This includes prediction of what will occur, and comparison of the outcome to the expected outcome. The ideas can then be amended as required. PDSA cycles are discussed in more detail in Chapter 6 and the details of measuring change in Chapter 7.
4. **Embedding the Changes:** When changes are found to bring an improvement, the team needs to embed the new method of working. Despite the reasons the change has been implemented, it is easy to slip back into long understood ways, particularly when under pressure. Methods of embedding change, including sharing the method with new staff and temporary staff, are reviewed in Chapter 8.
5. **Scaling up:** This will not be necessary in every instance, but in group practices, corporate groups, hospitals or community clinics, it may be necessary to spread the work to other settings, where the staff were not involved in the original trials of change. This requires appropriate caution to avoid staff feeling that a solution is being imposed on them, and ways of scaling improvement are explored in Chapter 9.

Whatever change is considered, and whatever the organisational situation, leadership will be needed. This is reviewed in the next section, and the roles of the wider team are considered later in the chapter.

Leadership

Leadership and management are related processes. Many managers provide leadership, but it is possible to lead on a project without also being a manager, and many clinicians find themselves in this situation. Leadership is a process by which an individual exerts an influence over others to structure activities and relationships in support of a task (Tang, 2019). Leadership can be at a strategic level, where it sets the direction of an entire organisation, or within a team.

Leadership Theory

Leadership was initially believed to be a characteristic of a person, an idea also known as 'the great man' theory of leadership. This idea has a long history and assumes that a single person can shape the destiny of an organisation, or even of a country (Harrison, 2018). This led to a search for the traits inherent in a person – at the time almost always assumed to be a man – which made them leaders. A long list of characteristics was suggested. These usually included characteristics such as intelligence, self-confidence, decisiveness, consistency and sociability, which included an ability to build relationships (Çoğaltay, 2015). Perhaps predictably, the exact traits identified changed over time and between studies, often reflecting the interests of the academic who undertook the research. No one person could conceivably have all the characteristics that have been identified in these numerous studies, and people with many of the characteristics identified did not always prove to be successful leaders. It also became apparent that even successful leaders do not always remain successful. They may have success in one situation, but not another. These problems resulted in a refocusing of research, although the idea of a single, innately talented individual remains popular (Willcocks 2016).

If leadership is innate, then there is little hope for the people who do not possess the precise mixture of traits that are popular at a particular time. This imagines a binary situation where people are either a leader or a follower. The limitation of this position results in a move to looking at leadership skills with the idea that if the skills of successful managers could be identified, then other people could be trained to develop them. There was also interest in looking at how leaders behave towards those they lead, and a range of behaviours and approaches were identified. One of the most popular theories sought to distinguish leaders by looking both at their degree of focus on results and their concern for their staff (Blake and Mouton, 1964).

Despite this, it was apparent that leadership styles could vary markedly but still be successful, and that a leadership approach could work in one situation but not another. This resulted in work on situational leadership and produced the idea that while individual skills are important in leadership, matching the leader, or the approach to the context is also required. This can include adopting different leadership styles with different staff members, depending on their personality and needs. For example, the management style that can be effective for a practice owner who recruits and employs their staff may not prove appropriate for a hospital department where there are separate routes of professional management for nurses, dentists, receptionists and so on. The extent to which decision-making is shared by the leader and the team can also vary depending on context (Cullen, 2015). Decision-making in an emergency will often need a different approach from a measured decision about long-term strategy in a practice or department, and some well-established teams with experienced practitioners may be more willing to share decision-making than a new or inexperienced team.

Managing groups of professional staff with their own caseloads who are making highly nuanced decisions that reflect individual clinical need is not the same situation as the management of staff who are undertaking very repetitive tasks with well-understood requirements. The idea that some leaders may fit one type of service better than another, and that leaders may need to alter their approach in different situations, moves a long way from the idea of natural leaders who will be successful because of innate talent, no matter the situation.

More recent developments in leadership theory identify other approaches to leadership, although they build on the earlier phases of work, rather than replace them. Some of the approaches are more relevant to dentistry than others. Some ideas relevant to both dentistry and leadership in quality improvement include:

Transactional Leadership: In transactional leadership, the leader sets clear expectations of what is to be delivered and uses rewards and sanctions depending on whether tasks are delivered as expected (Richards, 2020). The transaction is that the staff obtain the benefit – such as their salary – in return for meeting the leader's requirements. If outcomes are delivered, then the manager leaves the staff to get on with work. Staff can be expected to surrender their own decision-making and to subordinate it to that of the leader, creating a difficult situation for professional staff who have their own ethical requirements (Smircich and Morgan, 1982).

A focus on staff training and wellbeing is to allow the work to be delivered, rather than because of any great investment in the staff. This type of management can be effective in maintaining an existing service, but is less suited to making major changes. It also has limitations with dental professionals, who are likely to be internally motivated to deliver a good service, rather than driven by external pressures, and able to move if they do not like the work environment. There is also a potential for unethical practices to be followed if the leader will brook no dissent with a 'my way, or the highway' approach, with staff seeing no option but to follow the required approach to avoid censure (Rendtorff, 2020).

Servant Leadership: Leaders focus on the needs of the wider team, with positive effects on team and organisational culture. If the team members are happy and fulfilled, the theory suggests, they will be empowered to deliver good-quality autonomous care (Langhof and Güldenberg, 2020). This differs from transactional leadership as staff wellbeing is seen as having a value rather than only being a stepping stone to better performance. Many healthcare managers and staff find the idea of focusing on supporting teams to enable them to develop and to deliver good-quality care intuitively appealing. The downside of the approach is that some staff will see the efforts to support them rather than direct them as weakness and may take advantage of the leader (McDaniel, 2023). There is also some evidence of higher rates of burnout in leaders who use this approach (Panaccio *et al.*, 2015).

Transformational Leadership: The leader describes a clear vision for the organisation or team that appeals to positive characteristics of team members and motivates them to achieve. Team members look to the leader as a role model, whom they respect and trust (Ytterstad and Olaisen, 2023). In turn, the leader pays attention to the development and needs of their staff members (Dorjgotov, 2024). This relates to ideas of charismatic leadership, which can feel like a very high bar for other members of a dental team to reach if they are going to take a leadership role. Transformational leadership also carries the risk that the relationship may be abusive or otherwise manipulative, such as an expectation of very long work hours.

Authentic Leadership: Given the obvious risk that transformational leadership could become manipulative, in the authentic leadership model, the leader is careful to keep their actions aligned to their personal values and to apply ethical standards to their decisions. Leaders are inclusive and support diversity (Shaw, 2023). As with servant leadership, this will have appeal to many healthcare professionals, but authenticity does not automatically produce leadership. Leadership requires other skills including understanding the position of other people (Biehl, 2021).

Distributed Leadership: This concept can be implemented under various models of leadership but is more likely when managers are willing to share leadership, which is not always the case. In this approach, leadership functions can be spread across a wider group of individuals, either as a leadership group or a wider spread of leadership authority for specific activities. This is discussed in greater detail below.

Considering these approaches to leadership, it is evident that there is no single accepted way of leading, and that both fashion and circumstance have an impact (Hanks *et al.*, 2020). Organisations with one person who leads on all matters regardless of topic have a single point of failure and place enormous pressure on the individual. If good leaders are assumed to have a natural talent for it, then the opportunity is lost to learn leadership skills or to take on leadership functions over time, supported by others.

Some approaches to leadership are likely to have a resonance for dental professionals, who generally want to help and support others. These are not clear-cut choices, however. Some functions in dentistry, like patient safety matters, must be done and cannot be topics for debate, except in the detail of how to discharge the responsibility. Other decisions are less clear-cut and inevitably depend on professional judgement. No leader can be everywhere at once, so some degree of mutual trust between a leader and their staff is required in professional situations. The dichotomy of leaders and followers is less sustainable in many dental situations, where clinicians have areas of expertise, and may have special interests, for example in dental education or patient safety.

Leadership Skills in Dentistry

Busby (2012, p. 437) defines leadership in dentistry as 'the ability to continuously define a future practice vision which inspires you and your dental team towards success'. The section above describes how leadership was long thought of as a personal characteristic with an assumption that some people are leaders, while others are not. This underestimates the importance of context, and of acquired skills (Wardman 2020). The creation of programmes to develop leadership skills in dentistry reflect an understanding that leadership can be learned (Bedi and Wordley, 2019). This also relates to the 'post heroic' phase in thinking on leadership, with a move away from the idea that one individual must know everything, and do everything (Barnas, 2014, Svensson and von Knorring, 2025).

Given that no one can be everywhere at once, this means that in anything other than the smallest organisation, leadership must be provided by more than one person, although what a person leads on will vary by their organisational position. Dentists and members of the dental team can provide leadership at various levels from the strategic to work in an individual team (Grocock, 2020). What works, and what is required, will vary depending on the clinical and organisational context (Modha, 2020). Despite this, leadership training for dentists is often limited and variable (Mara, 2024).

Programmes of leadership training for dental professionals are beginning to appear, although opportunities are still limited (Power *et al.*, 2017, Danesh and Huber, 2021, Park *et al.*, 2022). Taichman and colleagues (2012) reviewed training for dental and dental hygienist students and suggested that at undergraduate level, training is required on:

- **Communication Skills**: Written and verbal communication skills are relevant to all members of the dental team. In quality improvement work, being able to work with people and to manage concern and disagreement is very useful.
- **The ability for Self-reflection**: Taichman and colleagues were thinking about the ability to set priorities and to create a leadership vision. This ability applies no less to quality improvement work, because being able to step back from a problem and to separate people from processes is valuable.
- **Critical Thinking and Problem-solving Skills**: Dental practice changes constantly, and the pace of technical developments has never been faster. The ability to analyse problems and to seek structured solutions has obvious relevance to quality improvement practice.

- **Professionalism, Ethics and Social Responsibility**: These are key skills for any dental professional and are as applicable in quality improvement work as in any other aspect of dental health practice.

There are challenges for dental professionals in providing leadership. Dentists and lead nurses are well used to managing their team. This involves setting clear expectations of behaviour and actions, deciding on care plans and processes, and implementing them (Brocklehurst *et al.*, 2013). Dentists generally value their clinical autonomy and do not expect to be challenged. This is compounded because dentists often have limited clinical contact with one another, with each responsible for what happens in their treatment room with their own patients and for the quality of care delivered. This type of leadership will be familiar to most dental teams (Nalliah, 2016).

Although this individual leadership is often thought of as the norm, hybrid roles are common in healthcare (McGivern *et al.*, 2015, Moore *et al.*, 2015). In dental care, clinicians often combine clinical work with management roles, whether they are dental nurses, dental technicians or dentists. These hybrid roles, where clinicians manage a team, supervise education, or take responsibility for an aspect of team practice, are frequent and reflect the complexity of contemporary dental practice. These roles often come with an assumption that people in these hybrid roles will lead all work in their area of responsibility, but appropriate delegation is also possible. Leadership teams are also common, where a group of staff come together to provide joint leadership, although there will often be an identified manager within the group. Examples in a private dental practice could include a senior team with the owner, a practice manager, a lead nurse and often a senior dentist. In a hospital setting, a similar arrangement with a manager, senior dentist and a senior dental nurse would be common. This demonstrates that while the one dentist – one nurse – one treatment room model is common, many dentists and dental nurses also work in wider team contexts that mean the move to team working on quality improvement is not as large as it might initially seem.

Leadership in Quality Improvement

Friman and colleagues conducted a systematic review of the leadership factors associated with successful quality improvement (Friman *et al.*, 2025). There was no single leadership approach that was required for effective change, but their work suggests common themes that support success and can be incorporated into leadership for quality improvement across a range of different personal styles.

- **Senior Support:** At organisational level, senior leaders show that they pay attention to quality. The aspects of quality that are important to the service and their patients are clear and consistent.
- **Makes Use of Evidence:** Healthcare professionals expect decision-making and prioritising to be evidence-based. Showing the use of evidence for change, including the use of guidelines, structured methods and appropriate measurement helps to reassure staff that there is evidence to support change.
- **Participation:** Team involvement is discussed further below. Demonstrating that the views, experiences and potential of team members to engage in change are both valued and taken seriously supports engagement. This includes listening to staff, including giving them the opportunity to express any concerns.

- **Shared Values:** Leaders demonstrate that they want the same things as the wider team, such as improved patient safety and effective care.
- **Staff Support:** Helping to prioritise work on quality improvement, coaching new skills and, where relevant, providing training both shows commitment and the value placed on staff. Letting people problem-solve, rather than dictating the direction of response, can also help.

There is a difference between leadership and management in quality improvement (Boguslavsky et al., 2019). In dental care, team leaders, service managers, practice managers and practice owners play influential roles. In many cases, a first-line or service manager will also lead improvement work, but this is not always the case. As with clinicians, managers have many demands on their time, and it may be impractical to look after the day-to-day process of improvement. It is also the case that many managers have limited training or experience in quality improvement, while a team member may have an interest in the process of improving service delivery. This may mean that the work of leading a quality improvement project may be better to sit with another member of staff.

When managers do not lead the day-to-day work of improvement, they can still provide leadership direction. How managers act, and what they prioritise, has an enormous impact on their staff. If managers show interest and support, then staff absorb a positive message about quality improvement. On the other hand, if managers tolerate quality improvement activities rather than advocate for them, staff get the message. This does not need to be active hostility. Teams are quick to pick up on the matters to which managers pay attention, and to give them additional weight, and to identify issues about which a manager rarely asks, comments, or celebrates. Managers are in a good position to enable quality improvement work, or to suppress interest and enthusiasm.

Clinicians also have a valuable role in extending quality improvement beyond their own immediate area of control. Clinicians can act across groups of practices, commissioned by a funder such as the UK's National Health Service or a Health Maintenance Organisation or in a group of related practices which are in common ownership, or which have agreed to work on a common interest. There is great scope to share teaching, learning and information across teams (Bridgman and McGrady, 2015). This can have a significant impact: in one example in England, a service redesign in three practices was then extended, with public funding, to 70 dental practices, with the dental team from the original three practices contributing to the training (Bridgman and McGrady, 2015, p. 8–9).

Distributed Leadership

A problem with the traditional hero-leader model where one person is responsible for all leadership functions, and all others follow, is that it places enormous pressure on the identified leader, while also encouraging passivity in everyone else (Gemmill and Oakley, 1992, Bass *et al.*, 2022). Distributed leadership is the idea that people throughout an organisation can adopt leadership roles with team agreement (Gronn, 2002, Fitzgerald *et al.*, 2013). This role may be for a specific task, for a short or long period, or can be a wider leadership role. This model already exists in most dental teams with examples of plural leadership where more than one person leads in different situations (Boak *et al.*, 2015).

In private practice, a practice manager may be responsible for leading a recruitment process, a practice owner can be responsible for leading training events, an associate dentist responsible for ordering new equipment, and a senior dental nurse may be responsible for the supervision of new nurses. This may be a set and understood leadership group with roles that continue over time, sometimes for many years, and in which the people in the leadership group, and the wider service team, have a good understanding of who is responsible for which aspect of practice.

Leadership can also change very quickly; for example, with a dentist leading the assessment and care of a patient who has collapsed in the waiting room, taking over from the receptionist who identified the problem. Some roles will be formal, recognised roles, such as a Patient Safety Lead or an Audit Lead, while other roles are informal and adopted as required. In practice, most dental teams and services recognise this way of working, even if they do not make use of the 'distributed leadership' term.

In quality improvement work, distributed leadership occurs when a team agrees to make an improvement and create a shared understanding of what roles each person will undertake (Braut *et al.*, 2022). Distributed leadership can occur as part of a structured change programme but can also happen within teams (Toma *et al.*, 2020). It is important not to leave ambiguity, and leadership for each component of a project needs to be clear (Chreim and MacNaughton, 2016) with no key aspect left uncovered, and no dubiety about who is leading which element. It is important to revisit roles if the project changes or personnel alter to avoid confusion creeping in (McKee *et al.*, 2013, Carstensen *et al.*, 2024). Distributed leadership necessarily means that if leaders change, then some people who usually act as leaders may find themselves as followers in relation to a specific task, or part of a project (Clark and Buljac-Samardžić, 2018). This also requires clarity on roles for everyone involved.

Distributed leadership in quality improvement can be used at scale. Improvement collaboratives, discussed in Chapter 9, involve teams across an organisation, or in different organisations, working on broadly similar issues simultaneously. This requires coordination but could be a suitable method for independent dental practices to share teaching and learning. In hospital settings, or in corporate chains, there is great scope to use a collaborative approach.

Teams

Dental teams depend on collaboration. While dental staff have different roles, little can be accomplished without teamwork. Quality improvement is a good example of an area where collaboration brings dividends. Components of quality improvement where team involvement helps include:

Identification of Problems: Staff in different roles experience the service in varied ways. Problems may be invisible to a dentist but cause constant irritation to a receptionist. A dental nurse may have to take repeated steps to work with a supply problem, but because they work to resolve it every time, the problem is not visible to others. Dentists may manage to work within time pressures caused by scheduling problems, but at considerable cost to their well-being. Patients can also provide valuable insights. As well as the technical aspects of dental care to which they are exposed, they experience the booking system and information provision in a different way from staff. The more sources that can be used, the wider a view of the system that is available to the team.

Understanding the Nature of a Problem: When problems are identified, it is easy to make assumptions about what may be the cause. This can set the team off on a direction of change that does not address the root causes. Involving the wider team in exploring a problem brings different perspectives. There is a risk that the initial view of the most senior person, a team leader, manager or practice owner, is taken as the last word. Stepping back and discussing a problem with the wider team helps to reach a rounded view of the issue.

Mapping Processes: Drawing a diagram of a process is easy. This does not mean that it is correct. There are two main risks. One person may describe the whole process, even when they do not undertake some of the steps. For example, a clinic lead may assume that they understand booking procedures, but their knowledge may be outdated or inaccurate. Asking the staff members who undertake the work to describe it usually brings more detail and more information on problems. The second risk is that people describe what they believe should happen rather than what happens in practice. Avoiding this depends on the team knowing that personal blame will not be allocated and that getting to the bottom of a problem is the most important thing.

Generating Options for Improvement: More people generate more ideas. Being an excellent clinician does not automatically bring an eye for improvement options. Sometimes people less involved in a process may be able to see it more clearly because they have less personal stake in the issue. People who have worked in other places, or whose training is less constrained, can generate good ideas. Involving the team in the production of possible options also reduces the risk of going down the same line on every occasion.

Testing out Changes: The spirit of how Plan-Do-Study-Act (PDSA) cycles are conducted is no less important than the technical aspects of a PDSA cycle. Teams need to be engaged, and their feedback on small tests of change is essential. Testing out changes with one person, on one patient or occasion, and then spreading as experience is gained, as described in Chapter 6, involves more staff, and assures people that change is not being imposed without their involvement and attention to their feedback. When an improvement cycle does not yield the anticipated results it is essential that this is not interpreted as a failure of the person or people conducting the change: getting the tone right, showing respect and placing value on staff views and feedback not only promotes engagement but also leads to a better product, because problems are identified earlier in the work.

Embedding the New Approach: Imposed changes work less well than changes that have buy-in. Many management ideas are greeted with nods, implemented half-heartedly and then quietly dropped. The engagement in the improvement process described above will do much to give people confidence that an improvement makes sense and works. Keeping it going can be a different matter. There is a natural tendency to drop back into well-worn patterns when under pressure. As pressure is a constant in dental practice, teams need to build in steps to avoid an unconscious return to previous practices: if it had worked, the team would not have changed it in the first place.

Documenting the new work is a good place to start. This needs to be easy to explain, straightforward to understand, and practical to teach to others. This is discussed further in Chapter 8. Having an agreed description means that there is a baseline against which any change can be compared, and a record of the agreed process. Building in checking mechanisms that are proportionate to the issue is valuable. Constructing a time-consuming measurement process around a relatively small change does not balance effort against gain, but clarity on what is required, knowledge of who is responsible for using the new process, and a mechanism to raise problems, for example at a regular quality improvement meeting, can go a long way to avoid unintended drift.

Conclusions

Quality improvement and audit are closely related. Audit is a traditional approach to analysing and improving a situation where there is a structured issue with existing standards and often existing guidelines. Many problems are less well-structured and have no guidelines on which a team can fall back. In this situation, teams need to analyse problems carefully to generate options for improvement. Using Plan-Do-Study-Act cycles then allows them to test out changes in a measured manner.

Managers can help quality improvement work to thrive or ensure that it fails. Showing interest, engagement and support increases the likelihood of success. Managers can provide leadership, but other team members can also offer leadership, either for components of a process or across the range of quality improvement. Dentists and senior dental nurses have important roles, as disinterest from them would reduce the likelihood of other team members engaging with the work: active engagement and leadership will increase the possibility of success, and of longevity for the work.

The style of leadership influences how staff respond. All dental teams require decisions on direction at times, and some work, such as attention to a patient safety issue, cannot be optional. For involvement in quality improvement, supporting leadership styles that increase involvement and encourage active participation makes a difference and signals to staff that they are important and that they can play a key role in producing improvement for themselves, their team, and their patients. Tips on team involvement are given in Box 4.1.

BOX 4.1 TIPS ON TEAM INVOLVEMENT IN QUALITY IMPROVEMENT

- Be clear on why the work is being done. Separate system problems from staff performance. People did not design the system in which they work.
- Show senior engagement. Staff take an interest in the things on which senior staff focus.
- Harness team experience. No one knows a service as well as the staff who work in it, and the patients who use it.
- Show interest and respect. If team members feel that their views and inputs are not taken seriously, they will stop offering them.
- Make it easy for team members to contribute. Use existing meetings where necessary.
- Wrap a structure around the work and stick to it. Having regular updates lets staff know that the work is ongoing and that their involvement is making a difference.
- Think about leadership style. Signpost the reasons for the work and model the engagement and attitude you want to see.
- Make it possible for team members to take on leadership roles that are relevant to their career stage, experience and confidence.
- When tasks are delegated, agree clear roles, check in regularly and offer coaching as required.
- Celebrate success. Teams can take pride in what they achieve.

References

Alexander C., Tschannen D., Hays D., Clouse M., Zellefrow C., Amer K., Lambert-Davis J., Watson T., Tovar E., Milner K. (2022) An integrative review of the barriers and facilitators to nurse engagement in quality improvement in the clinical practice setting. *Journal of Nursing Care Quality*, 37; 1: 94–100. https://doi.org/10.1097/NCQ.0000000000000562

Barnas K. (2014) *Beyond Heroes: A Lean Management System for Healthcare.* Appleton, WI: Thedacare Center for Healthcare Value.

Bass A. E., Milosevic I., Uhl-Bien M., Nadkarni S. (2022) Shared accountability in distributed leadership for improved healthcare access: A study of a US dental institution. *Leadership in Health Services*, 35; 4: 595–610. Available at: https://doi.org/10.1108/LHS-03-2022-0019

Bedi R., Wordley V. (2019) Education and training for dental leadership – A case study of the Senior Dental Leadership programme. *Journal of Dentistry*, 87: 36–39. Available at: https://doi.org/10.1016/j.jdent.2019.05.007

Biehl B. (2021) *Leadership in Game of Thrones*. Wiesbaden: Palgrave Macmillan.
Blake R. R., Mouton J. S. (1964) *The Managerial Grid*. Houston, TX: Gulf.
Boak G., Dickens V., Newson A., Brown L. (2015) Distributed leadership, team working and service improvement in healthcare. *Leadership in Health Services,* 28; 4: 332–344.
Boguslavsky V., Gutierrez R., Holschneider S. (2019) *Effective Leadership for Quality Improvement in Health Care: A Practical Guide*. USAID ASSIST Project. Chevy Chase, MD: University Research Co., LLC (URC).
Braut H., Oygarden O., Storm M., Mikkelsen A. (2022) General practitioners' perceptions of distributed leadership in providing integrated care for elderly chronic multi-morbid patients: A qualitative study. *BMC Health Services Research*, 22; 1: Article 1085. Available at: https://doi.org/10.1186/s12913-022-08460-x
Bridgman C., McGrady M. G. (2015) Clinical leadership and prevention in practice: Is a needs led preventive approach to the delivery of care to improve quality, outcomes and value in primary dental care practice a realistic concept? *BMC Oral Health,* 15; (Suppl 1): S2. Available at: https://doi.org/10.1186/1472-6831-15-S1-S2
Brocklehurst P., Nomura M., Ozaki T., Ferguson J., Matsuda R. (2013) Cultural differences in clinical leadership: A qualitative study comparing the attitudes of general dental practitioners from Greater Manchester and Tokyo. *British Dental Journal*, 215: E19. Available at: https://doi.org/10.1038/sj.bdj.2013.1096
Busby M. (2012) Follow the leader: Part 1 – What is leadership? *Dental Update*, 39; 6: 437–441. Available at: https://doi.org/10.12968/denu.2012.39.6.437
Carstensen K., Kjeldsen A. M., Nielsen C. P. (2024) Distributed leadership in health quality improvement collaboratives. *Health Care Management Review*, 49; 1: 46–58.
Chreim S., MacNaughton K. (2016) Distributed leadership in health care teams. *Health Care Management Review*, 41; 3: 200–212. Available at: https://doi.org/10.1097/HMR.0000000000000073
Clark M. A., Buljac-Samardžić M. (2018) From followership to shared leadership: The changing role of the patient in the healthcare team. In Chatwani N. (Ed.), *Distributed Leadership: Palgrave Studies in Leadership and Followers*. Cham: Palgrave Macmillan. Available at: https://doi.org/10.1007/978-3-319-59581-8_4
Çoğaltay N. (2015) Conceptual perspectives on leadership. In Karadağ E. (Ed.), *Leadership and Organizational Outcomes: Meta-Analysis of Empirical Studies*. Cham: Springer International Publishing.
Cullen, J. (2015) Leading through contingencies. In Carroll B., Ford J., Taylor S. (Eds.), *Leadership: Contemporary Critical Perspectives*. London: Sage, pp. 45–69.
Danesh D. O., Huber T. P. (2021) A literature review of leadership training and a novel conceptual model of leader-member exchange theory for new dentists. *Journal of Health Organization and Management*, 36; 4: 417–427. Available at: https://doi.org/10.1108/JHOM-05-2021-0192
Dorjgotov B. (2024) *Enhancing Organizational Effectiveness through Knowledge Management and Transformational Leadership*. Singapore: Palgrave Macmillan. Available at: https://doi.org/10.1007/978-981-97-8039-6
Fitzgerald L., Ferlie E., McGivern G., Buchanan D. (2013) Distributed leadership patterns and service improvement: Evidence and argument from English healthcare. *The Leadership Quarterly* 24; 1: 227–239. Available at: https://doi.org/10.1016/j.leaqua.2012.10.012
Friman S., Maijala R., Eloranta S., Suominen S., Ikonen T. (2025) The characteristics of leadership and their effectiveness in quality management in healthcare – A systematic literature review and a content analysis. *Health Services Management Research*, 38l; 1: 37–49. Available at: https://doi-org.uhi.idm.oclc.org/10.1177/09514848241254921
Gemmill G., Oakley J. (1992) Leadership: An alienating social myth. *Human Relations,* 45; 2: 113–129.
Grocock R. (2020) Leadership in dentistry. *British Dental Journal*, 228: 882–885. Available at: https://doi.org/10.1038/s41415-020-1633-4
Gronn P. (2002) Distributed leadership as a unit of analysis. *Leadership Quarterly*, 13; 4: 423–451. Available at: https://doi.org/10.1016/S1048-9843(02)00120-0

Hanks S., Cotton D., Spowart L. (2020) Leadership in dental practice: A three stage systematic review and narrative synthesis. *Journal of Dentistry*, 102: 103480. Available at: https://doi.org/10.1016/j.jdent.2020.103480

Harrison C. (2018) *Leadership Theory and Research: A Critical Approach to New and Existing Paradigms*. Cham, Switzerland: Springer International Publishing. Available at: https://doi.org/10.1007/978-3-319-68672-1

Langhof J. G., Güldenberg S. (2020) Servant Leadership: A systematic literature review—toward a model of antecedents and outcomes. *German Journal of Human Resource Management / Zeitschrift für Personalforschung*, 34; 1: 32–68. Available at: https://www.jstor.org/stable/26906026

McDaniel M. (2023) Servant leadership and its vulnerability: Walking the fine line of servant leadership. In Dhiman S. K., Roberts G. E. (Eds.), *The Palgrave Handbook of Servant Leadership*. Cham: Springer Nature. Available at: https://doi.org/10.1007/978-3-031-01323-2_2

McGivern G., Currie G., Ferlie E., Fitzgerald L., Waring J. (2015) Hybrid manager– professionals identity work: The maintenance and hybridization of medical professionals in management contexts. *Public Administration*, 93: 412–432.

McKee L., Charles K., Dixon-Woods M., Willars J., Martin, G. (2013) New' and distributed leadership in quality and safety in health care, or 'old' and hierarchical? An interview study with strategic stakeholders. *Journal of Health Services Research & Policy,* 18 (2 suppl): 11–19. Available at: https //doi.org/10.1177/1355819613484460

Mara M. D. (2024) Training future leaders: A qualitative study exploring leadership development in predoctoral dental curricula. *Journal of Dental Education*, 88: 596–605. https://doi-org.uhi.idm.oclc.org/10.1002/jdd.13465

Modha B. (2020) Leadership and management culture within dental practice: A case study. *Leadership in Health Services*, 33; 4: 417–428. Available at: https://doi.org/10.1108/LHS-04-2020-0018

Moore D., Saleem S., Hawthorn E., Pealing R., Ashley M., Bridgman C. (2015) Healthy gums do matter: A case study of clinical leadership within primary dental care. *British Dental Journal*, 219; 6: 255–259. Available at: https://doi.org/10.1038/sj.bdj.2015.712

Nalliah, R. (2016) Do dentists make poor leaders? *British Dental Journal*, 220: 389–391. Available at: https://doi.org/10.1038/sj.bdj.2016.292

Panaccio A., Donia M., Saint-Michel S., Liden R. C. (2015) Servant leadership and wellbeing. In Burke R. J., Page K. M., Cooper C. (eds) *Flourishing in Life, Work and Careers*. Cheltenham, Gloucester: Edward Elgar Publishing.

Park S. E., Chung D., Giannobile W. V. (2022) Professional leadership training programs for dental faculty: Perspectives of the US dental school deans. *Journal of Dental Education*, 86; 6: 670–676. Available at: https://doi.org/10.1002/jdd.12887

Power A., Allbutt H., Munro L., MacLeod M., Kennedy S., Cameron D., Scoular K., Orr G., Gillies J. (2017) An evaluation of experiences and views of Scottish leadership training opportunities amongst primary care professionals. *Education for Primary Care*, 28; 3: 159–164. Available at: https://doi.org/10.1080/14739879.2016.1266239

Rendtorff J. D. (2020) *Moral Blindness in Business: A Social Theory of Evil in Organizations and Institutions*. Cham: Palgrave Macmillan.

Richards A. (2020) Exploring the benefits and limitations of transactional leadership in healthcare. *Nursing Standard*, 35; 12: 46–50. Available at: https://doi.org/10.7748/ns.2020.e11593

Shaw S. (2023) *The Philosophy of Authentic Leadership*. Cham: Springer Nature. Available at: https://doi.org/10.1007/978-3-031-29650-5_1

Smircich L., Morgan G. (1982) Leadership: The management of meaning. *The Journal of Applied Behavioural Science*, 18; 3: 257–273. Available at: https://psycnet.apa.org/doi/10.1177/002188638201800303

Svensson I., von Knorring M. (2025) Connecting distributed leadership and leadership-as-practice to increase understanding of leadership as distributed in healthcare practice. *Journal of Change Management*, 25; 1: 1–20. Available at: https://doi-org.uhi.idm.oclc.org/10.1080/14697017.2025.2453136

Taichman R. S., Parkinson J. W., Nelson B. A., Nordquist B., Ferguson-Young D. C., Thompson J. F. (2012) Program design considerations for leadership training for dental and dental hygiene students. *Journal of Dental Education*, 76; 2: 192–199. Available at: https://doi.org/10.1002/j.0022-0337.2012.76.2.tb05246.x

Tang K. N. (2019) *Leadership and Change Management.* Singapore: Springer Nature.

Toma M., Blamey A., Mahal D., Gray N. M., Allison L., Thakore S., Bowie P. (2020) Multi-method evaluation of a national clinical fellowship programme to build leadership capacity for quality improvement. *BMJ Open Quality*, 9; 4. Available at: https://doi.org/10.1136/bmjoq-2020-000978

Wardman M. J. (2020) *Rethinking Leadership for Dentistry: A Critical, Exploratory Approach.* PhD Thesis, University of Leeds School of Dentistry [Accessed 5 March, 2025] Available at: https://etheses.whiterose.ac.uk/id/eprint/28040/1/Wardman%20MJ%20Dentistry%20PhD%202020.pdf

Willcocks S. G. (2016) Exploring leadership in the context of dentistry in the UK. *Leadership in Health Services*, 29; 2: 201–216. Available at: https://doi.org/10.1108/LHS-02-2016-0009

Ytterstad S., Olaisen J. (2023) *Learning Transformational Leadership: A Pedagogical and Practical Perspective.* Cham: Palgrave Macmillan. Available at: https://doi.org/10.1007/978-3-031-21824-8

Further Reading

Langley G. J., Moen R. D., Nolan K. M., Nolan T. W., Norman C. L., Provost L. P. (2009) *The Improvement Guide.* San Francisco: Jossey-4+Bass.

Chapter 5

Scoping a Problem

Introduction

When problems arise, it is necessary to reach a shared view on their nature and likely causes. Every issue exists in a context. Some issues are too large to be resolved by a single team and would require organisational attention (Batalden, 1991, Roehrs, 2018). Knowing this at the start can save a lot of effort by steering the clinical team onto issues that are likely to have a greater yield. It is easy to jump to conclusions about the nature of a problem, its potential causes, and therefore its likely solutions. Taking time to explore an issue pays dividends. Teams also need to decide what issues they want to prioritise. While not all decisions are within the control of individual clinical teams, knowing why a topic is being selected for improvement work and being able to contribute views supports ownership. When there are choices about countermeasures to a problem, taking a team perspective helps to avoid blind spots in understanding, and therefore increases the likelihood of identifying testable solutions. This chapter explores how teams can work together to identify problems and to understand the underlying issues.

Where to Start

Many issues are manageable by a team, and it is these issues that most services will want to address in their first phase of familiarity with quality improvement methods. Teams often come to quality improvement because they have already identified a problem on which they want to work. When this first issue is resolved, or the team are beginning quality improvement with no fixed issue in mind, taking stock of what issues cause problems for the team works well. This can be done in a group session, or by collecting ideas first, for example, by having a sheet staff can write ideas on, or to which they can add a sticky note, and then talking about the issues.

A prioritisation matrix can be a good way of doing this. The team chose two dimensions and then rated ideas on these dimensions. The team can use any dimensions that make sense to them,

DOI: 10.4324/9781003493532-5

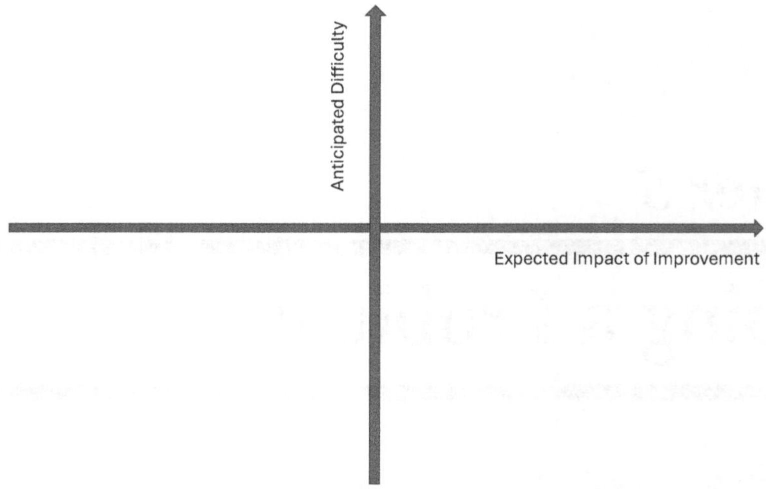

Figure 5.1 Example of a prioritisation matrix

but it is common to use the likely impact if the problem is resolved as one axis, and how difficult the team expects the work to be as the other axis (Figure 5.1).

The team places items on the matrix as a group process. This is also useful in identifying when staff have very different views of either the impact of the problem or the likely difficulty in resolving it. This provides an opportunity to share ideas and to understand how the issue affects different people in the team, often because of their differing responsibilities. The team may choose to pursue a more difficult project in search of bigger gains or choose to focus on smaller improvements that they see as achievable, particularly in the early stages of experience with quality improvement.

Defining the Problem

Defining a problem sounds straightforward but can be more difficult than expected. This is usually because different staff members vary in their view of possible causes, which pushes them down different lines when thinking about options for improvement. It can also arise because of different understandings of broad aims. Looking at the example later in the chapter, a team might agree that overrunning clinical sessions is an important issue to tackle but still expect very different improvement work because of the many possible contributing causes.

Lack of clarity on the issue being addressed causes confusion. It can be particularly disruptive if different staff members have varying constructions of the problem. This relates to the problem itself, its possible causes, and to generating testable solutions. If there is disagreement about the problem and its causes, it inevitably produces different views on possible solutions. Taking time to develop a shared understanding is a good investment of effort.

In some instances, the selected problem dissipates when examined and proves to be more imagined than real. In most other cases, there is a real issue of concern, and showing interest in understanding it is powerful. Staff often experience problems at work and put up with them or work around them. This can be because they are used to it and accept it as part of business as usual; because they do not believe it will have any result if they draw it to a manager's attention;

are concerned that they may be blamed for the problem; are too stressed to have time to think about it, or because they do not think it is possible to improve the situation, often because they see it as a resource problem.

Agreement on a problem is best reached as a team. This can be helped by gathering information in advance of a discussion. Ways of doing this are considered in the next section.

Gathering Information

In quality improvement, triangulating information is valuable. Triangulation in research involves looking at results from different types of studies, each with its own inherent biases (Hibbert *et al.*, 2016, Lawlor, Tilling and Davey Smith, 2016, Hessen *et al.*, 2019, Guttierrez, Glymour and Davey Smith, 2025). The same principle is applicable when understanding a service problem. Views and experiences from staff and patients, data from routine monitoring or one-off pieces of work, and information from other sources such as complaints can be combined to obtain a rich view of the issue.

Data

What data is applicable depends on the issue being reviewed. There may be routinely collected information that can be accessed, such as for waiting times or appointment cancellations. Other information, such as complaints, may be useful in some situations. For many quality issues, there will be a problem for which no data is routinely collected. Examples include the clinic overruns discussed later in the chapter, unless the electronic system used by the team allows this to be accessed. Other matters, such as the causes of delays, are very unlikely to be recorded. This means that one-off data collection may be needed.

As with other aspects of measurement discussed in Chapter 7, it is important not to put more work into data collection than is needed for the purpose. Clinically trained staff often default to methods used in research projects, which is usually unnecessary for local quality improvement work. The clinic overruns example later in the chapter gives an example of a locally developed data collection sheet. Other types of data collection can be very simple. For example, if a service looked at late cancellations, then a tally chart would give the required information, with a mark on the chart made for each instance. Using five bar gates, with four vertical marks and then a fifth diagonal line, make them easy to count and to compare.

Staff Views

The people who have the best knowledge of problems are the people who work in the system and the people who use it. The closer the proximity to the issue, the more information people will have. It is easy for service heads or practice owners to assume that they have a good understanding of every aspect of their service. That may be true in the smallest practices, but in larger practices, group practices and hospital services, no one can know every detail. Hospital services are likely to use intersecting systems that may not be designed for dental services alone. Interactions between software systems, or even between ways of working in different departments, can cause problems, and often no one person has detailed knowledge of every system.

Senior managers often come to a problem with the assumption that they know what the issue is, and they are best placed to resolve it. If someone has worked in a service very recently, that may be correct, but in most instances, the knowledge of the senior manager will be partial and incomplete. This issue can be elevated to a larger problem when managers feel they are responsible for fixing things. Staff are often promoted because they are good at problem solving in their own area, but this does not automatically carry across to new areas of work. The idea that they may have to admit to less than complete knowledge can be challenging for managers who believe that they may lose respect from staff if they do not offer instant answers.

A good response to this is to consciously apply the principles of humble inquiry, regardless of whether the person or group gathering information is managers. Humble inquiry is an approach to gathering information you do not know by asking questions in a respectful manner (Schein and Schein, 2021). The approach is underpinned by interest and curiosity, and an aim to reach a shared understanding (Moffett *et al.*, 2019). It is risky to approach a problem with a pre-existing view of the problem, even if the expectations are based on previous experience in similar situations.

Asking questions allows everyone to reflect on the issue and often helps to structure the problem (Kon *et al.*, 2023). If staff feel there is a preferred explanation for the problem, they are likely to suppress facts and views that may run counter to the apparent preferred narrative. It can be satisfying for the interviewer to have their opinion supported, but it is much more important to reach a full understanding of the issue. For that to happen, it must be clear that questions are being asked to reach understanding, rather than because the questioner is looking for evidence of individual failure. As discussed in Chapter 1 and 2, many problems in healthcare arise from systemic issues, rather than from individual error, and if it is apparent that the inquirer is starting from an assumption of error, it generates immediate defensiveness. Avoiding this demands genuineness from the inquirer. Staff are quick to see through a veiled attempt to gather evidence of blame while claiming otherwise, which is why genuine interest and engagement are required.

This does not mean that there is never individual failure or systematic inadequate performance in health care systems, but the route to address these requires other considerations such as human resource issues. In some cases, the performance problem will prove to be related to organisational conditions such as inadequate staffing, unreasonable demands, unclear or conflicting processes, in which case a quality improvement approach may be appropriate.

Observation

If a member of the team is taking a lead in gathering information, they may choose to watch the process. This is easier for a specialist quality improvement worker in a larger service who can use dedicated time for the work, but clinicians or administrators can often find time to make observations if they use a structured approach. For example, if the team wants to look at problems with a booking process, the observer can watch the relevant staff member using the software. This usually intersects with other processes as it may be necessary to move information from one electronic system to another. Seeing this being done and having the staff member explain what they are doing often allows problems to be observed directly and then reflected back to check understanding.

In work looking at management of emergencies, for example, it may be necessary to look at different days of the week. The team may want to explore how emergencies are triaged and allocated to treatment slots. Many services find they have more calls about emergencies on Mondays after the weekend, and on Fridays because patients are conscious that they may not be able to access dental care over the weekend. In a situation like this, having observations only on a Tuesday or Wednesday is unlikely to paint the whole picture. Knowing that the team needs to include a Monday and a Friday in observations allows a systematic approach to be taken.

If observations are being conducted, it is essential that the whole team understands that this is not an attempt to catch people out but rather to identify problems with the system that the team can work together to address. Getting the tone right is important. As was discussed in Chapter 1 and Chapter 4, an adversarial culture is much less likely to encourage staff engagement. The people who undertake tasks day in and day out will have a good understanding of the process and often have good ideas for improvement. Keeping staff onside and comfortable yields dividends.

If it is not practical for one person to follow a whole process, as might happen in a dental group with different branches, then a group can work together to undertake and share observations. This can be organised using online conferencing and messaging. This type of arrangement may be required when spreading work from one area to another (see Chapter 8) or when taking part in large-scale collaborative work (Chapter 9).

Describing a Process

When describing a process, visual representation usually works best, although it may need to be supplemented by notes or tables. When describing a process, think about:

- What steps are undertaken.
- Who undertakes each step.
- What materials and information are needed for the step.
- What software or equipment, if relevant, is used.
- How long each step takes on average, and the range of times for that step. Some steps have a commonly occurring time but may have much longer times in some cases because of a complication in some patients or situations. If this is the case, then taking stock of how common the longer times are is useful as it steers the group in whether it must be addressed immediately or whether the group can look at common pathways first.
- Any qualitative observations, such as problems that commonly arise.
- The waits between each step.

There are common ways of drawing processes, and details are available online and in books and papers. For most purposes, the form illustrated in Figure 5.2 works well. Each step is represented by a box with the name of the step, who undertakes the work, and the main actions that occur in that step. Arrows joining the boxes show the handovers. Numbers adjacent to the arrows can be used to show how many people are normally waiting for the next phase of the process, if that is useful. In some cases, a process will be branching rather than linear; although if some options are uncommon, it may not be necessary to show them all.

There are no rules about how a diagram should be done. A team should make it no more complex than is required for their purpose. The requirement is that it communicates the necessary information in an understandable way. Communication is more important than adhering to a Platonic ideal of a process diagram. If a hand-drawn diagram serves the purpose, no more is needed.

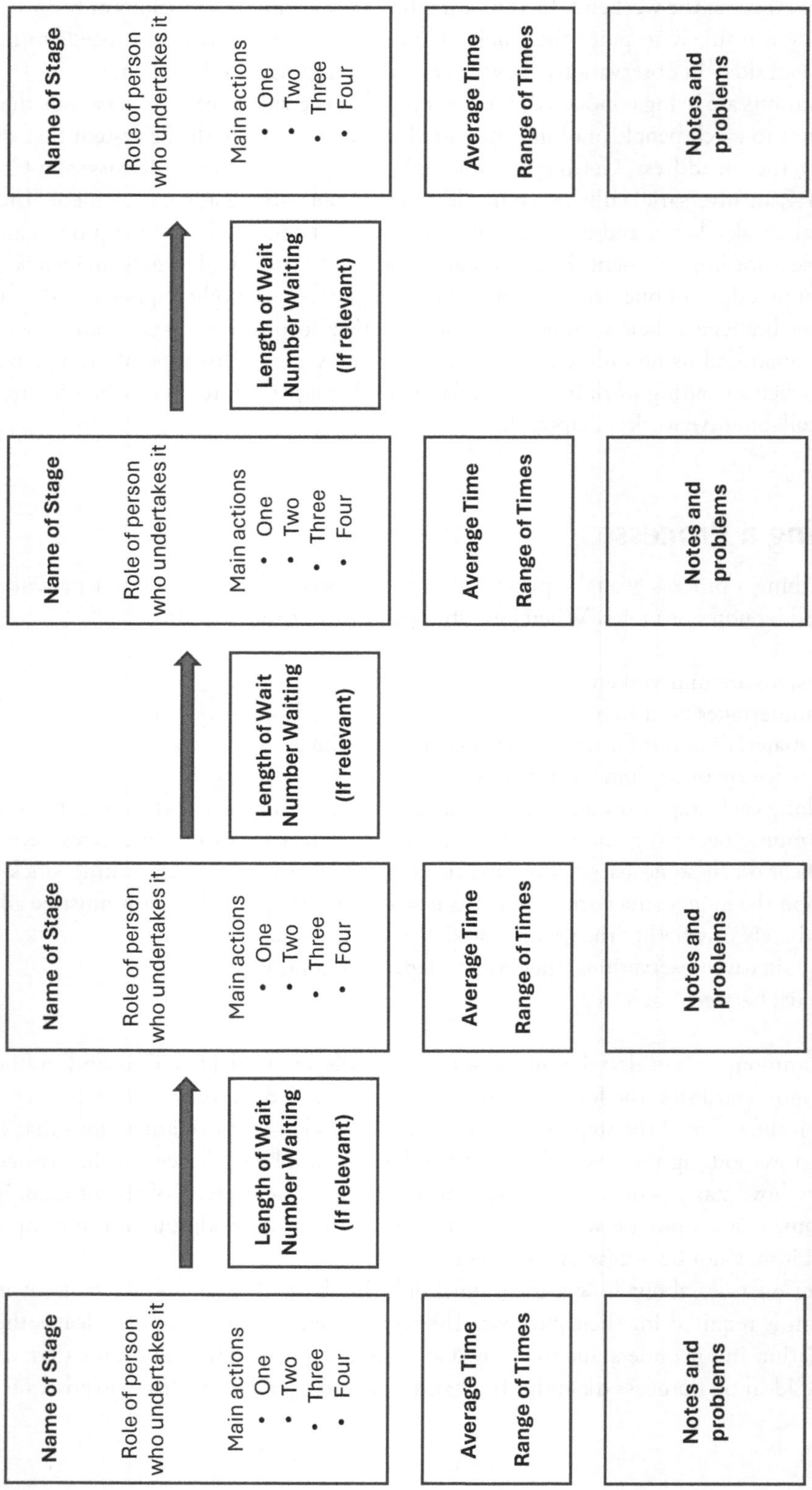

Figure 5.2 Drawing a process

Pareto Diagrams

Pareto diagrams are named after the Pareto principle, or 80/20 rule, associated with the Italian economist Vilfredo Pareto (Pyzdek, 2021). Pareto's initial observation was that 20% of Italians owned 80% of societal wealth. This was developed into a general principle by Joseph Juran, an influential management and quality theorist. Juran commented that it was possible to separate the 'vital few', these categories that had a major influence, from the 'useful many', the other causes of a problem that can be large in number without having a comparable influence (Juran, 1995, p. 17–18). He often presented the information in a diagram, now known as a Pareto Chart.

A Pareto Chart displays the numerical value of categories, placed in order from largest to smallest, in a bar chart. A second axis shows the cumulative percentage contributed by the categories. Figure 5.3 shows a Pareto Chart. This layout makes it straightforward to visualise the relative contribution of a problem to the overall frequency of problems. In dental care, it may still be appropriate to address a less common problem first because of its impact on services, patients or staff, but it becomes an explicit decision made after consideration of the options.

The next section shows an example of a team looking at an issue that concerns them.

Example of a Team Scoping a Problem

The senior staff of a dental practice, including the owner, other dentists, the practice manager and the head dental nurse, have a brief weekly meeting to deal with practice matters. One of the practice members has an interest in quality improvement and led an occasional session to discuss quality improvement possibilities.

At one session, the team discussed problems with clinic overruns. These over runs stressed the dentists, annoyed patients and caused problems in room cleaning for the next session. Dentists sometimes had to stay late or miss lunch to catch up. When this prevented administrative tasks happening in clinics, such as making referrals to external services, dentists found themselves having to work in the evenings or at weekends, with an impact on their personal life. Nurses' plans were disrupted by late-running clinics, and receptionists found themselves having to deal with annoyed patients. The team decided that this could be a priority for improvement work.

The team resolved to establish how common a problem this was. It is easy to overestimate the frequency of an issue because of the disruption it causes. If a problem is uncommon, it may still be worth addressing if its impact is large. Having knowledge of the baseline frequency helps to make this an explicit decision. It also gives a measurement against which to judge improvement.

The team agreed to record the start and end times of clinics for two weeks and developed a form for this purpose (Figure 5.4). The form was completed by the practice receptionist.

The information showed that overruns were common, sometimes because the clinic started late. Most overruns were short, but some were as long as 30 minutes. After reviewing the results, the team decided this was worth improvement action because of its frequency, and its impact on staff and patients.

The dentists and senior nurses had a weekly meeting in which any team issues were discussed. They expanded the next session to include all staff who were in the clinic at that time. The team discussed possible reasons for delays, including both issues identified during the baseline recording period, and other issues identified by the team members at the meeting. Team members wrote

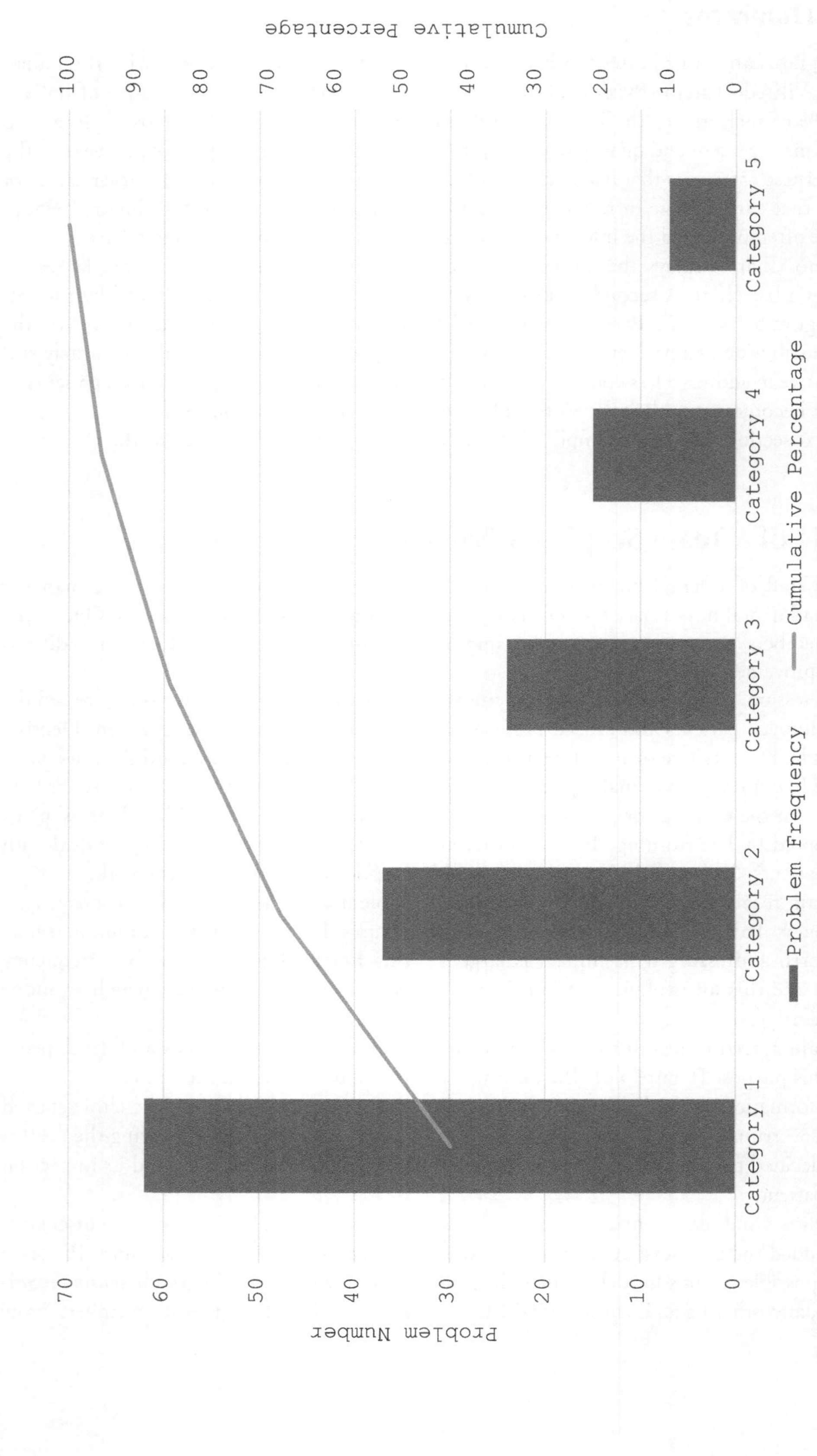

Figure 5.3 Structure of a Pareto chart

Date:

MORNING

Room 1	**Room 2**	**Room 3**	**Room 4**	**Room 5**
In use/not in use	In use/not in use	In use/not in use	In use/not in use	In use/not in use
Expected Start: Actual Start:	Expected Start: Actual Start:	Expected Start: Actual Start:	Expected Start: Actual Start:	Expected Start: Actual Start:
Expected End: Actual End:	Expected End: Actual End:	Expected End: Actual End:	Expected End: Actual End:	Expected End: Actual End:
Notes:	Notes:	Notes:	Notes:	Notes:

AFTERNOON

Room 1	**Room 2**	**Room 3**	**Room 4**	**Room 5**
In use/not in use	In use/not in use	In use/not in use	In use/not in use	In use/not in use
Expected Start: Actual Start:	Expected Start: Actual Start:	Expected Start: Actual Start:	Expected Start: Actual Start:	Expected Start: Actual Start:
Expected End: Actual End:	Expected End: Actual End:	Expected End: Actual End:	Expected End: Actual End:	Expected End: Actual End:
Notes:	Notes:	Notes:	Notes:	Notes:

Figure 5.4 Form used to record clinic overruns Note: Expected Start – booked time of first patient. Expected End – end of booking time. Actual Start Time – time first patient enters room. Actual End Time – time last patient leaves room.

their ideas down on sticky notes and added them to a large sheet of paper. The list produced is shown in Figure 5.5

The team grouped the issues into categories. As the original list was produced using sticky notes, it was straightforward for the team to group and regroup them until they were content with the categories (Figure 5.6). When undertaking this, the groupings did not have to be perfect. Different teams may choose different categories or allocate issues to different categories than would happen with another team. The main requirement is that the categories make sense to the team, and that they are willing to work with them. The diagram produced by grouping facts or issues in this way is known as an Affinity Diagram (Mizuno, 1988).

• Patient arrives late. • Working in a clinic with a new trainee nurse. • Equipment or materials not available. • Technical difficulties resulting in longer treatment times, such as a more complicated root canal than expected, or an extraction turning into a surgical procedure. • Having to take a call from a laboratory. • A network problem preventing or slowing access to the computer system. • Discovering that a material or drug is out of date when checking at the chair side before treatment.	• Helping a vocational trainee, therapist, or hygienist. • Anxious patient needing more time. • Long discussions about treatment options. • Issues clarifying consent, such as concerns about possible cognitive impairment. • Receptionist coming into treatment room with a query. • Computer rebooting. • Problems with Wi-Fi link to iPad for consent form completion. • A required procedure set not available because being used by another clinician. • Treatment set still in the decontamination process.	• A problem at the reception desk, such as a disruptive patient. • A patient taking ill in the waiting room. • A patient fainting or taking ill during treatment. • A request from the local ambulance service for a dentist to attend with the defibrillator. • Lengthy notes. • Having to write a referral. • Having to call or write for prior approval of a treatment. • Over run in the patient's previous treatment session, with the hygienist. • Patient changing their mind about their preferred treatment option.

Figure 5.5 Staff views on causes of clinic overruns

Category	Examples	Category	Examples
Patient-Related	• Late arrival. • Anxiety. • Change of mind about treatment preference. • Long discussion about treatment options. • Child's appointment taking longer than average because of limited compliance.	**Records and administration**	• Network problem. • Wi-Fi problem. • Computer rebooting. • Lengthy notes required. • Onward referral required. • Unexpected prior approval required.
Medical Emergency	• Emergency during treatment. • Emergency in waiting room. • Ambulance service request for dentist to attend.	**Technical**	• Extraction failed, surgical extraction required. • Treatment taking longer than expected, such as a root canal proving more difficult than anticipated.
Staff-Related	• Dentist working with a new trainee nurse. • Hygienist, therapist, or junior dentist requiring advice or help. • Call from laboratory that requires the dentist.	**Stock**	• Procedure set not available when needed. • Material out of date. • Required drug out of date. • Materials not in the room, must be sourced from the clinic central supply store.

Figure 5.6 Grouping causes into categories

The list can be recorded in a table, as show in Figure 5.6. Alternatively, they can be shown in a Fishbone Diagram (also known as an Ishikawa or Cause-and-Effect diagram) (Ishikawa, 1985, Stark and Hookway, 2019, pp. 136–138). The information in Figure 5.6 is shown in a Fishbone Diagram in Figure 5.7. Visual layouts such as this can work very well and are easy to share.

It may not always be necessary, but counting how often issues occur can be valuable. Some issues are less common than a team believes but have such an impact when they occur that they stick in people's minds. Other issues are less dramatic but can have a major impact because of their frequency and may be overlooked. It is also possible that a team member can have a particular interest in one issue, and this can come to dominate conversation even when it may not be the biggest priority when considered dispassionately.

Obtaining numerical information can be very helpful. The degree of sophistication of the data collection does not need to be high: the information must be accurate, and the team must agree that it represents the problem. Tally charts are often fine. It is not necessary to create a new electronic data collection method or to have an existing software system revised to allow additional data collection or access.

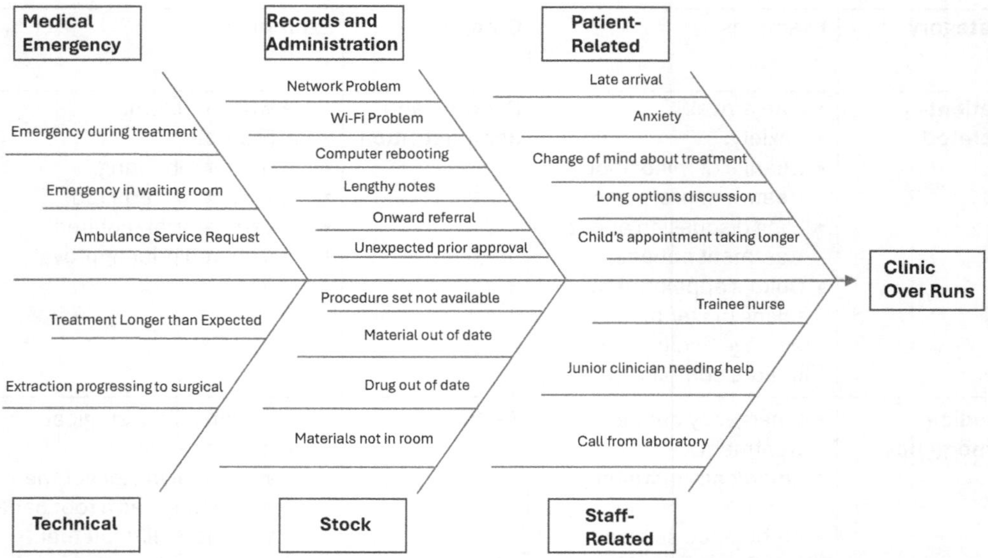

Figure 5.7 Fishbone Diagram of reasons for clinic over runs.

In the example above, the team took the category list from their meeting (Figure 5.6) and amended it to allow easy data collection (Figure 5.8). It would also be possible to record the time of each delay depending on what is important to the team.

When using this table, staff added the room number and the date, and then added a tally for each occurrence. When the data was collated after two weeks of collection, a Pareto Chart was produced showing the relative frequency (Figure 5.9).

Taken together, this information gave the team a firm basis on which to agree priorities and where to direct their initial improvement efforts.

Further Tools

Root Cause Analysis

Some factors require further exploration. Root cause analysis that seeks to identify the underlying cause or causes is one option that teams may regard as attractive. Formal root cause analysis is a useful method that can be applied in dental care (Kalenderian *et al.*, 2023, Sedlock, Halpin and Walji, 2025). The method was developed in industry but has been applied in healthcare for decades. The most recent healthcare iteration of the method is RCA^2, Root Cause Analysis and Action (National Patient Safety Foundation, 2015, Balakrishan *et al.*, 2019). RCA^2 is often used in patient safety. It requires a team approach and uses a structured method for which additional training is recommended, and its application benefits from coaching (Institute for Healthcare Improvement, 2019). RCA^2 is commonly used in large healthcare organisations to investigate patient safety incidents.

The method is part of an organisational approach. It requires:

- Senior organisational commitment and involvement.

Clinic Room:		Date:	
Category	Frequency	Category	Frequency
Patient Issue		Records and administ·ation	
Late arrival.		Network problem.	
Anxiety.		Wi-Fi problem.	
Change of mind about treatment preference.		Computer rebooting.	
Long discussion about treatment options.		Lengthy notes requir-d.	
Child's appointment compliance issue.		Onward referral required.	
Other patient issue.		Unexpected prior approval required.	
		Other Records or Admin Issue.	
Medical Emergency		Technical	
Emergency during treatment.		Extraction failed, surgical extraction required.	
Emergency in waiting room.		Treatment taking longer than expected.	
Ambulance service request for dentist to attend.		Other treatment issue.	
Other Medical Emergency Issue.			
Staff -Related		Stock	
Dentist working with a new trainee nurse.		Procedure set not available when needed.	
Hygienist, therapist, or junior dentist requiring assistance.		Material out of date.	
Call from laboratory that requires the dentist.		Required drug out of date.	
Other staff-related issue.		Materials not in the room.	
		Other stock-related ssue	
Notes			

Figure 5.8 Data collection tool expanded from category list

- Creation of a culture that focuses on understanding causes in preference to blaming individuals.
- Four to six-person teams.
- Clear agreement on what incidents are suitable for RCA[2].
- Agreement on how incidents will be identified is usually based on a risk-based prioritisation method. This may use a formal trigger tool (Hibbert *et al.*, 2016).
- Gathering of data and creation of flow diagrams.
- Production of Cause-and-Effect diagrams.
- Identification of remedial factors
- Development and implementation of solutions.

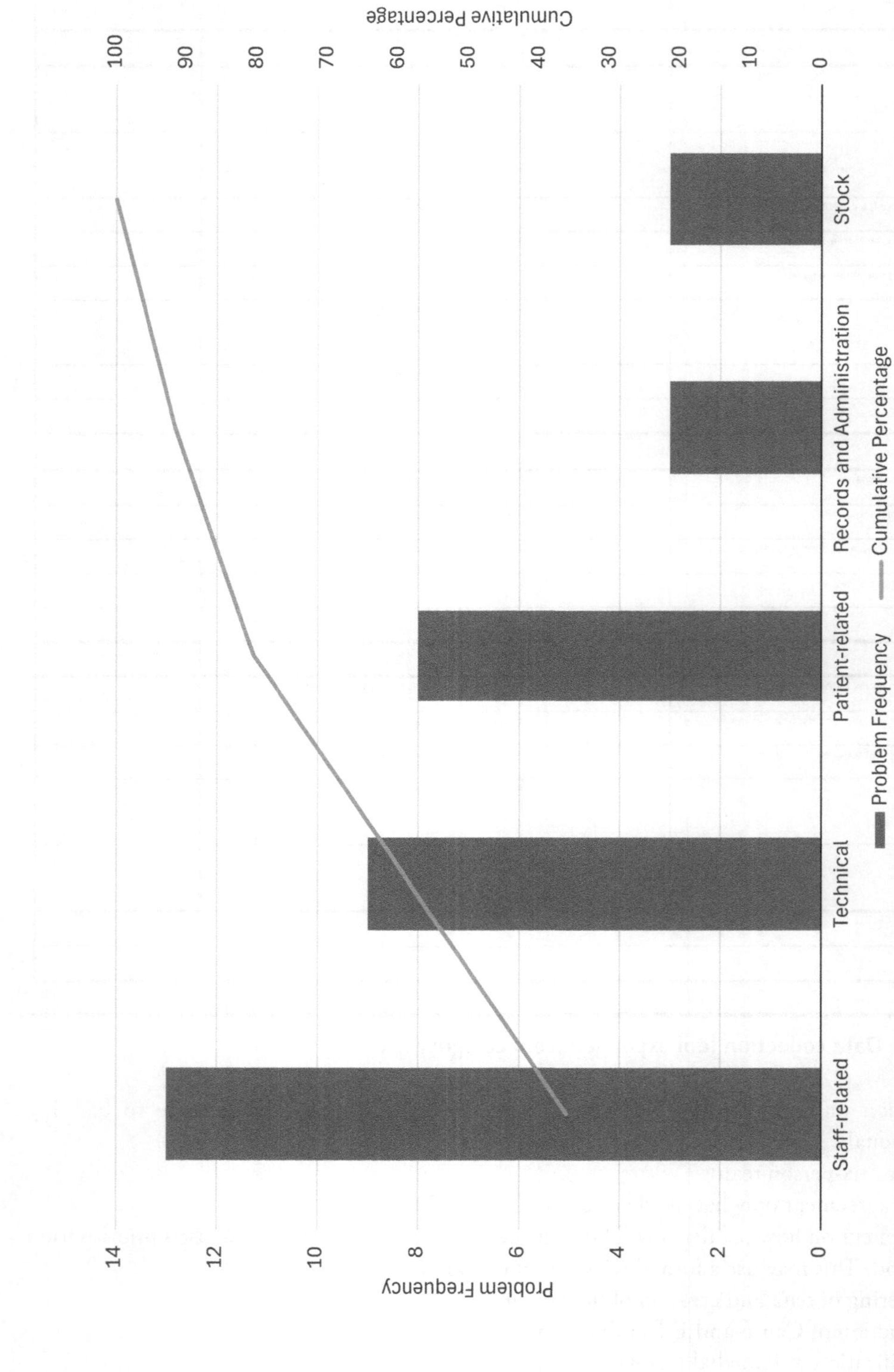

Figure 5.9 Pareto chart of problem frequency

Applying the entire method is better suited to organisational use than introduction in a single team, but many of the individual techniques are useful and can be applied in any improvement work. Having someone with training in RCA^2 can be very useful to a team.

Five Whys

One useful option is to use the '5 Whys' technique when exploring an incident. This involves asking why the issue happens and keeping going until it seems likely that the underlying cause has been reached. There are limitations to taking this too literally. There is no magic in the number five, and a root cause can be reached in two steps, or seven. It is also possible that there is more than one important underlying cause. The approach, however, is often useful.

In the example above, where surgical sets are not always available, the following sequence could occur:

Problem: Surgical sets are not always available when required.

Question 1: Why are surgical sets not always available?
Answer: The kit may be in use by another clinician.

Question 2: Why does this happen?
Answer: Similar procedures are scheduled at the same time in different rooms, or unexpected problems requiring a surgical kit arise at the same time.

Question 3: Even if there is no other procedure underway, the kit may not be available. Why is this?
Answer: The kit has not been cleaned and re-stocked.

Question 4: Why does this happen?
Answer: The autoclave may be in use; a nurse may not be free to take the kit to the washer and disinfector, to transfer the kit to the autoclave, or to take the kit from the autoclave and make up the set.

Question 5: Why does the kit have to be cleaned and sterilised urgently?
Answer: There is only one set of surgical tools for a surgical extraction.

In this example, the question the team stop at will influence the decision for improvement action. For example, if the team stop at question two, the answer is likely to be to create a system that avoids scheduling similar procedures in different rooms at the same time. This could be effective but would not address the less common issue of two emergency surgical extractions arising at the same time.

If the team stop at question three, this may seem like a problem of nurse behaviour. Drilling down further, nurses may not be free to return kit during a treatment session or there may be no one free to move the kit to the next stage of the cleaning, sterilisation and re-stocking process. This suggests creating standard work for the process, creating a mechanism to alert nurses to move the kit to the next stage, and altering nurse duties to make the sterilisation process a priority.

This omits the issue of timing. Figure 5.10 shows the timings of the process; even if everything goes well with no delays, it still takes about two hours to clean the kit, even if staff are immediately

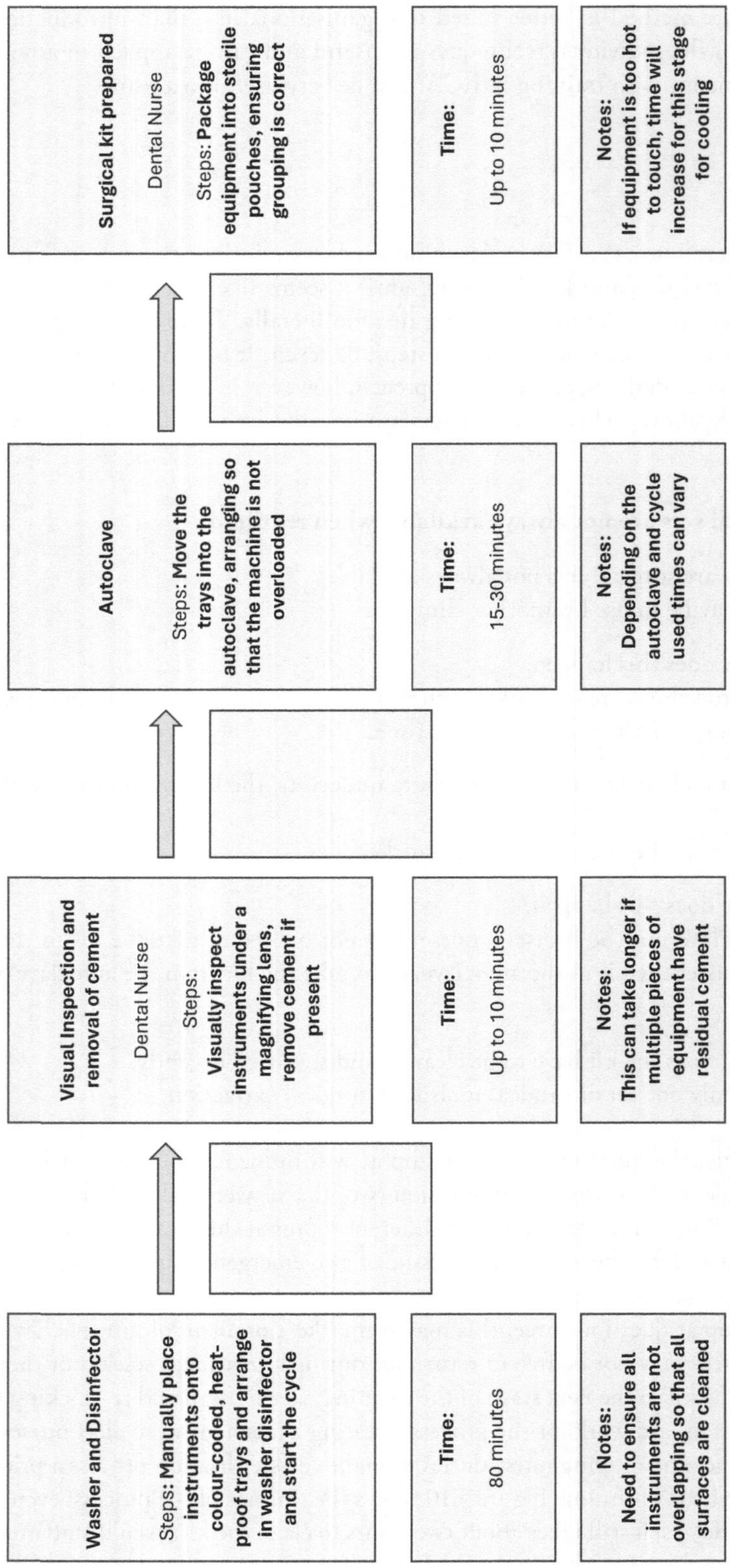

Figure 5.10 The cleaning and decontamination process Source: Rhona Günhan

available to move it on to the next stage. This could take it out of circulation for a significant amount of time.

Taking this into account, the team may conclude that the key issue is that there is only one set of tools for a surgical extraction. This would not mean that none of the other issues remain important. Even with two sets, things could go wrong. An extraction needing to progress to a surgical procedure is always possible. Even if there are two sets of instruments, avoiding scheduling two procedures known to require the same materials makes sense when the kit may also be required unexpectedly. In this practice, materials are cleaned in the evening and at lunchtime, and a clear protocol for unexpected additional cleaning would again be helpful.

Capacity is not always the final issue. In other cases, issues such as booking processes, work processes, or training may be the root cause of the issue. The key point is that the team should seek to look past the first obvious cause to assure themselves that there are no further issues that they need to consider. Even when underlying causes are identified, if these are out with the direct control of the team, then the team may find issues they can improve in their own area of control that can ease the problem while they seek to influence the underlying issue. It is also possible that a resource issue cannot be resolved because the capital is not available to resolve it. In that case, the team can again look at what they can control that will improve the situation.

Conclusions

Dental teams are busy and want to get on with things. Taking time to review what feels like well-understood problems can feel like unnecessary effort that creates a delay. Despite this, it is worthwhile ensuring that the team have a collective understanding of the problem. This helps to keep efforts aligned and avoids any staff members being confused by what is happening.

As discussed in other chapters, it is important to get the tone of the work right and to engage people without criticism. Seeking collective understanding is more productive and helps the team on to discussion of possible solutions. This then leads on to testing of the options, discussed further in the next chapter.

References

Balakrishnan K., Brenner M. J., Gosbee J. W., Schmalbach C. E. (2019) Patient safety/ quality improvement primer, part II: Prevention of harm through Root Cause Analysis and Action (RCA2). *Otolaryngology-Head and Neck Surgery*, 161; 6: 911–921. Available at: https://doi.org/10.1177/0194599819878683

Batalden P. B. (1991) Building knowledge for quality improvement in healthcare: An introductory glossary. *Journal for Healthcare Quality*, 13; 5: 8–12. Available at: https://doi.org/10.1111/j.1945-1474.1991.tb00195.x

Gutierrez S., Glymour M. M., Davey Smith, G. (2025) Evidence triangulation in health research. *European Journal of Epidemiology*. March 27. Available at: https://doi.org/10.1007/s10654-024-01194-6 Epub ahead of print.

Heesen R., Bright L. K., Zucker A. (2019) Vindicating methodological triangulation. *Synthese*, 196; 8: 3067–3081. Available at: https://doi.org/10.1007/s11229-016-1294-7

Hibbert P. D., Molloy C. J., Hooper T. D., Wiles L. K., Runiman W. B., Lachman P., Muething S. E., Braithwaite J. (2016) The application of the Global Trigger Tool: A systematic review. *International Journal for Quality in Health Care*, 28; 6: 640–649. Available at: https://doi.org/10.1093/intqhc/mzw115

Institute for Healthcare Improvement (2019) *Patient Safety Essentials Toolkit: Action Hierarchy Tool.* Boston, MA: Institute for Healthcare Improvement.

Ishikawa K. (1985) *What is Total Quality Control?* Englewood Cliffs, NJ: Prentice-Hall Inc.

Juran J. M. (1995) *Managerial Breakthrough.* 2nd Edition. New York, NY: McGraw-Hill.

Kalenderian E., Bangar S., Yansane A., Tran D., Sedlock E., Xiao Y., Urata J., Olson G., Franklin A., Kookal K., Ibarra-Noriega A., Tungare S., Tokede O., Spallek H., White J. M., Walji M. F. (2023) Identifying contributing factors associated with dental adverse events through a pragmatic electronic health record-based root cause analysis. *Journal of Patient Safety,* 19; 5: 305–312. Available at: https://doi.org/10.1097/PTS.0000000000001122

Kon S., Fisher S., Ngo N., Craig R., Gunter C., Bessesen M., Gilmartin H. (2023) Utilization of a novel humble inquiry interview approach in assessing implementation barriers to a nurse-driven Clostridioides difficile test order set. *American Journal of Infection Control,* 51; 11: 1288–1290. Available at: https://doi.org/10.1016/j.ajic.2023.05.012

Lawlor D. A., Tilling K., Davey Smith G. (2016) Triangulation in aetiological epidemiology. *International Journal of Epidemiology,* 45; 6: dyw314–1886. Available at: https://doi.org/10.1093/ije/dyw314

Mizuno S. (1988) *Management for Quality Improvement. The Seven New QC Tools.* Cambridge, MA: Productivity Press.

Moffett S., Anand A., Walsh I. (2019) Does humility facilitate Knowledge Sharing? Investigating the role of humble knowledge-inquiry and response. *Journal of Knowledge Management,* 23; 6: 1218–1244. Available at: https://doi.org/10.1108/JKM-06-2018-0353

National Patient Safety Foundation (2015) *RCA²: Improving Root Cause Analyses and Actions to Prevent Harm.* Boston, MA: National Patient Safety Foundation.

Pyzdek T. (2021) Pareto analysis. In *The Lean Healthcare Handbook. Management for Professionals.* Cham: Springer. Available at: https://doi.org/10.1007/978-3-030-69901-7_14

Roehrs S. (2018) Building of profound knowledge. *Current Problems in Pediatric and Adolescent Health Care,* 48; 8: 196–197. Available at: https://doi.org/10.1016/j.cppeds.2018.08.013

Schein E. H., Schein P. A. (2021) *Humble Inquiry: The Gentle Art of Asking Instead of Telling.* 2nd Edition. San Francisco, CA: Berrett-Koehler.

Sedlock E. W., Halpin R., Walji M. F. (2025) Teaching root cause analysis to dental and dental hygiene students: Interactive case study. *Journal of Dental Education:* e13881. Available at: https://doi.org/10.1002/jdd.13881

Stark C., Hookway G. (2019) *Applying Lean in Health and Social Care Services: Improving Quality and the Patient Experience at NHS Highland.* New York, NY: Routledge / Productivity Press.

Chapter 6

PDSA Cycles

Introduction

A PDSA cycle, or Plan-Do-Study-Act cycle, is a way of structuring small cycles of change. The method can work well in a clinical environment (Campbell and Tickle, 2013). By working through four stages, changes can be developed, tested and applied to enable the best outcome. PDSA cycles can be first used at a small scale, and each cycle builds upon what was learned in the last. Eventually, these cycles can be applied to larger, more extensive settings. This chapter should be read in conjunction with Chapter Three on audit, as many of the issues discussed there on conducting audit are also applicable to PDSA cycles.

Starting at a small scale allows the user to evaluate the outcome before implementing it across a wider setting. In a dental setting, an example would be running PDSA cycles in one surgery, then moving to other surgeries in the same practice and then on to a second practice. Working through the four stages gives flexibility to adapt the changes and ensure the systems are fit for purpose. In larger change programmes, PDSA cycles can be more extensive from the beginning, but in projects run by clinical teams, an incremental approach works well.

Use of PDSA Cycles in Dental Care

PDSA cycles are beginning to be reported in dental and oral health care. A selection is shown in Table 6.1. Compared to published audit reports, PDSA papers tend to cover a wider range of topics. The PDSA method, described later in the chapter, lends itself to application in a variety of situations. Dental PDSA publications are dominated by academic departments. This may be because staff in academic departments are both more likely to publish and because they may have better access to relevant support services. The examples in Table 6.1 demonstrate the wide applicability of the method to a variety of topics.

Positive results are more likely to be published, so the reports will not be representative of all PDSA cycles. They do demonstrate that the technique can be applied to many different issues. The

DOI: 10.4324/9781003493532-6

Table 6.1 Examples of PDSA cycles used in dental care

Authors	*Setting*	*Topic*	*Notes*
Campbell *et al.*, 2016	Dental Hospital, Dundee, Scotland.	Residual cement contamination on instruments.	The team used five PDSA cycles. Reduction of examination kits with a contaminated instrument from 27% to 7%.
Sudhanthar *et al.*, 2019	Academic dental practice, Michigan, United States of America.	Fluoride varnish application in a paediatric service.	Three PDSA cycles. Began with educational interventions and later introduced changes to electronic systems. Fluoride varnish application increased from 14% to 55% of eligible patients.
Nic Iomhair and John, 2020	Community Dental Service, Belfast, Northern Ireland.	Planning and preparation for appointments in the Special Care Dentistry service.	Two PDSA cycles. Assessment of relevant care needs increased from 30% to 90%. The average time taken to obtain the information decreased from 2 minutes 31 seconds to 17 seconds.
Barratt *et al.*, 2020	Dental Hospital Cardiff, Wales.	Management of diagnostic specimens.	Four PDSA cycles. Most frequent issue was samples with no patient details. Days between incidents increased from less than 50 to an average of over 150.
Qabool *et al.*, 2022	Aga Khan University Hospital, Karachi, Pakistan.	Donning and doffing of personal protective equipment (PPE) during the COVID pandemic.	Educational intervention. Variable results. 44% improvement in handwashing before donning PPE.
Alkarimi *et al.*, 2025	King Fahd Armed Forces Hospital, Jeddah, Saudi Arabia.	Access to preventative dental services for children in paediatric wards.	Four PDSA cycles, including development of a system (cycle 1) and ongoing monitoring (cycle 4). No referrals at all in the baseline period, increasing to between 80% and 100% of eligible children being referred by cycle 4.

studies listed also show work in which the organisation has produced its own topics for improvement and where there is no established standard. This is different from the audit studies shown in Tables 3.1 and 3.2 which tended to use a national or international standard, or one derived from published literature. It is also notable that many of the studies outlined in Table 6.1 report several cycles, in some cases distributed over long periods of time. This demonstrates the importance of incremental change and the potential value of linking PDSA cycles together in the same manner as an audit spiral.

Application of PDSA Cycles

The PDSA cycle is particularly suitable for use in dentistry when testing small changes aimed at improving patient care, safety in the workplace, or operational efficiency. This includes situations where a healthcare team wants to implement evidence-based interventions but needs to tailor them to their specific setting, such as a dental practice or hospital-based dental service. The cycle allows for rapid, iterative testing of changes on a small scale before broader implementation, helping teams learn what works and what does not in real time. This approach is valuable when addressing complex processes like reducing practice waiting times, improving hand hygiene compliance, or enhancing communication between the team, where measurement is important for success, and several different strategies may need to be developed and tried out to achieve the desired result.

Questions Before Starting a PDSA Cycle

Associates for Process Improvement, a quality improvement consultancy service, developed the Model for Improvement. This model is used by the Institute for Healthcare Improvement, and this has helped to encourage its use in healthcare (Institute for Healthcare Improvement, No date). The model is straightforward and involves three questions combined with the use of PDSA cycles (Langley *et al.*, 2009, p. 5):

1. What are we trying to accomplish?
2. How will we know that a change is an improvement?
3. What changes can we make that will result in an improvement?

These questions seem obvious when set out on the page, but paying attention to them helps to maximise the time and effort that services put into quality improvement work. It is essential to be clear on the end goal for the quality improvement activity. This can be anything required to increase the productivity of the clinical environment and the welfare of staff and patients. It could be reducing waiting times, increasing patient satisfaction, reducing burdens and stresses on staff, increasing financial income or reducing errors, for example. Being explicit on the aim keeps the team focused and helps to avoid mission creep, when the work begins aiming at one problem but gradually changes direction to tackle other problems without the team making an explicit decision to do so.

Knowing what success will look like helps the team both to spell out what they hope to achieve and to consider what changes may contribute to it. To know if there is an improvement, the team must be able to identify measures related to the aim of the project. These can be process measures or outcome measures. Details are discussed later in the chapter, but outcome measures are used to analyse how effective the change has been. To know this, it is also necessary to know the current performance of the service. This is described as the baseline weith the measurement of the baseline being conducted in the ways as described for audit in Chapter 3. Agreeing on which measurable outcomes will be used beforehand will aid the team in judging their results and make the 'study' section of the PDSA cycle easier.

Identifying what will produce an improvement requires the team to have a theory of the nature of the existing problem. Causes may be obvious, but in other cases, work is required to gain a full understanding (see Chapter 5 for more details). Thinking this through also avoids bringing in unrelated issues. Teams often have many good ideas, but not all ideas will be linked to the problem they are addressing at any time. Knowing what should change helps to make it easier to identify what can plausibly contribute to the hope for improvement. This does not mean that other issues are unimportant, but addressing problems systematically is more likely to produce and maintain gains than taking a scattergun approach.

Measuring Change

These factors mean that before beginning a PDSA cycle, or series of PDSA cycles, it is important to decide exactly how you are going to measure change. Setting out clear ways of measuring change will make the 'study' phase more efficient and save time during the process. Sometimes it is difficult to tell if a change is an improvement; deciding on the measuring outcomes beforehand will help in this scenario and show any improvements made.

Measurable Outcomes include:

Outcome Measures: Outcome measures reflect the aim of the improvement work, such as reducing waiting times, decreasing non-attendance or increasing patient safety.

Process Measures: Process measures relate to the processes that will impact the aim. For example, to reduce waiting times there may be changes to triage processes, or to how clinics are booked. All the changes will be measurable. If the team's understanding of the problem is accurate and no other issues intervene, then they will contribute to the desired outcome.

Balancing Measures: Balancing measures are selected to monitor whether the changes may be causing undesired effects. For example, changes to the time available for an appointment may increase the proportion of patients who return later with adverse treatment sequelae, or staff morale may reduce because of increased workload.

Selecting measurements is discussed in greater detail in Chapter 7.

Stages of a PDSA Cycle

The stages of a PDSA cycle are (Figure 6.1):

PLAN – Design and agree the change to be tested based on your end goal.
DO – Conduct the PDSA cycle, collect information to assess the hypothesis.

Figure 6.1 Stages of a PDSA cycle

STUDY – Analyse the changes with data gathered before and after the cycle using the agreed measures.

ACT – Plan the next cycle for change based on what has been learnt from the improvement cycle, or implement the change achieved if satisfied with the result.

Figure 6.2 shows an example of a form that can be used when conducting PDSA cycles. Other examples of PDSA forms are available online. The Insitute for Healthcare Improvement offer a PDSA workbook for free download (Institute for Healthcare Improvement, 2017).

Important issues to consider in each stage are:

Preparation: The work undertaken in understanding the problem will help at each subsequent step. In some cases, further information gathered in a PDSA cycle will lead the team to review their understanding of the problem as new information is generated. Based on the team's new information, they may revise planned steps. Preparation is discussed in more detail in Chapter 5.

This is a good time to think about the scale of the change being tested. Identifying an idea that does not work as quickly as possible saves time and avoids disappointment. Generally, trying out an intervention with one patient and one staff member, or the equivalent in a non-clinical intervention, will identify any major issues, such as the instructions being unclear. If this is successful, or after any required adaptation, the new arrangements can then be tried out by one staff member for a longer period, such as a clinic. The third cycle could be for a different staff member or staff team to try it out in a different treatment room. Each stage helps to minimise disruption and maximise learning. In this sequence, the team would know by the end of the third cycle that they had a new method that could be applied by different staff members in more than one setting. Expanding PDSA cycles in this way is often termed 'PDSA Ramping'.

PDSA Worksheet Topic:

Location: Date: Cycle No:

What are we trying to achieve?:

Plan:
What change will be tested? Where will it be tested? How will it be recorded? Who will conduct the test?

Do:
Record the agreed measurements Are there any other observations?

Study:
What happened? How did it compare to expectations? What have we learned? What should we change?

Act:
Can we embed this change? If not, do we drop the idea, or make changes? If changes, what do we need to test in the next cycle?

Figure 6.2 Example of a PDSA Worksheet

In some cases, such as a booking system change, it may be more difficult to start small. It can also take longer to see the impact. In a situation such as this, process measures are likely to be very important as the new arrangements will have to bed in before there is any expectation of a change to the anticipated outcome.

Plan: The team agrees on the next test of change and how it will be conducted. The planned change should be as clear as possible so that there is no doubt about what has been tested. If there are different understandings of what was tested, the results will be interpreted differently by different team members. It helps to write it down. For example,

> 'Jeff and Stacy will try the new process with every patient in Consulting Room One, on Thursday morning.'
>
> 'On Monday, Myra will use the new flow chart with every patient calling reception to ask for an emergency appointment.'
>
> 'Every dentist and dental nurse in the practice will use the new surgical checklist with every patient for the next week.'

Having a written statement of what will be tested helps to avoid confusion. Testing out written checklists, flow charts, etc. also means that the layout and wording can be reviewed by the people testing them out. This is valuable in identifying any problems, most of which can be quickly resolved.

Being clear on what outcome is anticipated and how and when that outcome is going to be measured is essential. This may be 'the new pre-surgical checklist will be used by every team with every patient', as recorded by each clinical team. In this example, it would be important for each team to make a brief note of why they did not use it in a particular instance, such as a time constraint. As well as the numerical information there will also be important qualitative information to capture, such as how the staff member(s) found the change, how patients reacted, and how easy any guidance was to follow.

Do: This stage sounds self-explanatory. It is important, however, to capture as much relevant information as possible. Unexpected things happen and these can provide the team with a lot of information on what may need to change. For example, patients may consistently misunderstand a new question that the team thought was clear; a process that seemed to work well in one treatment room may not work in another because of layout, or a staff member with less experience may find a process more difficult than anticipated. Recording these issues at the 'Do' stage greatly helps with later analysis.

Study: In the study phase the team takes stock of whether the test of change performed as expected, and whether the desired outcome occurred. It is important to be honest about this. In the Sunk Cost fallacy, people sometimes persevere with something because they have already invested time and effort. A PDSA cycle should be the antithesis of this behaviour. It is an opportunity to take stock of the impact of a change using objective information. If the change did not perform as expected, this is not a criticism of the team. It is an opportunity for new learning, and the team must review it honestly and in good faith. This also means that any team member that opposed the change must be as honest as possible with themselves about what worked, as well as what did not. The team should consider whether the size of the change is commensurate with the work required to undertake the new process, once it is in routine practice. It is also important to consider whether there were any unintended consequences that need to be taken into account in the next cycle of change.

Often there are issues that need to be tweaked, such as changes to instructions or to the layout of a new checklist. In other instances, there may be something that no one thought of before the trial that needs to be taken into account, or which can be applied to improve the process further. Each time the team discovers a problem it is an opportunity to improve the process further to ensure that kg is effective in as many situations as possible. These reviews are best done in a group where possible to keep everyone in the team involved.

Act: In this phase, any required changes are incorporated into the next PDSA cycle. In some cases, the initial test of change will have delivered exactly what is required, but it is common to find other issues that need to be considered. When the team reaches a state where they are happy with the changes, they need to consider how to embed it in their routine practice. This is likley to involve writing down the new process so that it can be shared. This also allows any drift from the agreed method to be identified, and for the steps to be easily shared with new staff. Other methods, including using checklists, diagrams or visual controls may supoort the change depending on the improvement and the context.

Larger Scale Applications of PDSA Cycles

PDSA cycles do not have to be run on one issue at a time or be ramped up in the manner described above. The method can be used for large, complex changes as part of a larger process (Reed and Card, 2016). Running parallel PDSA cycles can be an effective strategy in dentistry when multiple aspects of a process need improvement simultaneously. This approach allows teams to test different interventions at the same time, either in separate locations or on different parts of a workflow, accelerating learning and generating a broader understanding of what changes are most effective.

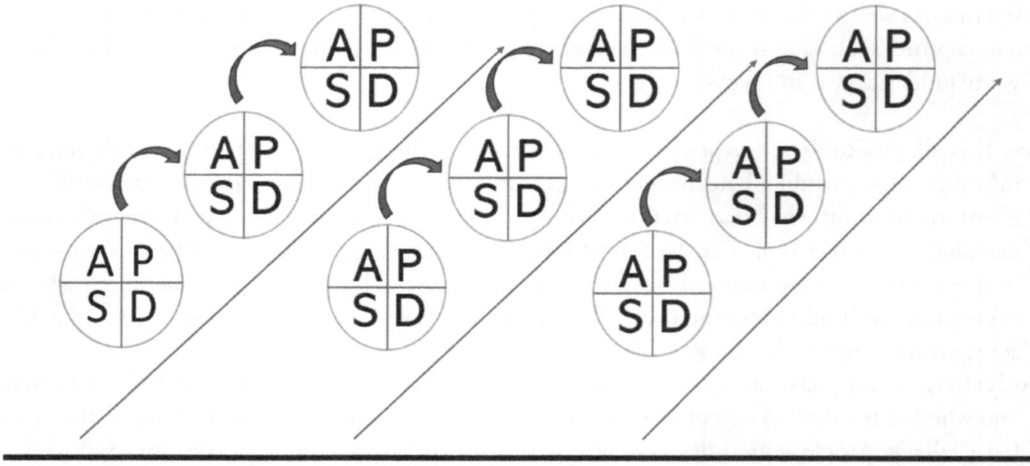

Figure 6.3 Diagram of running parallel PDSA cycles

For example, in an improvement project intended to avoid runing out of required supplies, dental nurses might test a new stock management checklist in the surgeries while the reception team test a new system for ordering supplies at the front desk.

The decision to conduct parallel PDSA cycles requires careful consideration. For many teams, working on one PDSA cycle at a time, focused on one issue, is the best choice. This concentrates effort and makes it clear that the service or team is prioritising a particular piece of work. It also helps to clarify what has produced any identified improvement. If a team has little or no experience of running PDSA cycles, this is a better option. Using the method in a manageable way and securing successes can lead on to other uses of the approach in the future.

In a larger service, or in the context of a major improvement project supported by improvement coaches, conducting several PDSA cycles at once may be practical (Stark *et al.*, 2024). Doing this will require coordination to avoid duplication of effort or contradictory changes. Clear communication and structured oversight are essential to ensure that each cycle remains focused, data is collected consistently and learnings are shared across teams. A centralised tracking system such as a shared notice board and regular meetings can help monitor progress and ensure alignment with overarching improvement goals. Without proper coordination, teams may become overwhelmed or confused by the volume of changes, which can reduce the overall effectiveness of the initiative and potentially compromise patient care.

Parallel PDSA cycles do offer the benefit of testing ideas more rapidly and identifying scalable solutions more efficiently (Figure 6.3). They can also enhance team engagement by giving more staff the opportunity to lead and contribute to improvement work. When well managed, this approach can accelerate progress and strengthen the setting's capacity for continuous learning. To succeed, however, it requires strong leadership, sufficient resources and a culture that supports collaboration and transparent evaluation. Most teams will take one thing at a time and evolve to dealing with parallel PDSA cycles once they have developed some experience and comfort with the method.

Importance of Staff Engagement

Staff engagement is an important aspect of running PDSA cycles, as it directly influences the effectiveness and sustainability of quality improvement efforts. When frontline staff are actively involved in the planning and implementation of changes, they are more likely to feel a sense of ownership and accountability for the outcomes. This engagement encourages a collaborative environment where team members contribute their firsthand knowledge of clinical workflows and patient needs, helping to design interventions that are practical and relevant. Engaged staff are also more motivated to identify problems, suggest solutions and support the testing of changes, leading to more meaningful and lasting improvements.

Involving staff in the PDSA process helps bridge the gap between theory and practice. Staff who are regularly engaged in testing and evaluating changes develop a deeper understanding of improvement science and the reasoning behind proposed interventions. This not only builds capacity for future quality improvement initiatives but also reduces resistance to change, as staff can see the direct impact of their work. When team members are encouraged to share feedback and data during the 'Study' phase, they become active participants in decision-making, promoting transparency and a shared commitment to patient safety (Batalden and Davidoff, 2007).

Considerations Before Expanding to a Second Setting

Expanding PDSA cycles to a second setting, such as a different service or a second practice, can experience challenges. Initial results may be different from those in the original setting. Differences in staff culture, patient demographics, workflows and available resources between the original and new settings can contribute to differences in the replication of results (Coles *et al.*, 2020). Professional organisations and trade unions can also influence uptake and may require to be engaged (McBride and Martínez-Lucio, 2018). Pre-existing professional practice can be very difficult to change (Grove, 2023).

What worked well in one practice or department may not translate seamlessly to another, especially if there is insufficient engagement or understanding among staff in the new setting. Sending an e-mail to another practice or department requesting a change to how they work is unlikely to be effective (Kellogg *et al.*, 2017). As noted above, improvement work has greater impact when staff are involved in deciding and testing interventions (Wolak *et al.*, 2020). If moving to a second location has always been likely, a staff member from the second site can be involved in the work from the beginning. If not, it is helpful to identify and support a local champion of the work. In cases where spread is within a hospital, or in a geographically spread corporate practice, creating a group to oversee the spread of quality improvement initiatives can work well. The group can consider the appropriateness of spreading the intervention more widely; help to share supporting materials from the pilot units, and identify people to champion the changes in each collaborating unit (Wolak *et al.*, 2020). In making a locally developed solution fit in a new setting, it may be necessary to run some local PDSA cycles to iron out the detail of the process in the context of any local constraints, such as different dental chairs, room layout, or software packages. Spreading interventions is reviewed in more detail in Chapter 9.

Limitations of PDSA Cycles

While PDSA cycles are widely used in healthcare improvement, they have limitations. One significant challenge is the variability in how PDSA cycles are understood and applied (Taylor *et al.*, 2014). Without the necessary discipline, teams may skip essential steps, rush through the process, or fail to collect meaningful data, reducing the quality and reliability of the outcomes. In some cases, PDSA cycles become a box-ticking exercise rather than a thoughtful approach to improvement. This can lead to superficial changes that do not address root causes or result in sustainable improvements.

Another limitation is the time and resource constraints often faced in healthcare settings. Staff are frequently under pressure from clinical demands, making it difficult to allocate the necessary time for planning, data collection, analysis and reflection. As a result, PDSA cycles may be cut short or conducted without adequate efforts, undermining their effectiveness. Additionally, the small-scale nature of initial tests can limit the generalisability of findings, particularly if background factors unique to one setting are not considered before broader implementation (Kaplan *et al.*, 2011). This raises the risk of interventions failing when scaled up without good planning.

Finally, organisational culture and leadership support play a crucial role in the success of PDSA cycles, as in any improvement project. In environments where hierarchical structures discourage open communication or where leadership is not committed to quality improvement, staff may feel reluctant to participate fully or to share honest feedback about what is and is not working. These issues are discussed in more detail in Chapter 1. Without a culture that values experimentation and learning from failure, teams may struggle to embrace the nature of the PDSA approach. While PDSA cycles offer a powerful framework for improvement, their success depends on thoughtful execution, adequate support and a culture that fosters collaboration and continuous learning.

Box 6.1 gives tips for the use of PDSA cycles that help to reduce some of these risks.

BOX 6.1 TIPS ON USING PDSA CYCLES

- PDSA cycles make sense to dental teams. Dental professionals are used to the idea of gathering evidence and using it to change practice, so the approach is a good fit.
- Be clear on the aim of the work. Any vagueness results in confusion and makes mission drift more likely.
- A team cannot solve every problem at once. Dealing with a manageable issue and addressing it thoroughly is better than spreading limited capacity across many topics.
- Do not rush the preparatory work. The pressure to get on with a test of change can be hard to resist, but time spent understanding the problem is never wasted.
- Involve staff from the beginning. The more that people are involved and see what is happening, the more they will trust the method.
- Think about ramping up in a measured manner. It is easier to start small and then spread, reflecting and adapting to the results of each PDSA cycle.
- Measure – Measurement is core to the PDSA method. Identify measures that can be easily counted, reported and shared.
- Complete the cycle – Services often undertake repeated 'Plan – Do' cycles without the study and act steps. This leaves them with no notion of whether the change has worked, and if it has worked, why it has worked. This makes it impossible to build on knowledge gained and devalues the method.

Conclusion

The PDSA cycle offers a practical and structured approach to driving continuous improvement in dentistry. Whether enhancing patient safety, streamlining clinical workflows, or improving communication within the dental team, the iterative nature of the PDSA model allows for small, manageable changes to be tested and refined before wider implementation. This reduces the risk associated with large-scale changes and helps ensure that interventions are tailored to the unique needs of a dental practice or department, which can be very different from a larger institution like a hospital. When applied thoughtfully, PDSA cycles empower dental professionals to take an active role in quality improvement, fostering a culture of learning, reflection and patient-centred care.

The successful application of PDSA cycles in dentistry depends heavily on staff engagement, consistent data collection and a supportive organisational environment. Limitations such as time constraints, inconsistent methodology and scaling challenges must be acknowledged and addressed to maximise the model's impact. As dental teams continue to face evolving challenges in service delivery and patient expectations, embracing the PDSA approach can serve as a valuable tool for navigating change, enhancing care quality and ensuring long-term improvement. By embedding continuous improvement into everyday practice, dentistry can remain responsive, efficient and committed to excellence.

References

Alkarimi H. A., Jawadi A., Tayeb S., Ismail R., AlShareef E. J., Sherbini N. (2025) Implementing the Child Oral Health Initiative (COHI): Improving access to preventive dental care to achieve Saudi Vision 2030 healthcare goals. *BMJ Open Quality*, 14; 2: e003070. Available at: https://doi.org/10.1136/bmjoq-2024-003070

Barratt O., Simms M., John M., Lewis M., Atkin P. (2020) Improving diagnostic specimen management systems in an oral medicine department. *BMJ Open Quality*, 9; 3: e000926. Available at: https://doi.org/10.1136/bmjoq-2020-000926

Batalden P. B., Davidoff F. (2007) What is 'quality improvement' and how can it transform healthcare? *Quality and Safety in Health Care*, [online] 16; 1: 2–3. Available at: https://doi.org/10.1136/qshc.2006.022046

Campbell L., Barton A., Boyle R., Tully V. (2016) Improving the inspection and manual cleaning of dental instruments in a dental hospital. *BMJ Quality Improvement Reports*, 5: u205075.w2305. Available at: https://doi.org/10.1136/bmjquality.u205075.w2305

Campbell S., Tickle M. (2013) How do we improve quality in primary dental care?. *British Dental Journal*, 215: 239–243. Available at: https://doi.org/10.1038/sj.bdj.2013.831

Coles E., Anderson J., Maxwell M., Harris F. M., Gray N. M., Milner G., MacGillivray S. (2020) The influence of contextual factors on healthcare quality improvement initiatives: A realist review. *Systematic Reviews*, 9; 1. Available at: https://doi.org/10.1186/s13643-020-01344-3

Grove A. (2023) Micro-clinical cultures, group mindlines, and evidence-based practice. In Burgess N., Currie G. (Eds.), *Shaping High Quality, Affordable and Equitable Healthcare*. Cham: Springer Nature, pp. 67–91.

Institute for Healthcare Improvement (No Date) *Model for Improvement* [Online]. Available at: https://www.ihi.org/library/model-for-improvement [Accessed 21 August 2025]

Kaplan H. C., Provost L. P., Froehle C. M., Margolis P. A. (2011) The model for understanding success in quality (MUSIQ): Building a theory of context in healthcare quality improvement. *BMJ Quality & Safety*, 21; 1: 13–20. Available at: https://doi.org/10.1136/bmjqs-2011-000010

Kellogg K., Gainer L., Allen A., O'Sullivan T., Singer S. (2017) An intraorganizational model for developing and spreading quality improvement innovations. *Health Care Management Review*, 42; 4: 292–302. Available at: https://doi.org/10.1097/HMR.0000000000000122

McBride A., Martínez-Lucio M. (2018) Sustaining healthcare service improvements without collective dialogue and participation: A route to partial failure? In McDermott A., Kitchiner M., Exworthy M. (Eds.), *Managing Improvement in Healthcare: Attaining, Sustaining and Spreading Quality*. Cham: Palgrave Macmillan, pp. 155–168.

Nic Iomhair A., John M. (2020) Facilitating patient-centred care for special care dentistry patients: A Quality Improvement Project in the Community Dental Service. *BDJ Open*, 6; 1: 11. Available at: https://doi.org/10.1038/s41405-020-0038-4

Qabool H., Ali F., Sukhia R. H., Badruddin N. (2022) Compliance to donning and doffing of personal protective equipment among dental healthcare practitioners during the coronavirus pandemic: A quality improvement plan, do, study and act (PDSA) Initiative. *BMJ Open Quality*, 11; 3: e002001. Available at: https://doi.org/10.1136/bmjoq-2022-002001

Reed J. E., Card A. J. (2016) The problem with Plan-Do-Study-Act cycles. *BMJ Quality & Safety*, 25: 147–152. Available at: https://doi.org/10.1136/bmjqs-2015-005076

Stark C., Hookway G., McVicar G., van Woerden H. (2024) *The Field Guide to Rapid Process Improvement Workshops in Healthcare: Applying Lean to Improve Quality and Patient Experience*. New York, NY: Routledge.

Sudhanthar S., Lapinski J., Turner J., Gold J., Sigal Y., Thakur K., Napolova O., Stiffler M. (2019) Improving oral health through dental fluoride varnish application in a primary care paediatric practice. *BMJ Open Quality*, 8; 2: e000589. Available at: https://doi.org/10.1136/bmjoq-2018-000589

Taylor M. J., McNicholas C., Nicolay C., Darzi A., Bell D., Reed J. E. (2014) Systematic review of the application of the plan–do–study–act method to improve quality in healthcare. *BMJ Quality & Safety*, 23; 4: 290–298. Available at: https://qualitysafety.bmj.com/content/23/4/290

Further Reading and Resources

Langley G. L., Moen R., Nolan K. M., Nolan T. W., Norman C. L., Provost L. P. (2009) *The Improvement Guide: A Practical Approach to Enhancing Organizational Performance*. 2nd Edition. San Francisco, CA: Jossey-Bass Publishers.

The Institute for Healthcare Improvement offers free information and resources on PDSA cycles. They are available at: https://www.ihi.org/library/model-for-improvement

Chapter 7

Measurement

Introduction

Quality improvement depends on collecting and using evidence. This is required to create a shared understanding of the current situation, to generate options for improvement, and to establish whether the changes are for the better. Chapters 5 and 6 discussed the importance of using data to explore the problem and to identify and design options for improvement. This process also promotes team engagement. Using data to monitor the impact of a change is no less important. No one change is likely to solve all problems, so knowing what advances have been made and what is still to be done is essential. When teams become invested in a project, it can be difficult to step back and to objectively appraise the effectiveness of a change. Using data allows this to happen. As Chapter 6 discussed, quality improvement is a linked series of PDSA cycles producing a series of linked improvements, sometimes termed an improvement ramp, where the results from each cycle inform the next.

Teams sometimes feel that if they make a change they will know if an improvement results from their test of change without having to measure. Taking the time to establish measures and to record them helps because:

- With a small effect there may be disagreement about the existence of an impact, whether an improvement or a deterioration in the process. Also, knowing the size of a change as well as the direction of change makes it much more straightforward to decide whether further adjustments are required.
- A service can feel different to the staff without any change to the topic of interest. In a busy clinic session, the same process may feel more burdensome than in a quieter session. In a clinic with a medical emergency in the waiting room, a patient in the surgery who is disruptive or even verbally abusive, or a clinic with a higher load of more complex procedures that require great concentration, the cognitive and emotional load is higher, making comparisons to other situations challenging.

DOI: 10.4324/9781003493532-7

- Some staff members may prefer the old system. Even when there is an improvement, it may feel to them that the old arrangements were better. Equally, advocates for the change can be predisposed to detect an improvement when none objectively exists.
- Even if a change is made and the team agrees there has been an improvement, this performance may not be maintained over time. With no measures, it is difficult to be sure that the improvement has continued. Having an objective measure to which current performance can be compared makes this more straightforward.

Being able to measure change is therefore an integral part of the improvement process (Schroeder, 2021). This chapter reviews measurement in improvement.

Measurement Needs in Quality Improvement

Dental teams have undergraduate, and often postgraduate, training in research methods. Whether or not members of the team have conducted research of their own, they are aware of issues about consent; representativeness; testing for statistical significance and ensuring adequate power for statistical assessment. This means they bring a set of assumptions to evidence for improvement that are not always appropriate to the method (Institute for Healthcare Improvement, no date). Approaching a team-based quality improvement initiative as if it is a research project can slow progress significantly or even prevent the work from beginning. The data needed for quality improvement work are commensurate with the aims and the importance of the work: a small project changing a single process will not require the approach used in research, although appropriate rigour is still required (Wolfe *et al.*, 2021).

One issue that does need to be considered is ethical and legal requirements for data collection (Monsen, 2024). There are situations in which formal ethical approval for work is required. For example, if researching the improvement process itself, the participants become research subjects, and the work seeks to produce generalisable knowledge, and so appropriate review is required (Mormer and Stevans, 2019). This does not mean that there are no ethical considerations in generic quality improvement. Appropriate consideration of ethical issues needs to be applied by clinical teams, particularly around data collection and use, and information for patients (Hunt *et al.*, 2021).

In relation to the ethics of measurement, teams in the United Kingdom can review guidance from the Healthcare Quality Improvement Partnership (2017). There are similar statements in many countries that can be consulted (e.g. Nelson, 2014, Goldman, 2018, U.S. Department of Health and Human Services, no date). Some institutions will have internal guidance that teams should follow. In general, authorities recommend:

- Ensuring that all relevant guidance on information handling is met.
- Measurements should be in keeping with any organisational requirements.
- Protect patient confidentiality throughout the quality improvement project.
- Vulnerable patient populations may require additional actions.
- Where the organisation has a central record of quality improvement work, the project will need to be logged and the results added to the organisational database when available.

Clinical teams should check with their organisation whether there is any guidance they should follow. Making sure that clinical governance departments and audit teams in larger organisations know about the work can be very helpful in accessing advice and in spreading information on successful changes later in the life cycle of the improvement project.

Selecting Measures

The theory of change inherent in the quality improvement intervention helps to decide the measures. A theory of change is the description of the intervention and how and why it is expected to make a difference. A theory of change can vary from a grand construction underpinning a national programme to a local team's view of what change they can make to improve part of their own service. As Chapters 5 and 6 describe, the team need to investigate the problem and generate ideas for improvement. These ideas have an expected mechanism of action. For example, a change to booking processes may be intended to level workload by distributing cases more evenly or by better matching new patient referrals to available capacity. A new safety checklist may be intended to reduce the risk of wrong site surgery by checking patient identity and confirming the surgical site and procedure before any intervention commences. A revised layout to an instrument tray, or a new ordering procedure, will usually be intended to reduce delays by ensuring the right equipment is in the right place at the right time, and so on.

Each of these interventions, and any quality intervention, has a series of actions that need to happen for the desired effect to be achieved. For example, in a change to the ways supplies are ordered, the service needs to know what to order based on estimates of what will be needed, to make the order on the required date, and to stock the items in the correct location when they arrive. These steps provide potential process measures. There is no possibility of achieving the hoped-for benefit if these actions do not occur, other than by chance. This means that there are actions that can be identified, recorded and analysed. The selected measurements are based on the expected mechanism of action and are intended to support the improvement work.

The classic triad of measures in health service quality involve the consideration of structure, process and outcome (Donabedian, 1966). Structure relates to matters such as service organisation, capacity and culture. Process describes the activities that are undertaken by the service, and sometimes by patients, to achieve the desired benefit. Outcomes are the impact of the work that is done on health, illness or on another measure, such as waiting times, error rates or cost.

It is uncommon for quality improvement projects to be able to allocate new resources or to create new organisational structures or policies, although this can happen in large-scale projects or in those dealing with problems that are very significant to the organisation. Structural measures can also be relevant when changes to organisational culture are being sought as part of the change work, but this is less common. Measurement in quality improvement therefore usually involves process and outcome measures rather than structural measures. Measures of process and outcome are chosen to match the quality improvement project's aims. Services also should consider what unplanned impacts might occur, known as balancing measures.

Looking at process, outcome and balancing measures in more detail:

- **Process Measures:** Process measures track the activities or steps taken as part of the quality improvement intervention. These measures focus on whether the intended processes are being followed consistently and as planned. For example, in the stock ordering example described above, process measurements could include recording the day on which the order is made, and whether the items were received and stocked on schedule. If looking at patient safety, they could include recording the frequency of a surgical pause, or the use of a checklist. As described in Chapter 6, finding that something is not happening as expected is not a source of individual blame. Instead, the question becomes why the actions are not occurring, and what can be done to ensure they happen more consistently.

- **Outcome Measures:** Outcome measures in quality improvement are used to assess the impact of the intervention on the project aim. The outcome measure in many pieces of improvement work will be obvious. It is important to select something that can be counted, rather than an aspirational aim. In the stock example above, for example, the outcome measure is likely to be the number of occasions on which stock is not available, as the aim of the work is to reduce this.
- **Balancing Measures:** Balancing measures are included to keep track of any potential undesired consequences. Some adverse effects come out of the blue because of an unappreciated complexity in the system. Others come up as concerns early in the project, often in issues raised by staff. Common concerns include the time taken for a new process, a reduction in time available for talking to patients, or increased stresses, but there may also be issues specific to the project that also need to be considered.

Types of Data

In quality improvement work in dental care, we have found three types of information that are most used: count data, continuous data and information on what people think and feel.

- **Count Data:** This is information where items, episodes or people can be counted in whole numbers. Examples are the number of people who do not attend a treatment session without notification; the number of times in a week or a month that items expected from a laboratory are too late to be used in the planned treatment session, or the number of root canal treatments in a particular session.
- **Continuous Data:** Information that varies continuously. In dental services, this usually relates to times, such as waiting times, or the time taken for a procedure or clinic.
- **Information on What People Think or Feel:** This can be either count or continuous data depending on how it is collected. We have found it useful to think about it in a category of its own to ensure that a decision is made on whether it should be collected. Patient satisfaction with aspects of treatment, stress on staff and the impact of a change on work are the most frequent examples of this type of information.

Ways of recording data are described further below. Some electronic systems will output the required information in as much detail as can be required, but in other cases manual collection will be required, often using a tally chart or similar method. See below for more information. For the interested reader, much other information is available on data types and their management from statistical textbooks and specialist quality improvement texts (see for example, Langley *et al.*, 2009, Provost and Murray, 2011).

Creating a Measurement Plan

The measurement plan follows from the aim of the project and the agreed improvement steps. Creating a plan helps to avoid any confusion. It can also be shared, which helps to highlight the link between the original aims, ongoing work and the measurements and results. Figure 7.1

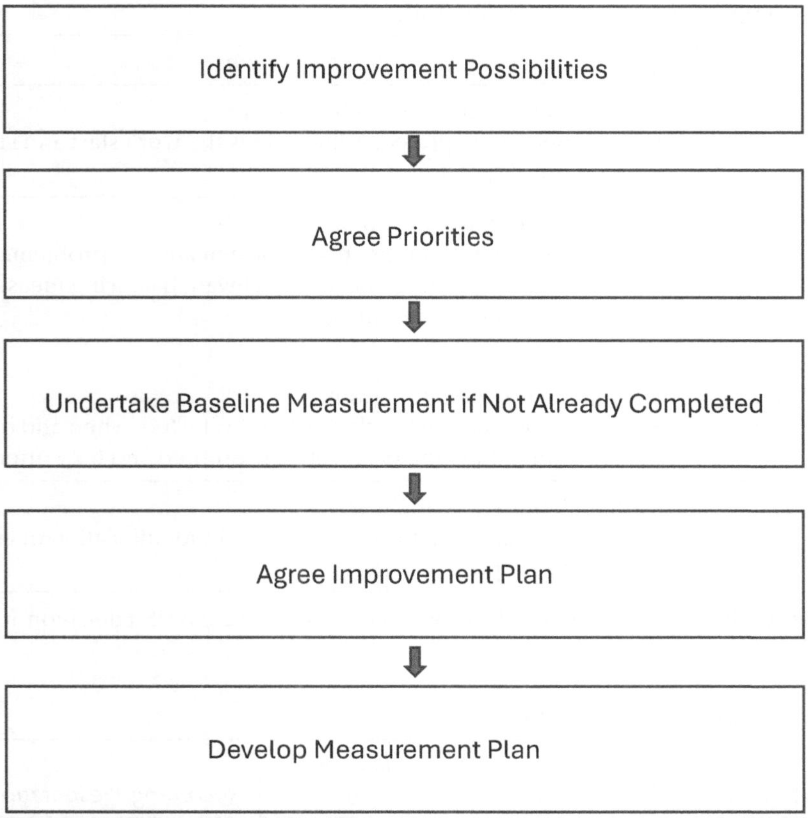

Figure 7.1 The link between project idea and measurement

illustrates that measurements follow from the earlier work in a logical sequence. It is not usually possible to identify process measures in detail before analysing the problem, although there may already be good ideas about outcome measures.

While measurement does not have to use the methods applied in research projects, this does not mean that it is not rigorous. Key features of a measurement plan include clarity on what is being measured; how it is defined; who will collect it; when it will be collected and for how long; and how it will be presented. Table 7.1 summarises some of the issues.

Other matters can be considered depending on the circumstances of the work. If work is taking place across several teams or units at once, then processes must work for all teams or be adapted as needed. This may require local adjustments to the measurement plan. In very large-scale projects, there may be a more detailed evaluation built into the work, sometimes from external researchers (Woodcock *et al.*, 2020). In most smaller-scale pieces of work, considering the issues in Table 7.1 will be adequate.

Table 7.2 has an example of the possible layout of a measurement plan document. The precise form of the document is not important, and the team can adapt the layout as needed to support their project. The main requirement is that it communicates the issues to the wider team, is easy to understand, and supports the team in their quality improvement work.

Table 7.1 Components of a measurement plan

Area	*Components*
Aims	• A statement of the aims of the project. • The scope of the project. Where does the work start and stop? • A numerical target.
Measurements	• Statement of measures to be used. • Linkage of the measurements to the aim and the problem. • Includes process, outcome and if relevant balancing measure(s). • Manageable number of measures.
Practical Aspects	• Definitions of measures. • Sampling process, if relevant. • Information on how the data will be collected, when and by whom. • Statement of how the data will be presented and how often.
Other Issues	• Time identified for the work. • If graphing or analysing data statistically, identification of any required support.

Source: Adapted from Langley *et al.*, 2009, Woodcock *et al.*, 2020, NHS Education for Scotland, 2025.

Table 7.2 Measurement plan structure

Measure	*Purpose*	*Definition*	*Collection Method*	*Recording/Presentation Method*

Sources: Langley *et al.*, 2009, Academi Gwelliant Cymru (No Date A); Clarke, Davidge and James, (No date).

Examples of Measurements in Oral Health Improvement Projects

Earlier chapters include examples of published audit and quality improvement projects which can also be reviewed. Table 7.3 shows examples of the outcomes used in a further selection of oral health-related projects in a variety of settings. Measures are mainly count data, sometimes then converted into percentages or rates. The projects often used data extracted from electronic

Table 7.3 Examples of measures in oral health projects

Study	*Setting*	*Aims*	*Measures*
Chate, 2010	72 general dental practices in the East of England.	Improve the quality of water from dental unit waterlines.	Outcome measure: Count of planktonic bacterial contamination, with *E. coli* and faecal coliforms separately identified.
Ng *et al.*, 2012	Dental services in two children's hospitals in the USA	Implement a disease management programme for dental caries in children aged under 60 months.	Process measures: number of visits per year, and length of follow-up. Outcome measures: Counts of new cavitation, pain and referrals for intervention with general anaesthesia, recorded and then calculated as a rate.
Myers, 2014	Public dental service, Eire.	Increase the recording of information in emergency dental visits.	Outcome measure: Count of completion of items in an electronic record system. Information presented as percentages by domains of information, by dentist. Balancing measure: Staff feedback on new prompt cards.
Jackson, 2015	Community paediatric clinic, South Carolina, USA	Increase screening for early childhood caries by paediatricians and nurse practitioners.	Process measures: Count of patients screened, calculated as a percentage of those eligible. Outcome measures: Count of high-risk patients referred to a dentist, calculated as a percentage.
Gnaedinger, 2018	Paediatric practice, Virginia, USA.	Increase the use of fluoride varnish in eligible children and increase income.	Process measure: Count of the application of fluoride varnish to eligible patients, then calculated as percentage of those eligible. Outcome measure: Count of billing of the procedures. Balancing measures: Time to apply the varnish. Staff feedback on the process of applying the varnish.

(*Continued*)

Table 7.3 Continued

Study	*Setting*	*Aims*	*Measures*
Miles and Shah, 2022	Oral surgery department, King's College Hospital, London.	Increase the confidence of dental nurses in managing patients undergoing intravenous sedation.	Outcome measure: Confidence measured on a five-point Likert rating scale from 'No Confidence' to 'Very confident'.
Hashemizadeh, Lyne and Liddicott, 2024	12 dental practices in North London, England.	Reduce the use of single use plastics in dental practice.	Outcome measure: Count of the number of single use plastics used in a routine patient appointment.

health records, but others collected data directly or in the waterline quality project (Chate, 2010), information from laboratory samples. The structure - process - outcome headings have been used although all three types are not present in every example. Some data could be a process measure in one improvement project, but outcome data in another. For example, increasing the number of childhood visits in a year could be a process measure or an outcome, depending on the aim of the work.

In these examples there is alignment between the aims of the work and the measures selected. Many of these projects used measures repeated once, or once in each improvement cycle depending on the design, length and complexity of the project. It is also possible to look at data over time, usually by using Run Charts.

Run Charts

Run Charts plot data over time and have the benefit of looking familiar and being easy to understand. Keeping track of results over a period using Run Charts helps to sustain quality improvement. These charts can be used both to detect change and to know whether a positive change is being maintained using a simple set of rules (Williams, 2018).

Constructing a Run Chart

Run Charts can be produced on paper or using a programme such as Excel. If using paper, it is helpful to use graph paper as it makes it easier to place points accurately and to draw lines. The process to create a Run Chart is shown below (Provost and Murray, 2011, Perla, Provost and Murray, 2011, Institute for Healthcare Improvement, 2017, Academi Gwelliant Cymru, No Date B).

When drawing the graph on paper:

1. Decide what data you need and agree how to collect it.
2. Decide on an x axis. In this context, the axis will represent time. Think through what increment is required. In most circumstances, this will depend on the data collection frequency.

Depending on the timing, this could be hours, days, weeks or months. Make the axis long enough that you have room to plot new data for the period you plan to use it without redrawing the graph.

3. Decide on the y-axis scale. Based on the initial observations, set the scale so that there is room for data to decrease or increase. Use whole numbers for the scale so that it is easy to read. Step Six involves creating a median, so set the scale so that the average observations collected in the baseline stage are roughly in the middle of the scale.
4. Label the axes, showing both the value that is being plotted and the increment.
5. Plot the available data on the graph. A dot represents the data point. It is usual to join them with a line to make them easier to follow.
6. Calculate the median of the observations so far and plot it on the graph as a line running through the graph. The median is the number in the middle when the observations are placed in order (Box 7.1).
7. Add data to the chart as it is collected. If appropriate, mark on the chart the dates of changes to the process so that the data can be compared to the improvement idea applied. Other information, such as a target, can also be added.

BOX 7.1 CALCULATING THE MEDIAN

The median is the central number in a series of numbers placed in numerical order. It is best to have ten or more observations before calculating a median. For example, if the sequence of data collected is:

18, 13, 23, 16, 19, 20, 17, 17, 21, 23, 14, 19, 20.

Then the data in order is:

13, 14, 16, 17, 17, 18, 19, 19, 20, 20, 21, 23, 23.

There are 13 numbers, and the central number is 19, so 19 is the median.

If there is an even number of observations, then the median is the average of the two middle numbers. So, if this data set was:

18, 13, 23, 16, 19, 22, 17, 17, 21, 23, 14, 19, 20, 15.

Then the numbers in order are:

13, 14, 15, 16, 17, 17, 18, 19, 19, 20, 21, 22, 23, 23.

There are 14 numbers in the data set. The 7th and 8th numbers are 18 and 19, so the median is 18.5.

A Run Chart can also be produced in an app such as Word or Excel. Guides are available online describing how to produce Run Charts in both programmes.

Figure 7.2 shows a Run Chart showing the percentage of patients who did not attend per week over a six-month period in a five-dentist practice in a deprived area of Scotland. Recording the percentage was prompted by a particularly high week, but the median non-attendance in the initial recording period was 12%, which prompted the practice to undertake two rounds of PDSA cycles to seek to reduce this proportion. The graph shows the baseline observations added, and a median calculated for the first ten observations, two working weeks, and shown on the chart.

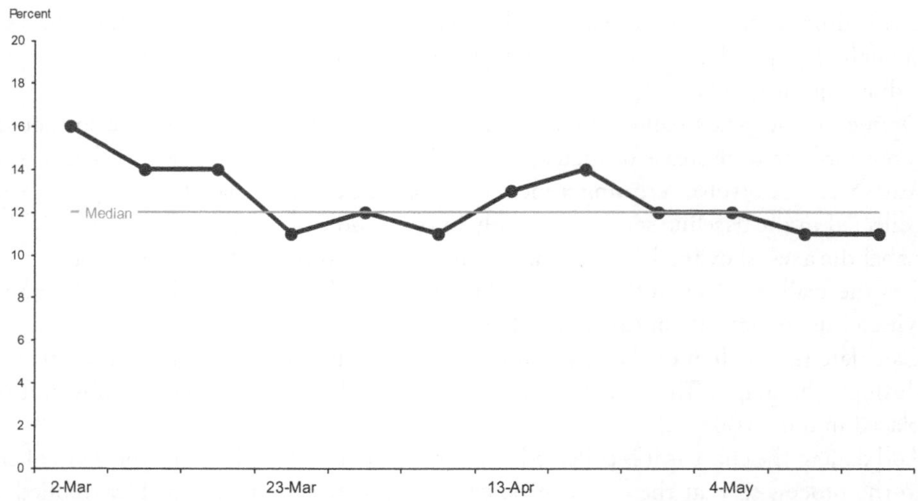

Figure 7.2 Example of a Run Chart

Interpreting a Run Chart

Run Charts have three purposes (Provost and Murray, 2011, p. 85):

- To share information so that the team can see performance over time.
- To establish whether the changes made have resulted in an improvement.
- To show whether the change has been maintained over time.

A major advantage of a Run Chart is that it can be used to determine if a change is random variation or a real change that is very unlikely to be explained by chance. This matters because it is easy to interpret randomness as a pattern. Pattern recognition is a key human attribute (Smith and Cordes, 2020). Without it, life would be very difficult as every situation would have to be tackled afresh. The downside of this is that people often detect patterns where none exist. Separating patterns from noise is not easy. Even when something is statistically unlikely, it is not impossible. A *p* value of 5% in a research study indicates that the result would be expected to happen by chance in less than 5 of every 100 times the study was conducted, which is why replication studies and appropriately powered trials are important.

For quality improvement work, staff want to be as sure as they can be that a change is real without having to invest the time for a research study. Run Charts provide a method of doing this and of being as sure as practically possible that a change is real. There are various ways of interpreting Run Charts, and the details are debated by statisticians who want to achieve the best possible interpretation. Most quality improvement organisations recommend applying a set of four rules.

These rules are shown in Box 7.2. They indicate, for example, that a shift in the data needs six consecutive points on the same side of the previously calculated median to demonstrate a shift. This seems a lot of points, but a helpful way to think about it is by using probability.

- If the numbers vary by chance, then there is a 50% chance of the next observation being above the median, and a 50% chance of it being below the median. (This is not completely true as the observation could be exactly on the previous median, but it makes the calculations easier to see if this possibility is set to one side in this description.)

- If the changes are random then the second observation also has a 50% chance of being above the median, and a 50% chance of being below the median.
- If random, the chance of two observations in a row being either both above or both below the median is 50% x 50% = 25%. If this is set out as a probability, then the calculation is 0.5 x 0.5 = 0.25.
- If this calculation is carried on, the chance of the next observation in a series being on the same side of the line continues to be 50%, or a probability of 0.5. As the sequence lengthens, the likelihood that the measurements continue a run on the same side of the median reduces steadily.
- By the sixth observation, the likelihood that the run of observations will be on the same side of the median is 0.5 x 0.5 x 0.5 x 0.5 x 0.5 x 0.5. This gives a probability of 0.016, or 1.6%, which is equivalent to a p value of $p < 0.05$. Thinking about it another way, this is a 1 in 64 chance. This can give teams reasonable confidence that their changes are having the impact they desire.

BOX 7.2 RUN CHART INTERPRETATION RULES

Rule 1: A Shift

A shift occurs when six or more consecutive points lie either above or below the median. Any measurement that falls exactly on the median is ignored for the purposes of identifying a shift and does not contribute to the six points or stop six points being counted. When a shift occurs, a new median can be added to the Run Chart.

Rule 2: A Trend.

A trend, either upward or downward, occurs when five consecutive points all go up or go down. If two consecutive points are identical, the second point is ignored for the purpose of calculating the trend and does not contribute to it.

Rule 3: Runs.

A run is a series of consecutive points that are all on the same side of the median. Fewer of these runs than expected, or more than expected, indicates non-randomness. The rule of thumb for calculating runs is to count the number of times the line crosses the median and to add one to the total. The number of runs is then compared to the number of observations using a Run Chart rules table, available online. The Institute for Healthcare Improvement provides a chart to check the number of runs, also available from other sites (Institute for Healthcare Improvement, 2019, link in reference list). Too few or too many runs is a sign that some factor is affecting the data in a non-random way and is an indication to investigate further.

Rule 4: An Astronomical Point.

There is no statistical rule to this. An astronomical point is one that anyone looking at the graph would identify as clearly different from the general run of the data. This does not mean that the highest and lowest numbers should be identified as such, as these will occur in any sequence. An astronomical point is one that is obviously different and requires exploration.

Sources: Provost and Murray, 2011, Perla, Provost and Murray, 2011, Institute for Healthcare Improvement, 2017.

To demonstrate the approach, the data from the example in Figure 7.2 can be extended. Figure 7.3 shows the new observations in the non-attendance example after two PDSA cycles.

Applying the Run Chart rules, there has been a shift in the data, allowing a new median to be calculated (Figure 7.4). The Run Chart allows a sustained shift to be demonstratefd visually, in a way that is easy to share.

Some teams find that looking at trends and shifts is enough for their purposes. Astronomical points are helpful in prompting thought about what might have caused the sudden change. Looking at signals in the data is helpful in interpreting what is happening. A trend in the direction the team expected, followed by a sustained shift, is powerful support for an impact of the quality

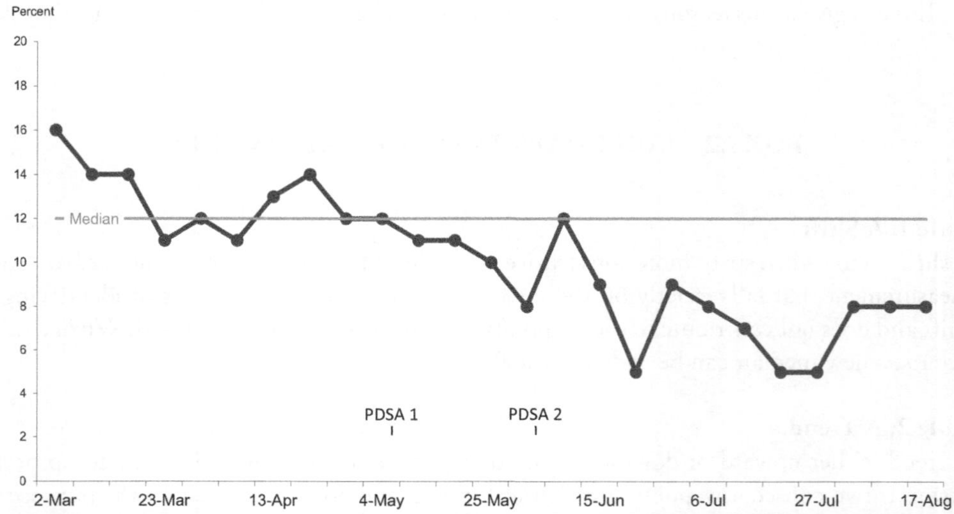

Figure 7.3 Non-attendance results after two PDSA cycles

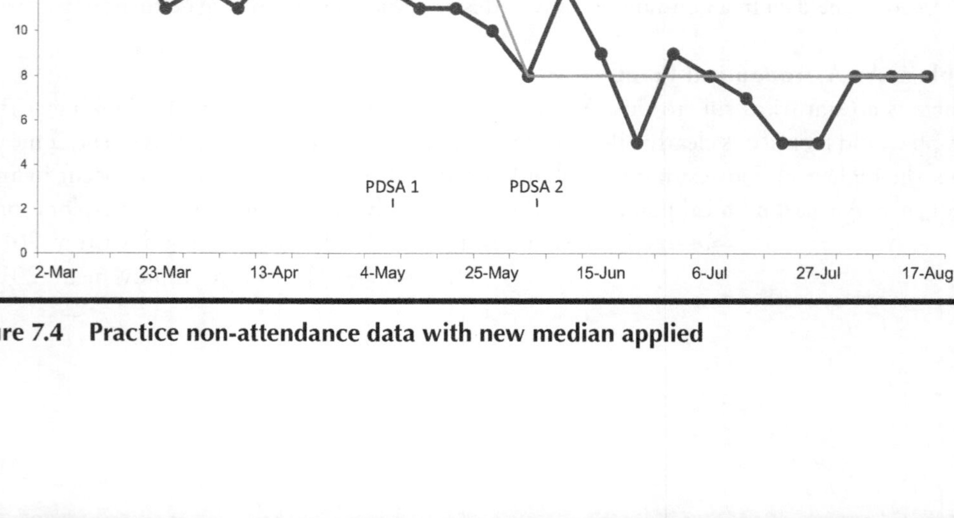

Figure 7.4 Practice non-attendance data with new median applied

improvement work. A trend without a sustained shift encourages the team to look at the problem again to look for unrecognised factors or for difficulty in sustaining consistent new work processes. Tips for using Run Charts are shown in Box 7.3.

BOX 7.3 TIPS FOR THE USE OF RUN CHARTS

Keep it real. The more concrete the data, the more confidence staff will have in the information. Recording patient numbers, waiting times, infections, etc. are real numbers that staff can check if they feel inclined. Seeing data created by their team and recorded directly from their work gives more confidence in the data than is accrued from more abstract data extracted only from electronic systems.

If there are fewer than 10 points of data in the initial observations, use what you have. If no improvement work has been conducted but a smaller set of baseline observations has been collected, then it is reasonable to use the available data to establish a baseline as it is likely to be typical of overall performance pre-improvement (Provost and Murray, 2011, p. 87–88).

Keep the baseline median unchanged. Teams sometimes want to recalculate the median each week or month. If the median is calculated for all the available data, and not just the baseline, then any improvement is averaged out. Best practice is to extend the original baseline median across the graph. This allows a shift from the original baseline to be seen.

Paper-based is fine. Run Charts hand-drawn on a sheet of paper can work well. Squared paper works best to ensure that the scale is consistent across the graph. Many teams use a spreadsheet. This is neat and easier to maintain over time, but is not essential.

Annotate the chart. Was the PDSA cycle one conducted in week seven or week eight? Was the new process introduced in week 12 or week 13? Remembering the detail is difficult. If a change is marked on the chart, it is easier for the team to recall when a change was made, and to see the recorded performance in the light of the change. This supports a sense of their work making a difference and helps to support enthusiasm for further quality improvement work.

Remember the goal. A change can be statistically significant and show a shift but not be clinically important. More often, a change is in the right direction but does not get the team to their initial goal. This is easier to see if the goal is marked on the chart. A new median that is lower than the goal is still an achievement to be celebrated but also indicates that further PDSA cycles will be required.

Statistical Process Control Charts

Some issues can be measured once but many healthcare processes have inevitable variation. It is easy to overreact to variation in measurements. Much variation is random. The number of emergency patients presenting day to day will vary. The average time to complete a procedure will alter depending on patient characteristics and technical difficulty. Senior managers often overreact to an increase or decrease in a measurement (Anhøj and Hellesøe, 2017). This can generate a great deal of effort with no benefit if the change is likely to be random variation rather than a systematic change (Wheeler, 2000, Graban, 2019).

Statistical Process Control (SPC) can be used to identify different types of variation and its likely significance (Gupta and Kaplan, 2020). SPC charts tended to be used mainly by statisticians, engineers and improvement specialists (Shewart, 1986). The development of apps and add-on modules for spreadsheets has brought them into more frequent use. SPC charts help to identify variation in data, and to separate random variation from a real change. The key distinction is between common cause variation and special cause variation (Provost and Murray, 2011).

Common cause variation is variation that occurs within a system for reasons related to the system itself. The data will change from day to day but will fall within a predictable band. It is important to note that a system operating within expected bands, described as being in control, does not mean that the system is producing the results that the team or service wants. It means only that the system is operating consistently. This could mean long waits, delays or other problems occur, but in a relatively predictable way.

Variation outside these expected performance limits is termed special cause variation. This means that something has happened outside the normal system. This could be a problem in a different department, something causing a change in demand, or some other unexpected change such as a staff capacity issue. Identifying special cause variation allows it to be investigated and the cause identified. If the variation is for the worse, the team can undertake PDSA cycles to bring the system back under control.

When a system is in control, also described as a stable system, there will still be scope for improvement. Much quality improvement work occurs in stable systems because there are ongoing problems that cause the system to produce a similar performance over time. If the team is using an SPC chart, it can also be used to show improvements. In this circumstance, the measurements would be expected to move in the direction the team expects from the improvement actions and then move outside the previous control limits as the process reaches a new state.

Software is available to construct SPC charts, either as a standalone programme, part of a statistics programme, or as a plug-in for Excel. They can also be constructed manually in a spreadsheet by inputting the relevant formulae. Several types of SPC charts are available. The X chart (Figure 7.5) is the most used. Some literature calls it an 'I' chart. This chart uses continuous data such as biological measures. It can also be applied to health service activity data (see Provost and Murray, 2011, p. 150 for details). Figure 7.5 shows fluoride varnishing treatments undertaken by a group practice per week. The chart indicates that the process is in control.

The X Chart format has a central line, which is the arithmetic average rather than a median. There are process limits which are calculated using a formula, or automatically using a programme, spreadsheet, or app. As with Run Charts, a set of rules are used to interpret the meaning.. In this type of chart special cause variation is indicated by any data point outside the limits; eight consecutive points on the same side of the line, or three out of four consecutive points that are closer to the control limit than to the central line (Graban, 2019, Academi Gwelliant Cymru, 2023). Variations of these rules are suggested by some authors. Some computer programmes will highlight these signals automatically.

There are different types of SPC chart available to suit most circumstances. Further reading is suggested at the end of the chapter for anyone who wishes to know more about these charts and their uses.

Example of a Measurement Plan

Chapter 5 described a situation where a team wanted to look at clinic overruns. The overruns were disruptive for patients, support staff and clinicians. The group identified a range of contributing

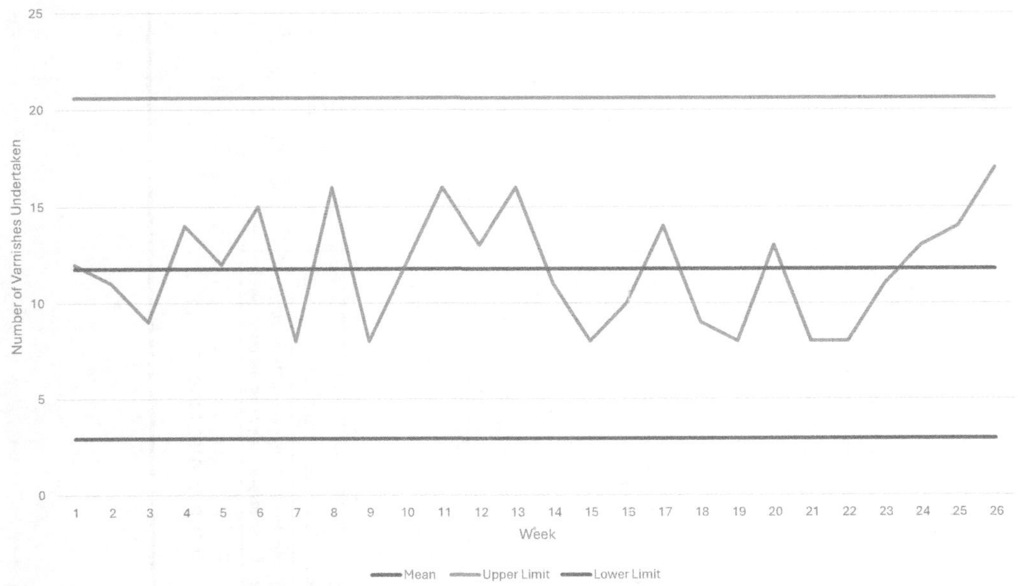

Figure 7.5 X-Chart of fluoride varnishing treatments per week

issues. Their Fishbone Diagram was shown in Figure 5.7. The team then quantified the issues, applied the methods described in Chapter 6 on PDSA cycles, and produced a plan to test out changes. As noted earlier in the chapter, this idea of what may produce improvement is also known as a theory of change.

A theory of change can be set out in several ways (Stadnick *et al.*, 2022). One option is to use a Logic Model that lays out the inputs, activities, outputs and short- and long-term outputs (Kellogg Foundation, 2004, Rajashekara *et al.*, 2020). This is a very good option in larger change programmes and makes linkage to evaluation explicit. This format is not usually required in a smaller project.

The team's overall model, in a form termed a Driver Diagram, is shown in Figure 7.6. The difference between a Fishbone Diagram and a Driver Diagram is that (Cox and Sandberg, 2018):

- A Fishbone Diagram shows what the team believes may be contributing to a problem.
- A Driver Diagram shows the team's view of what may produce a change.

The driver diagram can then be used to identify what can be measured to assess progress (Figure 7.7).

The example in Figure 7.7 shows that the team planned both an overall measure, the rate of clinic overruns and a series of process measures and balancing measures designed to identify progress and any unintended consequences. Information on the item, and on its method of collection, would supplement this using a measurement plan. Once change is achieved and maintained, the frequency of measurement can be reduced (Randolph *et al.*, 2009). The measurement can be changed to a maintenance objective, with regular checks to ensure that the change has been maintained.

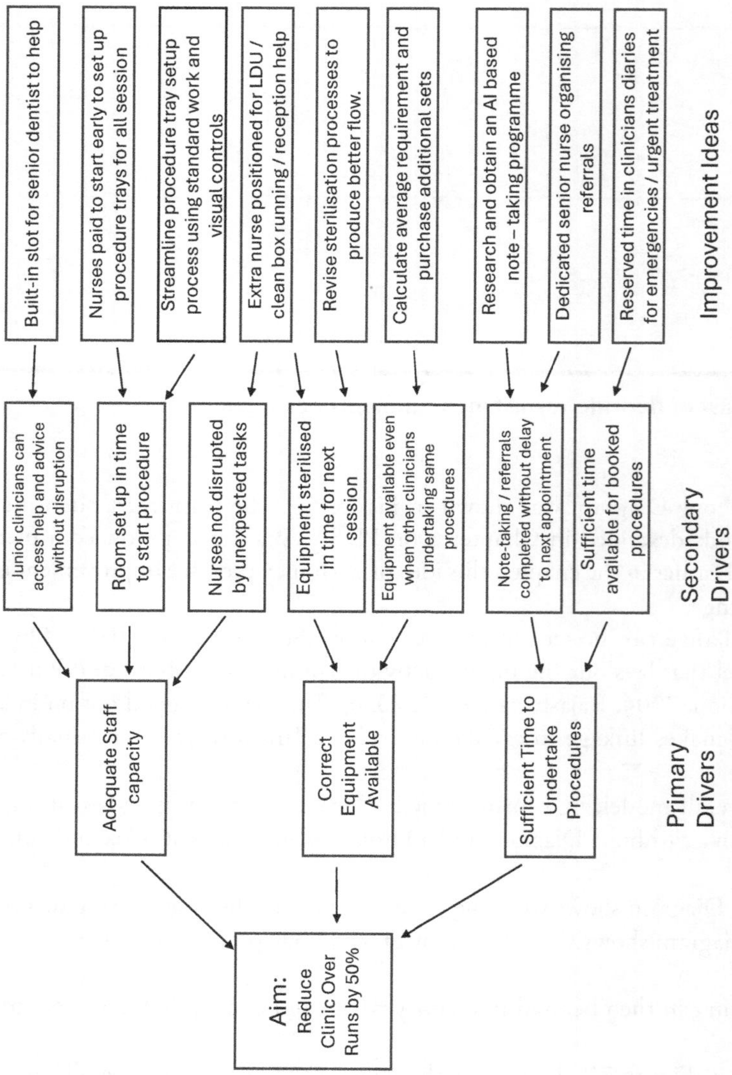

Figure 7.6 Example of a driver diagram developed to tackle clinic overruns

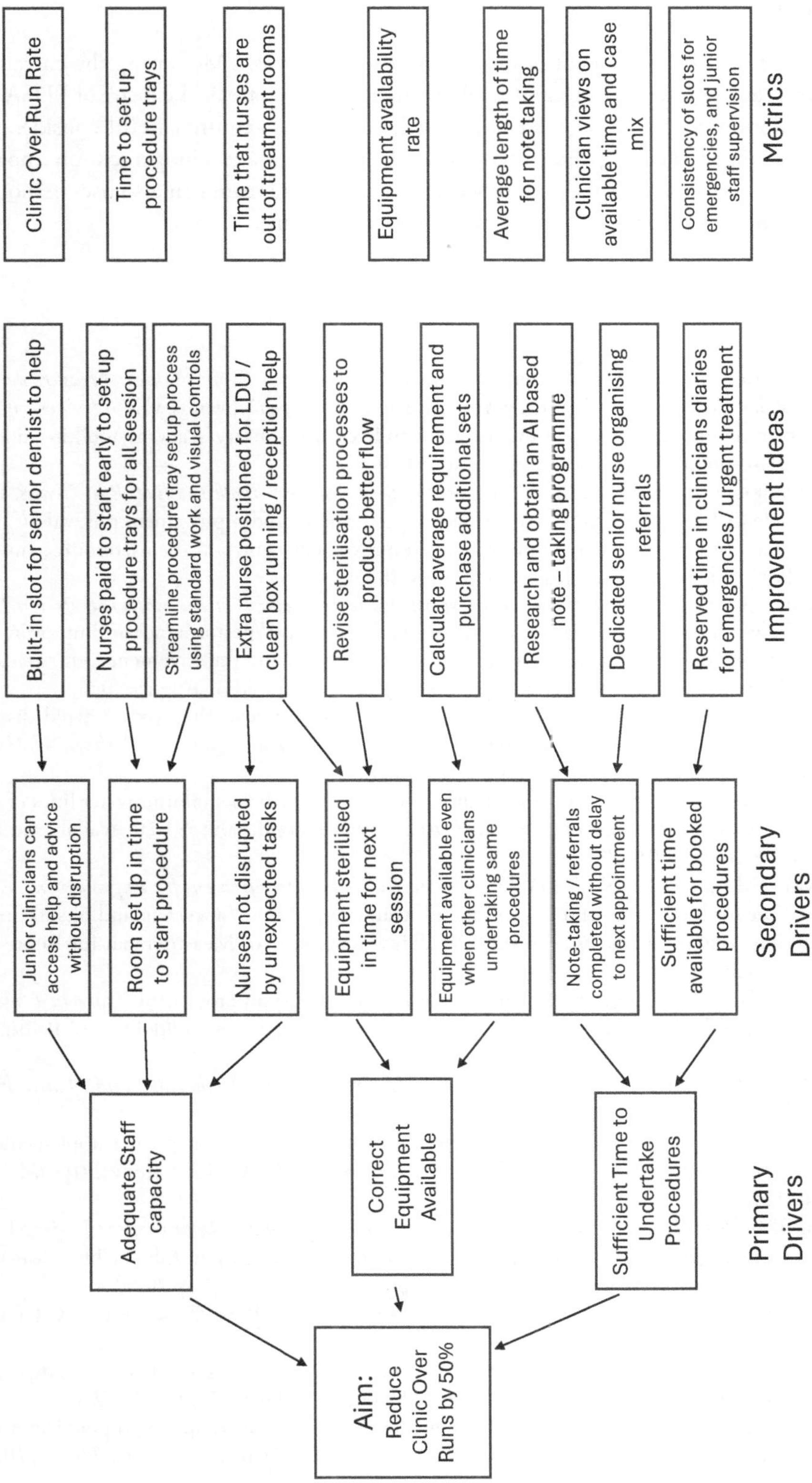

Figure 7.7 Driver diagram with measurements

Conclusions

Measurements are a core component of quality improvement work. Measuring the current state, developing and testing interventions and establishing the impact are at the heart of PDSA cycles. Measurement does not have to be overcomplicated, but it does require careful consideration to ensure that meaningful data is gathered that allow the team to make a judgement on impact and to plan further improvements. Once the process is improved the team can also use methods such as Run Charts and SPC charts to monitor performance over time.

References

Academi Gwelliant Cymru (No Date A) *Improvement Cymru Academy Toolkit Guide: Measurement Plan.* Cardiff, Wales: Academi Gwelliant Cymru. Available at: https://phw.nhs.wales/services-and-teams/improvement-cymru/improvement-cymru-academy1/resource-library/academy-toolkit-guides/measurement-plan-toolkit-guide/ [Accessed 30 July 2025]

Academi Gwelliant Cymru (No Date B) *Improvement Cymru Academy Toolkit Guide: Run Charts.* Cardiff, Wales: Academi Gwelliant Cymru. Available at: performanceandimprovement.nhs.wales/functions/quality-safety-and-improvement/improvement/improvement-cymru-academy/resource-library/academy-toolkit-guides/run-charts/ [Accessed 31 July 2025]

Academi Gwelliant Cymru (2023) *Improvement Cymru Academy Toolkit Guide: Statistical Process Control.* Cardiff, Wales: Academi Gwelliant Cymru. Available at: https://performanceandimprovement.nhs.wales/functions/quality-safety-and-improvement/improvement/improvement-cymru-academy/resource-library/academy-toolkit-guides/spc-toolkit-guide/ [Accessed 31 August 2025]

Anhøj J., Hellesøe A.-M. B. (2017) The problem with red, amber, green: The need to avoid distraction by random variation in organisational performance measures. *BMJ Quality & Safety*, 26; 1: 81–84. Available at: https://doi.org/10.1136/bmjqs-2015-004951

Chate R. A. C. (2010) An audit improves the quality of water within the dental unit water lines of general dental practices across the East of England. *British Dental Journal*, 209; 7: E11. Available at: https://doi.org/10.1038/sj.bdj.2010.885

Clarke J., Davidge M., James L. (No Date) *The How-To Guide for Measurement for Improvement.* London: NHS Institute for Innovation and Improvement. Available at: https://www.england.nhs.uk/improvement-hub/wp-content/uploads/sites/44/2017/11/How-to-Guide-for-Measurement-for-Improvement.pdf [Accessed 30 July 2025]

Cox M., Sandberg K. (2018) Modeling causal relationships in quality improvement. *Current Problems in Pediatric and Adolescent Health Care*, 48; 7: 182–185. Available at: https://doi.org/10.1016/j.cppeds.2018.08.011

Donabedian A. (1966) Evaluating the quality of medical care. *Milbank Memorial Fund Quarterly*, 44; 3 (suppl): 166–206.

Gnaedinger E. A. (2018) Fluoride varnish application, a quality improvement project implemented in a rural pediatric practice. *Public Health Nursing*, 35; 6: 534–540. Available from: https://doi.org/10.1111/phn.12522

Goldman D. (2018) *Dear IHI: Do I Need IRB Approval to Start My Quality Improvement Project?* Institute for Healthcare Improvement [Online] Available at: https://www.ihi.org/library/blog/dear-ihi-do-i-need-irb-approval-start-my-quality-improvement-project [Accessed 11 July 2025]

Graban M. (2019) *Measures of Success: React Less, Lead Better, Improve More.* Colleyville, TX: Constancy, Inc.

Gupta M., Kaplan H. C. (2020) Measurement for quality improvement: Using data to drive change. *Journal of Perinatology*, 40: 962–971. Available at: https://doi.org/10.1038/s41372-019-0572-x

Hashemizadeh A., Lyne A., Liddicott M. (2024) Reducing single-use plastics in dental practice: A quality improvement project. *British Dental Journal*, 237; 6: 483–486. Available at: https://doi.org/10.1038/s41415-024-7836-3

Healthcare Quality Improvement Partnership (2017) *Guide to Managing Ethical Issues in Quality Improvement or Clinical Audit Projects'.* London: Healthcare Quality Improvement Partnership. Available at: https://www.hqip.org.uk/wp-content/uploads/2017/02/guide-to-managing-ethical-issues-in-quality-improvement-or-clinical-audit-projects.pdf [Accessed 11 July 2025]

Hunt D. F., Dunn M., Harrison G., Bailey J. (2021) Ethical considerations in quality improvement: Key questions and a practical guide. *BMJ Open Quality,* 10: e001497. Available at: https://doi.org/10.1136/bmjoq-2021-001497

Institute for Healthcare Improvement (2017) *QI Essentials Toolkit.* Boston, MA: Institute for Healthcare Improvement. Available at: https://www.ihi.org/library/tools/quality-improvement-essentials-toolkit#downloads [Accessed 30 July 2025]

Institute for Healthcare Improvement (2019) *Run Chart Rules Reference Sheet.* [Online] Available at: https://www.ihi.org/sites/default/files/lms/legacy/education/IHIOpenSchool/Courses/Documents/11_RunChartRulesReferenceSheet.pdf [Accessed 30 August 2025]

Institute for Healthcare Improvement (No Date) *Model for Improvement: Establishing Measures.* Available at: https://www.ihi.org/library/model-for-improvement/establishing-measures [Accessed 13 July 2025]

Jackson E. B. (2015) Outcomes of a quality improvement project examining early childhood caries and improving identification of at risk patients in a pediatric medical home setting. *Journal of Pediatric Nursing,* 30; 4: 543–549. Available at: https://doi.org/10.1016/j.pedn.2014.10.020

Kellogg Foundation (2004) *Logic Model Development Guide: Using Logic Models to Bring Together Planning, Evaluation, and Action.* Battle Creek, MI: W.K. Kellogg Foundation.

Langley G. J., Moen R. D., Nolan K. M., Nolan T. W., Norman C. L., Provost L. P. (2009) *The Improvement Guide.* San Francisco: Jossey-Bass.

Miles E., Shah A. (2022) An audit of dental nurses' confidence with intravenous sedation within an oral surgery department at a UK dental hospital. *Primary Dental Journal,* 11; 3: 104–107. Available at: 10.1177/20501684221112509

Monsen K. A. (2024) *Intervention Effectiveness Research. Quality Improvement and Program Evaluation in Healthcare: A Practical Guide to Real-world Implementation.* 2nd Edition. Cham: Springer Nature.

Mormer E., Stevans J. (2019) Clinical quality improvement and quality improvement research. *Perspectives of the ASHA Special Interest Groups',* 4; 1: 27–37. Available at: https://doi.org/10.1044/2018_pers-st-2018-0003

Myers C. (2014) A quality improvement initiative for clinical records in the public dental services. [MSc Thesis]. Dublin: Royal College of Surgeons in Ireland. Available at: https://www.lenus.ie/server/api/core/bitstreams/1faed06b-4812-4cd9-a64e-cc6ccafc6e6a/content [Accessed 31 August 2025]

Nelson W. A. (2014) Proposed ethical guidelines for quality improvement. *Healthcare Executive,* 29; 2: 52, 54–55. Available at: https://www.ache.org/-/media/ache/about-ache/ethics/quality_improvement_ethics_reprint.pdf [Accessed 11 July 2025]

Ng M. W., Torresyap G., White A., Melvin P., Graham D., Kane D., Scoville R., Ohiomoba H. (2012) Disease management of early childhood caries: results of a pilot quality improvement project. *Journal of Health Care for the Poor and Underserved,* 23; 3 Suppl: 193–209. Available at: https://doi.org/10.1353/hpu.2012.0122

NHS Education for Scotland (2025) *QI Tools: Measurement Plan.* Edinburgh: NHS Education for Scotland. Available at: https://learn.nes.nhs.scot/3138/quality-improvement-zone/qi-tools/measurement-plan [Accessed 28 July 2025]

Perla R. J., Provost L. P., Murray S. K. (2011) The run chart: A simple analytical tool for learning from variation in healthcare processes. *BMJ Quality & Safety,* 20: 46–51. Available at: https://doi.org/10.1136/bmjqs.2009.037895

Provost L. P., Murray S. K. (2011) *The Health Care Data Guide.* San Francisco, CA: Josey-Bass.

Rajashekara S., Naik A. D., Campbell C. M., Gregory M. E., Rosen T., Engebretson A., Godwin K. M. (2020) Using a logic model to design and evaluate a quality improvement leadership course. *Academic Medicine,* 95; 8: 1201–1206. Available at: https://doi.org/10.1097/ACM.0000000000003191

Randolph G., Esporas M., Provost L., Massie S., Bundy D. G. (2009) Model for improvement – Part two: Measurement and feedback for quality improvement efforts. *Pediatric Clinics of North America,* 56; 4: 779–798.

Schroeder L. L. (2021) Using data to drive change. In Shah R. K., Godambe S. A. (Eds.), *Patient Safety and Quality Improvement in Healthcare.* Cham: Springer Nature.

Shewart W. A. (1986) *Statistical Method from the Viewpoint of Quality Control.* Mineola, NY: Dover Publications.

Smith G., Cordes J. (2020) *The Phantom Pattern Problem: The Mirage of Big Data.* Oxford: Oxford University Press.

Stadnick N. A., Cain K. L., Oswald W., Watson P., Ibarra M., Lagoc R., Ayers L. O., Salgin L., Broyles S. L., Laurent L. C., Pezzoli K., Rabin B. (2022) Co-creating a theory of change to advance COVID-19 testing and vaccine uptake in underserved communities. *Health Services Research*, 57; S1: 149–157. Available at: https://doi.org/10.1111/1475-6773.13910

U.S. Department of Health and Human Services (No Date) *Quality Improvement Activities FAQs.* Washington, DC: U.S. Department of Health and Human Services. Available at: https://www.hhs.gov/ohrp/regulations-and-policy/guidance/faq/quality-improvement-activities/index.html [Accessed 11 July 2025]

Wheeler D. J. (2000) *Understanding Variation: The Key to Managing Chaos.* 2nd Edition. Knoxville, TN: SPC Press.

Williams E. (2018) Understanding variation: Part 1- the run chart. *Current Problems in Pediatric and Adolescent Health Care*, 48; 7: 186–190. Available at: https://doi.org/10.1016/j.cppeds.2018.08.012

Wolfe H. A., Taylor A., Subramanyam R., Davidson A. (2021) Statistics in quality improvement: Measurement and statistical process control. *Pediatric Anesthesia*, 31; 5: 539–547. Available at: https://doi.org/10.1111/pan.14163

Woodcock T., Adeleke Y., Goeschel C., Pronovost P., Dixon-Woods M. (2020) A modified Delphi study to identify the features of high quality measurement plans for healthcare improvement projects. *BMC Medical Research Methodology*, 20; 1: Article 8. Available at: https://doi.org/10.1186/s12874-019-0886-6

Further Reading

Graban M. (2019) *Measures of Success: React Less, Lead Better, Improve More.* Colleyville, TX: Constancy, Inc.

A good introduction to the importance of variation and ways of using SPC charts to understand it. Uses healthcare examples.

Langley G. J., Moen R. D., Nolan K. M., Nolan T. W., Norman C. L., Provost L. P. (2009) *The Improvement Guide.* San Francisco: Jossey-Bass.

An excellent general introduction to measurements for quality improvement.

Provost L. P., Murray S. K. (2011) *The Health Care Data Guide.* San Francisco, CA: Josey-Bass.

Out of print but often available second hand. This book is filled with examples of measurements in quality improvement in health care. Includes a though discussion of Statistical Process Control charts.

Resources

The Institute of Healthcare Improvement provides an Excel workbook that includes a template to produce a Run Chart. The chart, and the instructions, are available in English, Spanish and Portuguese.

The chart is available at: https://www.ihi.org/library/tools/run-chart-tool

Chapter 8

Embedding Change

Introduction

Many dental teams will have experience of making changes and finding, a few months later, that they have inadvertently returned to the previous way of doing things. This can happen under pressure when staff tend to revert to well-rehearsed approaches, even if they know they are not optimal. It can also occur as an inexorable decline, with a gradual drift back to previous ways of working. This is inherently wasteful: if the problem was worth addressing, then a slide back to the pre-improvement situation is a loss of the effort invested, and a return to the situation that the team believed to be unacceptable. This chapter discusses ways of avoiding this and puts it in the context of a wider academic literature.

Sustaining Change

Quality improvement is about change. All change brings challenges, and this is no less the case in dental settings. Helping changes to stick requires careful attention. Failure to maintain an agreed change is a waste of resources, decreases the likelihood that changes can be spread from the original site, decreases team morale and their confidence in the value and applicability of quality improvement methods (Song *et al.*, 2022). This is the reason that academic models of change invariably include a maintenance component.

It is helpful to think about a consolidation phase in which change is embedded (Khali and Kynoch, 2021). Changes continuing over time are termed sustainment (Moulin *et al.*, 2020). Sustainment is taken to mean that changes continue to be used in routine practice. Definitions of sustainment accept that the changes may be amended in the light of experience, but for the change to be sustained, the outcomes must still be maintained by any adapted process (Moore *et al.*, 2017).

DOI: 10.4324/9781003493532-8

Building Sustainment into the Improvement Process

Many theories of change are linear. Models of how to apply evidence in practice usually assume that one step follows another in a planned progression (Khali and Kynoch, 2021) and the same assumption is often made in quality improvement. Many of the factors that affect the maintenance of evidence-based changes can also affect quality improvement change sustainment. For example, Bravata *et al.* (2022) reported that issues associated with a failure to sustain change in a clinical study included low motivation; inactivity by the person or group that had championed the change; a failure to reflect on performance data, and poor engagement by leaders.

These are familiar issues from the discussion in Chapter 4 and are reported in practice in quality improvement implementations. In one review of maintenance of improvements of processes in several addiction services, capacity, alignment between changes and existing business practices, availability of data and staff engagement in the initial work were all found to be associated with greater sustainability (Stumbo, Ford and Green, 2017). A clear understanding that healthcare staff groups are interdependent is important (Berwick, 2011). In dental care, dentists, therapists, dental nurses, administrators and technicians all play indispensable roles in many processes, and creating and sustaining change without joint involvement can be difficult or impossible.

A large-scale Canadian project in care homes where teams used quality improvement methods identified similar issues affecting sustainment at one and two years after the quality improvement work. The context often changed, because of staff changes and sometimes because of other changes in the workplace, such as management changes or other issues competing for attention. One of the insights offered by project participants was that sustainment was more likely if the team continued to adapt the work to the new context, so that improvements continued to be relevant and fit with the work of the team (Song *et al.*, 2022). A key insight from this is that the sustainment phase is both a continuation of the previous work and an additional phase that deserves consideration. How the initial improvement work is conducted in turn influences the chances of long-term impact.

Part of this work is thinking about what changes are likely to be sustainable. Any intervention that depends only on staff education is likely to fail over time. Staff change, people forget and other issues can crowd out the work. Where education is needed, it can be more effective if it is offered or reinforced by relevant staff in the course of the work, so that people embed it in practice (Mikkelsen and Holm, 2007, Fan-Lun *et al.*, 2019). Structural changes can help to promote sustainment of changes, such as prompts embedded in computer systems or case notes so that they are visible at the relevant stage of a clinical or administrative task. AIs embedded in clinical systems are likely to play similar roles by providing context-sensitive information and suggestions.

Changes that do not get to the root of a problem are often undercut by circumstance. For example, if the underlying cause of a system problem is lack of time, or an equipment problem, then making changes to the system can help, but the pressures themselves often remain, or recur. Aligning solutions with existing work processes and with the context of the team is also more likely to produce changes that stick (Burke and van de Mheen, 2021). This does not mean that a change that produces a short-term improvement cannot be worthwhile. A temporary improvement may come as a great relief to an embattled team. It may also give the space to identify larger changes that can tackle underlying problems. Even the experience of making a change that makes a difference to practice can act as a stimulus to further quality improvement work that can gradually chip away at a larger problem.

Learning from Other Areas

Evidence into Practice

All health care areas struggle with the shift of new evidence into use in routine practice. Early models assumed that if there was evidence of improved outcomes from research studies, then clinical services would adopt the new methods, assuming the change was affordable. Much evidence, and routine clinical experience, demonstrates that this is often not the case (Mitton *et al.*, 2007). The science of transferring knowledge into practice is termed implementation science (Westerlund, Nilsen and Sundberg, 2019). Dental teams often have a good understanding of research methods and of how research results are communicated, but the evidence of how to transfer knowledge is rarely taught in undergraduate training (Laurence, 2015).

Insights from implementation and translational research are relevant to embedding quality improvement work. Greenhalgh *et al.* (2004) suggested that the effectiveness of an innovation is a combination of the innovation itself, system readiness for change, the process of implementation, and the external context, such as current political and policy pressures. There are many theoretical approaches to implementation, and the best model is often chosen to be a good fit with the circumstances (Birken *et al.*, 2017).

In encouraging the implementation of research findings, early engagement of stakeholders is important, and taking a systematic and considered approach to change appears to help later uptake (Rutten, Ridgeway and Griffin, 2024).

Much implementation research has been conducted in general medical settings, which raises the question of whether the findings are representative of effects in dental services. Villarosa and colleagues undertook a systematic review of guideline implementation in dentistry. The studies they identified varied in quality but gave a good overview of current practice. Of 18 studies included in the study, 15 used a single implementation strategy, while five used combination approaches. The main approaches they identified were audit and feedback; reminders; education; patient-mediated interventions; payment for performance and multifaceted interventions (Villarosa *et al.*, 2019, pp. 11). All the approaches had at least some evidence of effectiveness to support them, although results were variable.

Learning Health Care Systems

As the speed of change accelerates with new technologies, translating knowledge into practice and embedding change will become ever more demanding (Chambers, Feero and Khoury, 2016). One option to tackle this is to create healthcare systems that make learning easier. A learning healthcare system 'generates and applies the best evidence for the collaborative healthcare choices of each patient and provider; drives the process of discovery as a natural outgrowth of patient care; and ensures innovation, quality, safety and value in healthcare' (Olsen, Aisner and McGinnis, 2007, pp. x). Creating a system that supports learning will help to support change (Mullins *et al.*, 2018).

A learning health care system approach envisages three loops: practice producing data for learning, this data being used to produce shareable learning, and the knowledge generated then producing a change in practice (Golburean *et al.*, 2024). Tokede *et al.* (2022) provide a dental example of the approach in work looking at routine data collected in the United States within three dental provider organisations. They were able to use routinely collected data to identify new diagnoses of periodontal disease and instances of periodontal disease progressing to tooth loss. In this unselected clinical population, they found that the risk of new periodontal disease was higher with male gender, older age, smoking, higher plaque levels and a diabetes diagnosis, as well as a longer time between dental visits. The highest relative risk of periodontal disease progressing to tooth loss was in men, older people, and people who smoked. This example demonstrates the first two loops identified above – practice to data, and data producing shareable learning – although, as this chapter has discussed, moving the findings to changes in practice is not straightforward. None of the periodontal findings will surprise dental teams. Being able to produce the information using routinely collected information from the services' own populations does seem likely to have a greater impact on clinical behaviour and the advice offered to patients than information from research papers unconnected to the service in which practitioners work. It also has the potential to generate new findings. Active use of data can be anticipated to increase interest in the regularity and accuracy of data collection.

There is good evidence that learning healthcare systems can produce benefits for both staff and patients, including improvements in efficiency (Enticott, Johnson and Teede, 2021). Clinical engagement is regarded as essential in learning healthcare systems. Clinical teams contribute to data collection, identification of important themes for investigation, interpretation of results and implementation of any changes. Learning healthcare systems raise issues about the blurring of research, with its ethical review processes and routine clinical practice (Hollestelle *et al.*, 2024). Data collection in learning healthcare systems has much in common with surveillance systems, and existing standards can be appropriately applied (Piaseck and Dranseika, 2019).

This is quality improvement on a grand scale using data collection and a sustained community of interest, but the principles are relevant to more locally based quality improvement. The two approaches can also be combined. Describing a learning healthcare system implementation in a mental health service, Sykes *et al.* (2025) comment 'the local agency staff are the experts on what changes may be necessary to improve the measured outcome … a continuous Quality Improvement (QI) framework is used to guide local QI efforts'. This ably demonstrates the interconnections between large scale improvement, discussed further in Chapter 9 and local change. Local improvements can both contribute to larger scale improvement and be supported by it. The infrastructure and organisational ethos that creates a learning healthcare organisation can also support local quality improvement work.

Reliability

High reliability is a recent term in dentistry, although its aim – to deliver consistently good care every time – is familiar to every dental team (Minyé and Benjamin, 2022). High reliability organisations are those that manage to deliver safe, error-free services despite the technological complexity of care (Roberts, 1990). In healthcare, high reliability is thought of in relation to patient safety where errors can be identified and recorded (Pronovost *et al.*, 2006, Martelli, Rivard and Roberts, 2018). The major challenge is thinking through how to learn when trial and error is not acceptable, because patient safety could be compromised.

Weick and Sutcliffe (2007) summarise the behaviours of high reliability organisations. Applied to dental care, they can be summarised as:

1. Look out for small problems, look for causes and fix them. A small problem this time can be a larger problem the next time it occurs.

2. Do not accept oversimplification. Simple explanations for problems are sometimes right, but it is easy to assume that you understand things. Bringing in colleagues to check your understanding and to avoid accepting the first explanation you think of can yield benefits and avoid complacency.
3. Keep focused on work with patients, and what you learn from it. If a problem appears but you avoid harm, it is still a problem even if it does not show up in the high-level monitoring data. As with point (1), take it seriously.
4. Pay attention to resilience. Organisations need to cope under strain, respond to problems, and bounce back. This includes acknowledging when problems happen and celebrating success when they are dealt with. Organisations need to think in advance about how to cope under pressure.
5. Put the right people in charge of a problem. Being senior is not always the right qualification to resolve something – consider expertise, influence and context.

Chassin and Loeb (2011, 2013) suggest a structured way of thinking about reliability principles in health care. They recommend examining how committed the leadership is to minimising patient harm; promoting a safety culture throughout the organisation and adopting the type of process improvement tools described in this volume.

For individual clinicians and smaller teams, Error Management Theory is worth considering (Guttman *et al.*, 2019). Most quality improvement coaches argue that errors are inevitable, so the approach to them is:

1. Reduce the likelihood of error by changing the circumstances, such as introducing Standard Work and Visual Management.
2. Make errors as easy as possible to identify. This includes making processes explicit and introducing routine checks, for example, at the beginning of the next stage of the process.
3. Encourage staff to stop when an error occurs and to correct it. This avoids passing it on to the next stage of the work, where it may be less obvious and can result in unexpected complications.
4. Revise the process to decrease the chance of the error occurring again.

This is sensible but is easier said than done. Many of the approaches identified in the Patient Safety chapter can be used, but staff may not think in terms of error. Some people assume that they do not make errors, ever. Observational studies suggest that errors are ubiquitous but that there are understandable reasons for hesitating to report them, even if they are identified, including fear of regulatory action (Chohan *et al.*, 2022). Error Management Theory argues that identifying errors is a mindset, and that staff are more likely to identify errors if they are supported, encouraged, and trained to do so.

There are obvious challenges in this. Dentists usually work alone, other than with a dental nurse. There is a power hierarchy here, particularly as the nurse may be employed by the dentist. Errors are bad for patients, however, and can be very costly, stressful and time-consuming for a practitioner. Supporting all the staff in a room to know what is happening, and to be willing to take discrete action to intervene, needs effort. Being aware of how to draw the dentist's attention to a possible issue without causing patient alarm, or practitioner offence, needs thought. Often there will be a good reason why a practitioner has omitted a step, or altered a process, but being willing to be queried about it becomes easier when clinical staff can move from the idea that they can never make a mistake, to accepting that dental care is complex and onerous, and that errors can and will happen. Preventing them from becoming defects in care is better than embarrassment at having an error gently drawn to one's attention. An example of this in clinical practice could be if a dentist and dental nurse are working on a patient to provide a new filling. During the placement of the filling, the dentist places a matrix band to create good contact points and contour. With the dental nurse sitting to the side of the patient and not behind, they see that the matrix band has slipped and is no longer in an optimal position, but the dentist has not noticed and begins to place the filling material. The dental nurse could bring this to the attention of the dentist by saying, 'from my position the matrix band looks like it may have moved a little, can you check it from your position to make sure?'. This approach would be subtle and not bring panic to the patient. This is an example of the team working together and the dental nurse not being afraid to point out a potential error. In the long run this could prevent patient discomfort and complaints, repeat treatment, and loss of earnings.

Minyé and Benjamin (2022) suggest that dental teams would benefit from the dentist moving from commanding to collaborating. This does not imply that the dentist has less responsibility or that they do not have the final decision in a clinical situation, but it does mean that the dentist has support. This links with to the literature on Crew Resource Management in aviation, principles that are now applied more widely and which are discussed in Chapter 2. Dreadful accidents have occurred because co-pilots deferred completely to the senior pilot in an aircraft, even when the co-pilot was aware of a real potential for an accident. This is often because of reduced situational awareness: the captain becomes focused on a problem when under pressure and may lose track of wider issues. This narrowing of focus will be familiar to every dentist (Green *et al.*, 2017). Having someone who is not as focused on the same task and who is more aware of wider issues – such as the approaching mountain – can be very valuable (Pinsky, Taichman and Sarment, 2010).

The impact of thinking about resilience is understanding that errors can and will happen, even in a redesigned system. Making it as easy as possible for people to understand the new process, and to be able to see when a problem occurs, is a valuable part of any quality improvement. Allowing clinicians to respond to a problem, and to feed back the information to support further change helps to further improve the system, and to create a more resilient response.

Standard Work

Dental teams can have a settled staff group for years or can be subject to rapid change. In the United Kingdom, dental practices that provide training have new Vocational Trainees each year, dentists in their first year after qualification. Dental nurses often arrive in a practice as trainees, with no previous experience of dental practice. New dentists, hygienists and therapists may be appointed, and specialists such as implant dentists may work in a practice for only a few days a week. Locum staff may arrive to cover maternity leave or as temporary replacements while new postholders are recruited to a vacancy. In hospital practice, trainees will arrive each year and staff may be rotated between teams. The effect of this is that there will often be staff who have worked in a service for some time, along with a group of staff who change frequently. Details vary by country and setting, but the experience of having staff of mixed experience and tenure is common.

This produces some staff who are very familiar with processes, and others who bring knowledge from elsewhere but will not know how the team in which they now find themselves implements their processes. When a team has engaged in quality improvement work, the new staff will not have gone through the process and so will be likely to feel less commitment to any methods agreed during the work. This means that there are three issues: how to maintain agreed changes with the existing staff, how to support new staff to apply the agreed methods and how to support further change when required.

Maintaining Agreed Changes

An underpinning step is for the team to be clear on what has been agreed. A useful way to do this is to record the changes made and to create a statement of the new process that the team has agreed to apply. This can feel bureaucratic, and dentists and other clinicians who are used to their own practice can chafe under the requirement. It is important for the team to recall that there was a problem that caused them to undertake the work, that they generated and tested changes, and that the new processes have been found to be an improvement on the initial ways of working, which reduce the original problem. Keeping in mind that the new processes are not set in stone and can be amended if new ideas emerge that are found to be better can also help to calm any concerns. Making changes to the new processes is discussed later in the chapter. It is also important for clinicians to keep in mind that they always have the clinical freedom to make a change that reflects a clinical need in their patient. As usual, they should record the reason they varied from an agreed process in case of any future challenge.

Recording the work that has been agreed also provides a base against which any future change can be tested. The team has created a new 'best way' of doing something, and this allows them to compare any future changes to this, knowing that it is already an improvement on the original process that resulted in problems. To do this, a clear record of the agreed work is required.

Teams and organisations have different terms for this record, including Standard Operating Procedures, Team Policies and Standard Work. Standard Work is the term used in this description, but departments and teams should use whichever term works best in their situation.

Creating Standard Work

The key is to have a step-by-step set of instructions that record the agreed process. Table 8.1 gives an example of the type of form that can be used. Many examples are available online, or teams can amend examples or create a template that fits with their own organisation and way of working. The Standard Work will also be used to support new staff, so as much clarity as possible is required when complete.

The form should describe the steps to be taken, the equipment to be used, and who is to undertake each step. This can include details such as which software system to use if that is relevant to

Table 8.1 Standard work form

Process Step	*What: Describe the process step*	*How: How will you accomplish this process step?*	*Why: What is the purpose of this process step?*	*Cycle time: How long does this step take?*
1				
2				
3				

Source: Adapted from Stanford Medicine Center for Improvement (Stanford Medicine, 2025).

the process. Table 8.2 gives an example of a completed Standard Work form used for setting up a trolley by a dental hygienist.

Table 8.2 Completed standard work form for setting up a dental hygienist's trolley

Process Step	*What: Describe the process step*	*How: How will you accomplish this process step?*	*Why: What is the purpose of this process step?*	*Cycle time: How long does this step take?*
1	Calculate how many of each procedure is booked in that session	Print out the day list with procedures listed and tally up how many of each are scheduled (Figure 8.1)	To know what will be neededn	5 minutes
2	Have the correct number of instruments and materials ready for the trolley	Gather the corresponding number of each instrument or material	To have enough of each item ready for the session	5 minutes
3	Set up the hygiene trolley for the session	Lay out the materials and instruments needed for each patient in corresponding order of appointments	To have the set-up complete for every appointment beforehand	5 minutes

Source: Adapted from Stanford Medicine Center for Improvement (Stanford Medicine, 2025).

Morning Session Schedule

Time	Patient	Procedure
9:00	Mrs B	Scale & Polish
9:30	Mrs K	Airflow Polish
10:00	Mr R	Scale & Polish
10:30	Miss O	Airflow Polish
11:00	Mr P	Periodontal Treatment
11:30	Mrs E	Periodontal Treatment
12:00	Miss I	Scale & Polish
12:30	Mr V	Periodontal Treatment
13:00	Lunch	------------------------------------

Tally of Procedures

Procedure	Number
Scale & Polish	3
Airflow Polish	2
Periodontal Treatment	3

Figure 8.1 Table and tally sheet for day list of procedures

When in doubt about what to include, try to think about someone who is completely new to the organisation, such as a person undertaking a temporary contract who arrives in the practice or department for the first time. Consider whether they could reasonably be expected to understand the work description. Asking someone unconnected to the process to read it and explain it back without consulting it can be a good test of whether it adequately explains what is needed.

Using Visual Controls

The purpose of visual controls is to make a situation visible (Stark and Hookway, 2019). This can include a process, such as which patients are in each treatment room, and which staff member is due to see them next; what dental supplies are awaited for patients, for example, dentures being sent from a laboratory in time for scheduled appointments, or to allow staff to see who is waiting in a waiting room.

In relation to Standard Work, visual controls help to make things visible related to the process that has been redesigned. For example, if a storage area has been redesigned to make items easier to find, or to co-locate items used in the same procedure, then it must be possible to restock it as easily as possible. This can be done by demarcating areas, for example, with tape and labels, subject to any relevant infection control requirements. It can also be done by providing a photograph of what the restocked area should look like. This is a very useful approach for the layout of items on a treatment tray, for example, and is a great help to new staff. A good example of this would be a surgical tray set-up, as many of the items are only used for surgical procedures, but should be available immediately if the situation arises. Figure 8.2 shows an example of a surgical tray set up, with the items required being shown in a photograph and labelled for new staff to follow and for more experienced staff to have available as a check.

This can be linked to Standard Work and forms part of it by showing in a visual fashion what is expected. This is also useful even when experienced staff may need to set up for a less frequently performed technique or to support a specialist clinician with whom they do not usually work, for example, an implant dentist.

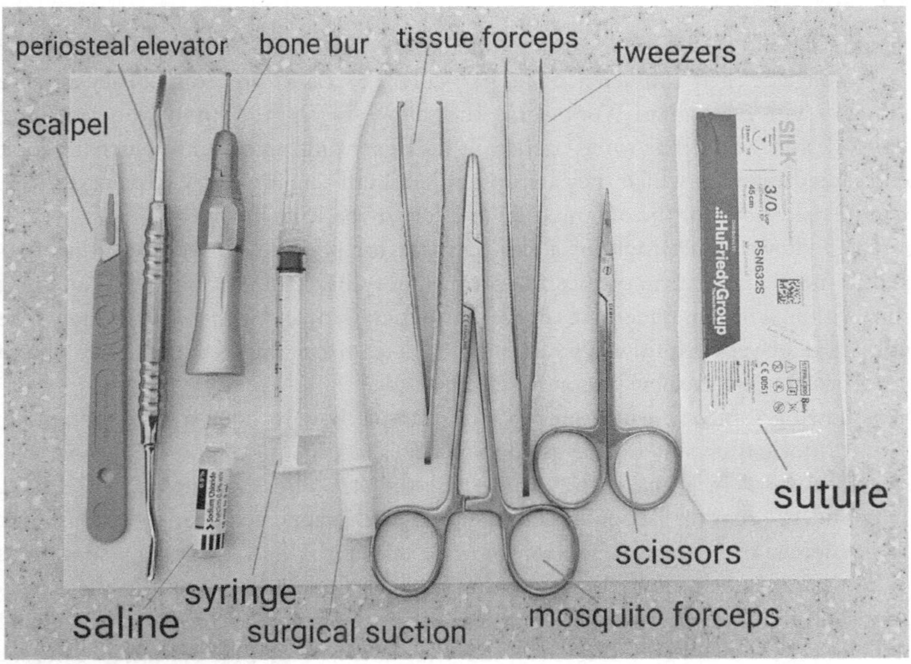

Figure 8.2 Surgical tray set-up

Other examples of visual controls include:

- **Demarcation Lines:** Lines on a surface showing where something should be located. Examples include the position of a waste bin, a cylinder or a trolley.
- **Tiger Stripes:** Hatched lines showing an area that should be left clear, for example, where a door might strike a person or an object.
- **Shadow Boards:** A laminated sheet that shows the position of each item, such as instruments. This also has the advantage that it is easy to spot a missing instrument. This is very useful when the person setting up for the procedure is unfamiliar with the work.
- **Location Boards:** These show where supplies are located, for example, when they may be spread out across several areas making checking difficult. These boards can reduce the time staff spend looking for supplies.
- **Process Boards:** These show the stage of a process. For example, if a dentist is working across several treatment rooms these can indicate what stage has been reached in the different rooms so that they know where to go next. This example is often used in dental school settings so supervising clinicians can keep tabs on which stage of a procedure their dental students have reached.
- **Kanban:** These are cards that show what supplies need to be reordered and where the items should be stored when they are resupplied. There are other types of kanban, and there is a large literature on their use. For more details see Stark and Hookway (2019, pp. 154–159).

Skills Matrices

Keeping track of who knows what can be difficult in a large team. A skills matrix is a form that shows staff alongside their competence in a particular process or procedure. They are often used in conjunction with a Standard Work form. They allow the team to know who can undertake a particular task and who needs to be trained in it. This avoids an assumption that people know how to do something with which they are unfamiliar. Staff sometimes try to persevere regardless, which can be risky both for the organisation and for any patients involved.

Figure 8.3 shows an example of a skills matrix for practice nurses, including two newly appointed trainees. There are many possible layouts, but this example shows who can do a process under supervision, who can undertake the work unsupervised, and who is able to show others how to do it. This can be very helpful when new staff join a team as it avoids doubt about who can offer training and what stage the new person has reached.

When showing someone a new process, for example how to book a new appointment into an electronic information system, the usual sequence is to explain it, have the person explain the process back to the trainer, and then to undertake the task while being observed. This can give the team confidence that the person has been appropriately supported to apply the task in the way the team has agreed is the current best way of undertaking the work. Making assumptions about who can do what is unhelpful: making sure that staff can undertake the task in the expected way produces a solid foundation. This does not mean that staff will never have to make changes in a particular clinical context, but it does mean that they have a good understanding of the stem process from which they have made a clinical decision to vary. Box 8.1 summarises issues to consider when maintaining improvements.

Completed on		Review date		Completed by	

⊕	No skill	◔	Minimal skills	◑	Some skills	◕	Highly skilled	●	Expert / can train others

Staff member	Surgical extraction	Orthodontics	Implants	Sedation	Taking x-rays	Intra-oral scanning
Stacey	●	●	●	●	◕	◕
Erin	●	◑	●	●	◔	◑
Kayley	◔	⊕	⊕	⊕	⊕	⊕
Taylor	◔	⊕	◔	⊕	⊕	⊕
Kelsey	◕	◑	◑	⊕	⊕	◑
Angela	●	◕	●	◑	◔	◔

Figure 8.3 Example of a Skills Matrix Showing Dental Nurse Experience in a Practice

BOX 8.1: TIPS ON SUSTAINING CHANGE

- Accept that changes are unlikely to stick without active effort.
- Don't see the need to build in maintenance steps as a failure: improvement science makes it clear that this is not a team problem, but rather good practice.
- Build in structural supports. These can include Standard Work descriptions and visual controls such as photographs and diagrams of how things should be laid out or where things should be stored.
- Remember that new and temporary staff will not know how the team wants things to be done unless the process is explained to them. This is made easier by the supports such as Standard Work descriptions and photographs where relevant.
- Consider using a skills matrix to keep track of who knows each process, and who can teach it to others.
- Creating an environment where staff can flag potential errors helps to maintain standards.
- Accept that nothing stays the same forever. Be prepared to adapt a process using the same steps as before. Creating revised Standard Work helps to maintain the new status quo.

Conclusions

Making change stick is difficult. Sometimes experience identifies problems with a new process that needs further revision. This is important but is not a good reason to revert to a situation that the clinical team already regarded as unsatisfactory. Maintaining improvements and developing them further requires careful attention. This is not unique to quality improvement: transferring new academic knowledge into practice faces similar challenges.

Being clear on the nature of the improvement and creating clear guidelines and expectations can go a long way to maintaining change. Using Standard Work to describe the updated process and ensuring all staff are familiar with them helps. It is also important to keep in mind that no process is perfect, and that further improvements are always possible. Rather than reverting to a previous unsatisfactory process, making further improvements and updating the Standard Work is a positive way to respond.

The culture of the team is also important. Where staff have been involved in changes, and feel like active participants, change is more likely to be maintained. Supporting staff to feel able to identify problems and to share them also helps with further quality improvement. Seeing maintenance of improvement as part of both delivering quality and improving it further helps to engage staff and to deliver for patients.

References

Berwick D. M. (2011) Observations on initiating systems change in health care: Challenges to overcome. In Claudia Grossmann C., Goolsby W. A., Olsen L., McGinnis J. M. (Eds.), *Engineering a Learning Healthcare System: A Look at the Future: Workshop Summary*. Washington, DC: The National Academies Press, pp. 53–61. Available at: https://www.ncbi.nlm.nih.gov/books/NBK61965/pdf/Bookshelf_NBK61965.pdf [Accessed 2 May 2025]

Birken S. A., Powell B. J., Shea C. M., Haines E. R., Kirk M. A., Leeman J., Rohweder C., Damschroder L., Presseau J. (2017) Criteria for selecting implementation science theories and frameworks: Results from an international survey. *Implementation Science*, 12: 124. Available at: https://doi.org/10.1186/s13012-017-0656-y

Bravata D. M., Miech E. J., Myers L. J., Perkins A. J., Zhang Y., Rattray N. A., Damush T. M. (2022) The perils of a "my work here is done" perspective: A mixed methods evaluation of sustainment of an evidence-based intervention for transient ischemic attack. *BMC Health Services Research*, 22; 1: 857. Available at: http s://dx.doi.org/10.1186/s12913-022-08207-8

Burke R. E., Marang-Van De Mheen P. J. (2021) Sustaining quality improvement efforts: Emerging principles and practice. *BMJ Quality & Safety*, 30; 11: 848–852. Available at: https://doi.org/10.1136/bmjqs-2021-013016

Chambers D. A., Feero W. G., Khoury M. J. (2016) Convergence of implementation science, precision medicine, and the learning health Care system: A new model for biomedical research. *JAMA*, 315; 18: 1941–1942. Available at: https://doi.org/10.1001/jama.2016.3867

Chassin M. R., Loeb J. M. (2011) The ongoing quality improvement journey: Next stop, high reliability. *Health Affairs*, 30; 4: 559–568. Available at: https://doi.org/10.1377/hlthaff.2011.0076

Chassin M. R., Loeb J. M. (2013) High-reliability health care: Getting there from here. *The Milbank Quarterly*, 91; 3: 459–490. Available at: https://doi.org/10.1111/1468-0009.12023

Chohan P., Renton T., Wong J., Bailey E. (2022) Patient safety in dentistry – The bigger picture. *British Dental Journal*, 232; 7: 460–469. Available at: https://doi.org/10.1038/s41415-022-4095-z

Enticott J., Johnson A., Teede H. (2021) Learning health systems using data to drive healthcare improvement and impact: A systematic review. *BMC Health Services Research*, 21: 200. Available at: https://doi.org/10.1186/s12913-021-06215-8

Fan-Lun C., Chung C., Lee E. H. G., Pek E., Ramsden R., Ethier C., Soong C. (2019) Reducing unnecessary sedative-hypnotic use among hospitalised older adults. *BMJ Quality and Safety*, 28; 12: 1039--1045. Available at: https://doi.org/10.1136/bmjqs-2018-009241

Golburean O., Nordheim E. S., Faxvaag A., Pedersen R., Lintvedt O., Marco-Ruiz L. (2024) A systematic review and proposed framework for sustainable learning healthcare systems. *International Journal of Medical Informatics*, 192: 105652-. Available at: https://doi.org/10.1016/j.ijmedinf.2024.105652

Green B., Parry D., Oeppen R., Plint S., Dale T., Brennan P. (2017) Situational awareness – what it means for clinicians, its recognition and importance in patient safety. *Oral Diseases*, 23; 6: 721–725. Available at: https://doi.org/10.1111/odi.12547

Greenhalgh T., Robert G., Macfarlane F., Bate P., Kyriakidou O. (2004) Diffusion of innovations in service organizations: Systematic review and recommendations. *Milbank Quarterly*, 82; 4: 581–629. Available at: https://doi.org/10.1111/j.0887-378x.2004.00325.x

Guttman O., Keebler J. R., Lazzara E. H., Daniel W., Reed G. (2019) Rethinking high reliability in healthcare: The role of error management theory towards advancing high reliability organizing. *Journal of Patient Safety and Risk Management*, 24; 3: 27–133. Available at: 10.1177/2516043518819952

Hollestelle M. J., Graaf R., Sturkenboom M. C., Delden J. J. (2024) An ethics framework for the transition to an operational learning healthcare system. *Learning Health Systems*, 8; 3: e10414. Available at: https://doi.org/10.1002/lrh2.10414

Khalil H., Kynoch K. (2021) Implementation of sustainable complex interventions in health care services: The triple C model. *BMC Health Services Research*, 21: 1. Available at: https://doi.org/10.1186/s12913-021-06115-x

Laurence B. (2015) Why introducing implementation science and stakeholder engagement belong in evidence-based dental education. *British Dental Journal*, 219; 6: 246. Available at: https://doi.org/10.1038/sj.bdj.2015.717

Martelli P. F., Rivard P. E., Roberts K. H. (2018) Caveats for high reliability in healthcare. *Journal of Health Organization and Management*, 32; 5: 674–690. Available at: https://doi.org/10.1108/JHOM-10-2017-0286

Mikkelsen J., Holm H. (2007) Contextual learning to improve health care and patient safety. *Education for Health*, 20; 3: 124. Available at: https://journals.lww.com/EDHE/fulltext/2007/20030/Contextual_Learning_to_Improve_Health_Care_and.11.aspx [Accessed 3 April 2025]

Minyé H. M., Benjamin E. (2022) High-reliability organisation principles implemented in dentistry. *British Dental Journal*, 232; 12: 879–885. Available at: https://doi.org/10.1038/s41415-022-4354-z

Mitton C., Adair C. E., McKenzie E., Patten S. B., Perry, B. W. (2007) Knowledge transfer and exchange: Review and synthesis of the literature. *The Milbank Quarterly*, 85; 4: 729–768. Available at: https://doi.org/10.1111/j.1468-0009.2007.00506.x

Moore J. E., Mascarenhas A., Bain J., Straus S. E. (2017) Developing a comprehensive definition of sustainability. *Implementation Science*, 12; 1: 110. Available at: https://doi.org/10.1186/s13012-017-0637-1

Moullin J. C., Sklar M., Green A., Dickson K. S., Stadnick N. A., Reeder K., Aarons G. A. (2020) Advancing the pragmatic measurement of sustainment: A narrative review of measures. *Implementation Science Communications*, 1: 1. Available at: http://dx.doi.org.uhi.idm.oclc.org/10.1186/s43058-020-00068-8

Mullins C. D., Wingate L. T., Edwards H. A., Tofade T., Wutoh A. (2018) Transitioning from learning healthcare systems to learning health care communities. *Journal of Comparative Effectiveness Research*, 7; 6: 603–614. Available at: https://doi.org/10.2217/cer-2017-0105

Olsen L., Aisner D., McGinnis J. M. (2007) *The Learning Healthcare System: Workshop Summary*. Washinton, DC: National Academies Press, Institute of Medicine. Available at: https://doi.org/10.17226/11903 [Accessed 1 May 2025]

Pinsky H. M., Taichman R. S., Sarment D. P. (2010) Adaptation of airline crew resource management principles to dentistry. *The Journal of the American Dental Association*, 141; 8: 1010–1018. Available at: https://doi.org/10.14219/jada.archive.2010.0316

Pronovost P. J., Berenholtz S. M., Goeschel C. A., Needham D. M., Sexton J. B., Thompson D. A., Lubomski L. H., Marsteller J. A., Makary M. A., Hunt E. (2006) Creating high reliability in health care organizations. *Health Services Research*, 41; 4p2: 1599–1617. Available at: https://doi.org/10.1111/j.1475-6773.2006.00567.x

Roberts K. H. (1990) Managing high reliability organizations. *California Management Review*, 32; 4: 101–113.

Rutten L. J. F., Ridgeway J. L., Griffin J. M. (2024) Advancing translation of clinical research into practice and population health impact through implementation science. *Mayo Clinic Proceedings*, 99; 4: 665–676. Available at: https://doi.org/10.1016/j.mayocp.2023.02.005

Song Y., MacEachern L., Doupe M. B., Ginsburg L., Chamberlain S. A., Cranley L., Easterbrook A., Hoben M., Knopp-Sihota J., Reid R. C., Wagg A., Estabrooks C. A., Keefe J. M., Rappon T., Berta W. B. (2022) Influences of post-implementation factors on the sustainability, sustainment, and intra-organizational spread of complex interventions. *BMC Health Services Research*, 22; 1. Available at: http://dx.doi.org.uhi.idm.oclc.org/10.1186/s12913-022-08026-x

Stanford Medicine. (2025) Stanford Medicine Center for Improvement. (online) Available at: https://smci .stanford.edu /toolkit -1 /standard -work -template [Accessed 27 August 2025]

Stark C., Hookway G. (2019) *Applying Lean in Health and Social Care Services*. New York: Routledge / Productivity Press.

Stumbo S. P., Ford J. H., Green C. A. (2017) Factors influencing the long-term sustainment of quality improvements made in addiction treatment facilities: A qualitative study. *Addiction Science & Clinical Practice*, 12; 26: 1–11. Available at: https://doi.org/10.1186/s13722-017-0093-x

Tokede B., Yansane A., White J., Bangar S., Mullins J., Brandon R., Gantela S., Kookal K., Rindal D., Lee C., Lin G., Spallek H., Kalenderian E., Walji M. (2022) Translating periodontal data to knowledge in a learning health system. *Journal of the American Dental Association*, 153; 10: 996–1004. Available at: https://doi.org/10.1016/j.adaj.2022.06.007

Villarosa A. R., Maneze D., Ramjan L. M., Srinivas R., Camilleri M., George A. (2019) The effectiveness of guideline implementation strategies in the dental setting: A systematic review. *Implementation Science*, 14: 106. Available at: https://doi.org/10.1186/s13012-019-0954-7

Weick K. E., Sutcliffe K. M. (2007) *Managing the Unexpected*. 2nd Edition. San Francisco, CA: Jossey-Bass.

Westerlund A., Nilsen P., Sundberg L. (2019) Implementation of implementation science knowledge: The research-practice ap Paradox. *Worldviews on Evidence-Based Nursing*, 16; 5: 332–334. Available at: https://doi.org/10.1111/wvn.12403

Chapter 9

Change at Scale

Introduction

Identifying problems is usually straightforward. Finding options for improvement, testing and implementing them, is manageable for a team. Sustaining change over time in the area that has led the work, as discussed in Chapter 8, is also practical, particularly when the dental team sees it as an opportunity to find further improvements. Spreading change to other areas, or making simultaneous changes across multiple settings, brings a different set of challenges. This chapter builds on discussions on change and leadership in Chapter 1 and Chapter 4.

Barriers to change can occur at patient level, team level; organisational level, or at regulatory level (Damschroder *et al.*, 2009):

- At patient level, changes that do not fit with patient expectations can cause unexpected issues, even when a process has been effective elsewhere.
- At team level, competing work demands on the team, team morale, team cohesion, previous experience of change and knowledge and experience of quality improvement methods are all significant factors.
- At organisational level, previous approaches to quality, management of change processes, knowledge and attitudes can all affect the ease and effectiveness of the spread of change.
- In very large-scale change, regulatory bodies may want to know about changes and tests of change. They are unlikely to want active involvement, but updates may be required.

This chapter discusses the spread of change to other teams and organisations. It introduces the idea of change readiness and considers likely team concerns about changes to established practices. In larger organisations, the Institute for Healthcare Improvement's Collaborative change model offers one approach to large-scale change, and many of its principles can be applied even if the precise approach is not appropriate for the setting. The chapter concludes by summarising issues that can be considered when thinking about the spread of change to a new team, area, or organisation.

DOI: 10.4324/9781003493532-9

Spreading Change

Spreading change can involve different settings in the same organisation, or other organisations (Song, 2022). Some of the same issues apply as in the spread of innovation from new research-based knowledge. In the spread of new research findings, there may be no central driver of the adoption of a new method or treatment. Change can happen in many places at once. This resonates with the spread of improvements between sites, although there will usually be greater coordination.

Roger's diffusion of innovation theory is the best-known model of innovation adoption and has been widely applied in healthcare (Roger, 2003, Harrison *et al.*, 2021). Discussion often focuses on Roger's idea of early and late adopters, but other parts of the model are relevant here. Roger made the point that staff need to become aware of a new method, at which point they can gather information on the new approach, helping them to decide on its use in their own practice. Implementation can still be difficult, and using a new clinical approach does not automatically result in its continuing use. Roger suggested that factors affecting adoption include perception of the advantage gained by adopting the new approach; how compatible the method is with existing approaches; the complexity and difficulty of the method and its adoption; and the ability to see gains when the method is used.

Change is ever present in dental care. Advances in digital processes like scanning, 3D printing and artificial intelligence suggest that change will continue to be rapid. Roger's model of innovation spread has endured because it has practical application. The approach has been useful in dental care, including examining factors likely to favour the use of case studies by dentists and dental hygienists (Cragun *et al.*, 2012); the spread of use of standard dental terminology (Ramoni *et al.*, 2017), and the use of new dental technologies (Matthews *et al.*, 2016).

Models of innovation help to inform methods of introduction of new approaches (van der Zande, Gorter and Wismeijer, 2013). Findings from the work on innovation in dental care largely support the importance of the factors identified by Roger. Research in dental settings confirms that change is more likely when clinicians are able to test out changes for themselves, changes are an evolution rather than a revolution in method; benefits are visible; the change is relatively easy to implement; there is discernible support from respected colleagues, and the perceived strength of the evidence for change is strong (Matthews *et al.*, 2016, Ramoni *et al.*, 2017). These factors identified in generic knowledge spread are useful to consider when spreading quality improvement initiatives across sites, including thinking carefully about channels used for dissemination (Balas and Chapman, 2018).

Further work is needed to better understand all the issues underpinning effective change in health services, including in quality improvement (Grol, Baker and Moss, 2002, Grol and Grimshaw, 2003). Technical interventions are subject to a further range of factors in relation to spread. Complex regulatory settings can cause problems, and a great deal of work is often required to succeed when multiple regulators and approval bodies are involved (Greenhalgh *et al.*, 2017). Changes produced by team-based quality improvement projects are unlikely to reach the same degree of complexity, but clarity on the value proposition – what the new approach offers to patients and to staff – remains important, and it needs to outweigh the work required to implement it. Big changes, rather than incremental improvement, often prove more difficult, as Roger's success factor on compatibility with existing processes suggests.

Knowledge transfer, discussed in Chapter 8, includes transmission of practices from one unit or organisation to another (Argote, 2024). This is relevant to individual practices or teams learning from others but is particularly important for dental organisations that are part of multi-unit dental chains. In theory, multi-unit chains have more capacity to benefit from the transfer of new practices because they should be able to share learning across their sites, but this often does not happen in practice. Reasons can include an unwillingness to accept that another team may have identified an improvement that has not been apparent to the first team; hierarchical differences between teams or units, and pressures or low morale that decrease the interest and ability of the receiving team to make changes in their own practice. Circumstances that are reported to increase the ease of spread of ideas include geographical proximity, similarity of aims between teams, units or organisations, organisational culture and strategic alignment.

Change Readiness

Staff are at the core of quality improvement work, so staff views have an enormous effect on the likelihood of any change taking root. Organisational change occurs in many contexts. This has driven research on Change Readiness, defined as staff 'beliefs, attitudes, and intentions regarding the extent to which changes are needed and the organisation's capacity to successfully undertake those changes' (Armenakis *et al.*, 1993, p. 681). Change Readiness can refer both to change driven by managers and leaders, and emergent change that arises within a team who identify a problem (Weiner, Amick and Lee, 2008, Weiner, 2009). The main context discussed here is when an organisation seeks to spread change from one site to another but many of the concepts are relevant to a clinician seeking to promote change within their own team. The ideas are directly relevant to practice owners, clinical leaders and group managers who want to support large scale quality improvement work.

The extent to which services see a need for improvement inevitably influences the climate for change (Maynard, Kennedy and Sommer, 2015). One of the best-known change models, discussed in Chapter 1, lists 'creating a sense of urgency' as the first component of producing change (Kotter, 1995, 2012a, 2012b). This links to the idea of a 'burning platform', a position that is so uncomfortable that change starts to seem inevitable. This can be taken to extremes, with managers deliberately creating adverse circumstances. In healthcare settings, this would be obviously unethical and very likely to be counterproductive. Losing trust in a change project is usually catastrophic.

Work on readiness for change initially focused on individuals (Cunningham *et al.*, 2002). The principle, that people must see the effort of change as being worthwhile is helpful to keep in mind. Individuals and teams exist on a spectrum of willingness to change, and change readiness will vary for different projects. Teams may be more inclined to change than larger groups, as they are confronted by problems in their day-to-day work that may be less visible at a corporate level. Team members are also likely to have the same, or at least similar, experiences of problems, contributing to cognate views on the severity of a problem. Understandings of a problem are socially constructed, and this can hinder or help a change programme depending on the priority a team accords to the issue, their view on the causes of the problem, and their collective belief that change is possible and within their scope to influence.

A dental study reviewed the readiness to change among staff working in a group of dental care providers. The work was conducted in a large for-profit group in the United States, with 42 group practices and around 200 affiliated primary care practices. The group wanted to introduce an evidence-based dental disease prevention protocol aimed at children. The protocol had three different levels of intervention depending on the estimated level of dental disease risk. A web-based questionnaire was used to assess readiness to change in participating staff (Cunha-Cruz *et al.*, 2017).

The survey response rate was 28%, which is lower than in many dental professional surveys, so this limits interpretation (Funkhouser *et al.*, 2017). The survey found that the dental staff who responded were generally in favour of the work and its aims. Commitment to the change project was associated with a belief in the need for caries prevention but was inversely related to a measure of 'office chaos'. Higher measures of burnout were associated with less belief that the project would be effective. This suggests that while professional investment in a project is important, the surrounding environment also has an impact on the likelihood of success. Notably, only 50% of respondents agreed that 'there is an open discussion of problems' in their practice, which suggests that quality improvement principles were a new notion, potentially making change more difficult. Where a substantial group of staff see their environment as chaotic, as reported in the Cunha-Cruz study, it may be difficult to muster the energy for improvement, even when the change could be of benefit to the staff working in the unit.

This emphasises that while attitudes and experience of quality improvement within individual clinicians are important, staff do not work in a vacuum. If staff perceive their organisation as having a focus on quality, then work on quality improvement will exist in a context. If instead they feel their employer's focus is on productivity and earnings, with limited attention to quality, then they are more likely to be suspicious of any new quality initiative that is being spread to their area. Lack of experience of any previous quality improvement work also makes things more difficult. In teams with positive previous involvement in quality improvement, the evidence of impact becomes a motivating factor for future work (Breckinridge *et al.*, 2019). Without previous involvement, it can be an uphill struggle, and concerns about change need careful consideration. Addressing them head on and discussing concerns is the best way to proceed. Worries about change are summarised in Box 9.1.

BOX 9.1 WORRIES ABOUT CHANGE

- Change that comes from somewhere else can feel threatening. Guidelines on technical aspects of treatment will be clear, but exactly how you do something in practice leaves more open to discretion. Part of being a professional is having the freedom to craft a solution for a patient. A team can feel that taking a process, such as a booking process, from elsewhere will interfere with their ability to make things work in their own context (Wutzke, Benton and Verma, 2016).
- Concerns about spreading changes include worry that a change might only be about productivity. Shorter waiting times are good, but squeezing down on clinical teams by changing a process could decrease the value for a patient that comes from interacting with clinicians in the dental team. Some clinicians worry that a focus on outputs – fillings, extractions, treatments undertaken – may lose understanding of what matters to patients.
- The idea of co-production is relevant to concerns about unthinking adherence to guidelines. Patients not only 'receive' a dental treatment, but they are also responsible for their own actions, such as tooth brushing and taking the dental team's advice on issues such as smoking. The patient and their actions affect the likelihood of success of many treatments, so they are not passive recipients of care (Batalden, 2018). Many social issues affect the probability that patients can or will follow advice, but the interaction with the dental team will also have an impact. Thought of in this context, time to speak to patients, listen to their concerns and address misconceptions are components of service quality (Choi *et*

al., 2024). They all provide something patients want and increase the probability of treatments being of lasting effectiveness.

- Multi-dimensional concepts of quality were discussed in Chapter 1. To engage staff, the team spreading ideas to new settings needs to make it clear that they are not overly focused on one dimension, such as efficiency or cost. There is nothing wrong with cost-saving measures, such as prescribing generic medicines, but for more complex changes the team needs to have confidence that changes will not make their working lives worse or harm their patients and their relationship with them.
- Staff can also worry that an improvement may be a fad. They can be concerned that management attention will move on to something else, leaving them with wasted effort. If they engage with the project and promote it to colleagues and patients, and managers later withdraw from the effort, they may be left exposed and even embarrassed. Signalling ongoing leadership support is important (Jackson *et al.*, 2017).
- Worry that it may be difficult or impossible to incorporate a change into normal practice without an unreasonable increase in work will also have an impact. Dental team members are willing to make an effort for the benefit of patients, but they understandably do not want this to be at the expense of their own wellbeing. Staff must feel there is time and support to let them apply new measures and to integrate them into their practice. This will interact with how supported staff feel in general; how organised the working environment is already, and how invested they feel in the team and organisation.

Worry that it may be difficult or impossible to incorporate a change into normal practice without an unreasonable increase in work will also have an impact. Dental team members are willing to make an effort for the benefit of patients, but they understandably do not want this to be at the expense of their own wellbeing. Staff must feel there is time and support to let them apply new measures and to integrate them into their practice. This will interact with how supported staff feel in general; how organised the working environment is already, and how invested they feel in the team and organisation.

Collaboratives

In health and social care, all quality improvement depends on collaboration, because services are delivered by teams of engaged individuals. Chapter 4 discussed the organisational features that make quality improvement more likely to be successful, and reviewed methods that can increase the likelihood of team participation. Collaboration can extend beyond teams, and having several teams working on quality improvement at the same time can produce considerable benefits.

The Institute for Healthcare Improvement developed the Collaborative series, a method by which groups of teams worked on the same quality improvement issues at the same time (Institute for Healthcare Improvement, 2003) and has also explored ways of spreading work (Massoud *et al.*, 2006). These approaches focus on teams and services working on similar quality issues at the same time. The teams are supported by quality improvement coaches, and the initiatives often extend for 9 - 18 months during which teams attend learning sessions to share their work (Kilo, 1998, Wilson, Berwick and Cleary, 2003). Much of the learning from them is applicable to the process of supporting multiple teams in dentistry, for example, across a community dental service, or in a corporate group with multiple practices.

Collaborative methods have been applied in many contexts since the original description by the Institute for Healthcare Improvement, but there are common features. In one review, the most frequently occurring components of the intervention were (Nadeem *et al.*, 2013):

- In-person learning sessions.
- Plan-do-study-act (PDSA) cycles.
- Multidisciplinary quality improvement teams.
- Data collection for quality improvement.

Reviews demonstrate that these collaborative quality improvement approaches can be effective in obtaining their intended quality improvement objectives (Schouten *et al.*, 2008, Wells *et al.*, 2018). There have been concerns that some published work may underestimate variability in outcomes between teams. The design of reported studies makes detailed interpretation difficult, but Zamboni and colleagues (2020) sought to tease out the impact of contextual factors on programme effectiveness. In producing a theoretical model to support further research on Collaboratives, they identified issues that may support change both within services and between multiple services involved in a Collaborative.

Within services, they suggest six broad approaches that increase the effectiveness of collaborative improvement work (Zamboni *et al.*, 2020, p. 12):

1. Increasing team confidence in identifying problems suitable for change and in using data in improvement work.
2. Increasing accountability by agreeing explicit standards.
3. Improving quality improvement knowledge and problem-solving skills.
4. Promoting teamwork and discussion.
5. Encouraging a climate of collective problem-solving.
6. Supporting adherence to evidence-based practices.

Their review also emphasises the importance of coaching and of appropriate leadership. In having an effect across teams and services, they note the likely benefits of a community of practice, the promotion of friendly competition and the impact of sharing methods of improvement and success stories (Zamboni *et al.*, 2020, pp. 14–15). Aunger *et al.* (2021) undertook a realist evaluation of the factors affecting general inter-organisational collaboration between healthcare organisations and identified very similar issues in this broader review. They suggest that synergy from partnerships is important and that this is underpinned by a range of factors including trust and good interpersonal communication.

When working across disparate practices or service settings, teams may not be working on identical issues at the same time, but they are applying the same improvement methods within the same structure, while making use of all the attributes that have proved to be important in Collaboratives. Taking Zamboni's structure of intra- and inter-team factors, the intra-team factors can be replicated in a single team. Introducing quality improvement across several teams begins to draw in many of the inter-team/inter-service issues by encouraging sharing, creating a community of practice and supporting the sharing of progress and method.

Systems to Support Changes in Multiple Sites

There are four common scenarios in which wider change may be required:

1. A private practice with multiple sites.
2. A private corporate organisation with many practices, and sometimes hundreds of dentists. In both (1) and (2), dentists may be employees or self-employed.
3. A government-funded public service, where dental staff are employees.
4. Working to spread a new practice across all dental settings in a region or country, usually supported by a professional or governmental organisation.

Scale is an important consideration in the support and infrastructure required. In the scenario with a private practice with a few other sites, there is no pressing need to create a specialist resource. A common situation is to have a practice identify a transferable improvement that is endorsed by the clinical team at the originating practice and by the owner. If the improvement has been appropriately evaluated and documented using the processes discussed earlier in the book, then having a clinician or project lead from the originating practice visit the other practices in turn and explain and preferably demonstrate the improvement may be all that is required. Identifying a named lead in each practice who will mentor the change is very helpful.

In a large group practice, having monthly quality meetings with the individual practice quality leads, usually in an online meeting, works well to keep track of progress and to identify and resolve any problems. Practices will often identify further improvements, and meetings like this are a good opportunity to share the new ideas, backed by evidence from Plan-Do-Study-Act cycles and appropriate evaluation.

For still larger groups in private or public practice, considerations of scale become more pressing. The four principal options are:

1. Encourage quality improvement but leave it to each unit to organise how it addresses this.
2. Create a network across practices to encourage quality improvement, for example by spotlighting good practice and innovative ideas.
3. Offer access to quality improvement training courses, usually combined with identifying a practice or unit quality improvement lead. Courses can be in-house or externally sourced depending on capacity and resource.
4. Create a quality improvement support capacity that works on corporate level quality improvement and supports individual units/practices. This can also be sourced externally, but larger organisations may find it more cost-effective to have an internal unit.

These are not all mutually exclusive options, and a mix and match approach that fits the organisation may be necessary. For example, in a corporate setting, having a Quality Improvement lead who commissions training from an external organisation, and who co-ordinates regular Quality Improvement meetings across settings, could be an appropriate response. If a full-time post, the duties might also include responding to audits and surveys on quality and safety required for practice approvals and registrations, and leading on patient safety.

For larger organisations that see quality as being at the core of what they do, and for whom the investment makes sense, an in-house resource can work well. This can vary from a single person who coaches quality improvement methods, runs courses and co-ordinates work across sites, to a larger team which may also have responsibility for audit, clinical governance and local and national reporting requirements. Organisations often start in a small way and scale up over time as they see and measure benefits.

Whatever route is chosen, maximising the benefit from the investment is essential. This needs active use of the evidence-based approaches discussed earlier in this chapter and a systematic approach to change, and to the maintenance of improvements.

Thinking About Spread of Change

Change has been discussed in earlier chapters, but it is useful to summarise aspects relevant to spread. Bringing these threads together, the following issues should be addressed when deciding to spread a quality improvement intervention.

1. The nature of the quality improvement intervention.

For a quality improvement intervention to be appropriate to spread, there should be persuasive data demonstrating its value. No issue absolutely rules out the spread of a quality improvement intervention, but taking stock of issues in teams and services will make it easier to identify what steps may be required to support the spread of the intervention and to increase its chance of success in the new setting. Consider:

- **Issue Recognition:** An intervention that tackles quality issues that are known to be widespread, or for which it is reasonable to assume that they will affect other teams. If teams do not recognise the issue, they are much less likely to engage with the work.
- **Changes that Have Good Evidence of Effectiveness in Their Original Setting:** This includes information on PDSA cycles that can be shared with the service that plans to adopt the work. The team developing the intervention will generally have Standard Work that can be shared. This will often include photographs and forms, and in some cases, computer files and adaptations to computer systems.
- **Evidence of Sustained Improvement over Time:** Changes that have continued to deliver the improvements expected, as shown by measurement, including the use of Run Charts or SPC charts (see Chapter 7 for more information).

2. The organisational context.

- **The Degree of Previous Focus on Quality Improvement:** If services are understood to support quality improvement efforts, and to prioritise quality, then the work is part of an understandable organisational orientation. Where this is a new focus on quality, it is probable that more work will be required to explain the process, the context and the value of engaging.
- **A History of Short-lived Initiatives:** Large services may have a track record of introducing new ideas and expecting staff engagement. As discussed in Chapter 4, if these have quietly faded to be replaced by later management interests, then staff may have learned to smile, nod and feign agreement while they wait for it to be replaced by another externally driven initiative. This will not work for quality improvement, as it depends on collaboration and participation. In this situation, effort would be required to give teams confidence that their input is essential, the effort is worthwhile, and that the work is going to be supported over time.

3. The team/area in which the change is to be implemented.

- **Existing Pressures on the Team:** Very few dental teams will feel they have time on their hands. Clinical and administrative pressures are unrelenting. Making changes to services can feel like just another demand on their time, particularly if they do not feel management is aligned with quality initiatives. Taking time to discuss how the planned improvement can benefit the team and their patients, and providing evidence from other sites, can go a long way to addressing this.
- **Team Understanding of Quality Improvement:** Staff have often participated in audit activities but may have limited experience of quality improvement. In some instances, staff members equate audit to a box-ticking exercise to meet regulatory requirements, rather than part of an improvement cycle. In other cases, staff may feel that quality improvement initiatives being spread to their area are a sign that they are believed to have failed in some way. Gaining a sense of local views on quality improvement and attending to any worries they create will be required.
- **Previous Experience in Quality Improvement:** If the team includes staff who have training or experience in the approach, they can be pivotal in the work. Existing team members know their team and their situation best. Having an internal leader for the work can be invaluable, and their time can be incorporated into the project in agreement with the relevant manager.

4. The support and quality improvement infrastructure.

- **Local Manager Views on Quality Improvement:** An engaged manager benefits any quality improvement project, while a disengaged, disinterested or hostile manager poses a significant challenge to progress. As discussed earlier in the book, staff are quick to pick up on the priority senior staff apply to a project. If the relevant manager asks about the work, shows interest and champions it, it signals to staff that the time they are investing in the project is valued. When deciding on an initial area of spread, the manager will be an important consideration. If a project is being spread organisation-wide, the co-ordinator of the work needs to consider how to ensure that managers engage. This can include advance briefings, explaining to managers how to support the work, and signalling from very senior staff that the involvement and support of managers is expected and required.
- **Available Quality Improvement Support:** Quality improvement is a participative activity. Although the methods are straightforward, they are often inadequately covered or omitted in undergraduate courses. This means that staff are often unclear on the differences between PDSA cycles intended to improve or redesign a process and research work intended to uncover new knowledge. Staff may seek a degree of rigour and statistical interpretation that is not practical and not required. Having any existing quality improvement infrastructure helps because it allows experienced people to support the team and allows the group to ask questions and challenge in a way that usually increases engagement. As mentioned in (3), team members with prior quality improvement experience are highly beneficial. Where this is not the case, but there is an organisational quality improvement capacity, or a person in a nearby team with experience, this can still work well. This can involve coaching, with perhaps an hour a week invested in supporting the clinician leading the process and the local manager. Where in-person meetings are not practical because of distance, regular online meetings can fulfil the same function. If they are spread to several teams, it can begin to introduce some of the

benefits of a Collaborative, discussed above. Absence of any local expertise or availability of wider organisational expertise is not a complete barrier to participation, but it does mean teams are likely to need more time to navigate the new concepts in a quality improvement project.

5. The opportunity for adaptation.

- **Build in Scope for Site-required Modifications:** Even when adopting an intervention spread from elsewhere, it is necessary for teams to be able to look at any adaptations required for local circumstances. This does not imply an option to opt out, but rather an opportunity to make it work in their own setting. This can include issues such as differences in software programmes; differences in room layouts, including location of supply cupboards, and the precise type and location of equipment. Some changes are straightforward substitutions, but larger changes will need PDSA cycles.
- **Feedback from Patients Is Always Valuable:** Even when a change is adopted wholesale, there can prove to be unanticipated issues when the new or revised process fits with existing working practices. Checking with patients where appropriate, such as in changes to booking processes, helps to identify any unexpected problems that may require local adaptations.

Conclusions

Change at scale ranges from extending an improvement from one team to a neighbouring team, all the way up to making evidence-based changes across the entire dental sector in a country. Many of the issues are similar no matter the scale, but complexity and unpredictability increase as more teams, settings and organisations are involved.

Most services will be extending a successful change within their own organisation. Careful attention to documenting the improvement and collecting information on benefits makes it easier to spread. When other teams or settings recognise the problem and identify it as an issue for themselves, this increases the likelihood of active engagement with the change. Services still need the opportunity to amend an idea to fit with their setting, as details of local organisation may make modifications necessary to make it work there.

At larger scale, organisations may seek to spread change across multiple sites, sometimes hundreds or thousands of miles apart. This is made easier by online communication and video conferencing, and implementation groups can work well together across large distances. Some organisations will have a dedicated quality improvement resource, such as a quality improvement lead or quality improvement office that can help to tie together the different sites. It is not practical to impose change, so staff must be engaged at each site and the considerations to allow this to happen will vary according to local circumstances.

The Institute for Healthcare Improvement's collaborative approach can also work well, particularly when the intention is for many sites to work on the same issue simultaneously. The established mechanisms for collaboratives give a roadmap that organisations can apply, particularly if quality improvement coaching is available to them.

Spread is no different from making the initial improvement. Careful attention is required to maximise the likelihood of successful spread. The research literature offers useful insights into issues that can help or hinder spread, discussed earlier in this chapter. Thinking about local circumstances, engaging local managers and staff, prompting ownership and perseverance over time allows major changes to be made, and to be sustained.

References

Argote L., Millar R., Greenhalgh J., Mannion R., Rafferty A., McLeod H. (2024) Knowledge transfer within organizations: Mechanisms, motivation, and consideration. *Annual Review of Psychology*, 75; 1: 405–431. Available at: https://doi.org/10.1146/annurev-psych-022123-105424

Armenakis A. A., Harris S. G., Mossholder, K. W. (1993) Creating readiness for organizational change. *Human Relations*, 46; 6: 681–703. Available at: https://doi.org/10.1177/001872679304600601

Aunger J. A., Millar R., Greenhalgh J., Mannion R., Rafferty A., McLeod H. (2021) Why do some inter-organisational collaborations in healthcare work when others do not? A realist review. *Systematic Reviews*, 10: 82. Available at: https://doi.org/10.1186/s13643-021-01630-8

Balas E. A., Chapman W. W. (2018) Road map for diffusion of innovation in health care. *Health Affairs*, 37; 2: 198–204. Available at: https://doi.org/10.1377/hlthaff.2017.1155

Batalden P. (2018) Getting more from healthcare: Quality improvement must acknowledge patient coproduction. *BMJ*, 362: k3617. Available at: https://doi.org/10.1136/bmj.k3617

Breckenridge J. P., Gray N., Toma M., Ashmore S., Glassborow R., Stark C., Renfrew M. J. (2019) Motivating change: A grounded theory of how to achieve large-scale, sustained change, co-created with improvement organisations across the UK. *BMJ Open Quality*, 8; 2: e000553. Available at: https://doi.org/10.1136/bmjoq-2018-000553

Choi H., Kim R. J., Park S. Y., Lee, J., Song, Y. (2024) Determinants of dentist-patient relationships: A scoping review. *International Dental Journal*, 74; 5: 1078–1088. Available at: https://doi.org/10.1016/j.identj.2024.02.015

Cragun D. L., DeBate R. D., Severson H. H., Shaw T., Christiansen S., Koerber A., Tomar S. L., Brown K. M., Tedesco L. A., Hendricson W. D. (2012) Developing and pretesting case studies in dental and dental hygiene education: Using the diffusion of innovations model. *Journal of Dental Education*, 76; 5: 590–601. Available at: https://doi.org/10.1002/j.0022-0337.2012.76.5.tb05293.x

Cunha-Cruz J., Milgrom P., Huebner C. E., Scott J., Ludwig S., Dysert J., Mitchell M., Allen G., Shirtcliff R. M. (2017) Care delivery and compensation system changes: A case study of organizational readiness within a large dental care practice organization in the United States. *BMC Oral Health*, 17: 157. Available at: https://doi.org/10.1186/s12903-017-0448-4

Cunningham C. E., Woodward C. A., Shannon H. S., MacIntosh J., Lendrum B., Rosenbloom D., Brown J. (2002) Readiness for organizational change. *Journal of Occupational and Organizational Psychology*, 75; 4: 377–392. Available at: https://doi.org/10.1348/096317902321119637

Damschroder L. J., Aron D. C., Keith R. E., Kirsh S. R., Alexander J. A., Lowery J. C. (2009) Fostering implementation of health services research findings into practice: A consolidated framework for advancing implementation science. *Implementation Science*, 4: 50. Available at: https://doi.org/10.1186/1748-5908-4-50

Funkhouser E., Vellala K., Baltuck C., Cacciato R., Durand E., McEdward D., Sowell E., Theisen S. E., Gilbert G. H. (2017) Survey methods to optimize response rate in the national dental practice–based research network. *Evaluation & the Health Professions*, 40; 3: 332–358. Available at: https://doi.org/10.1177/0163278715625738

Greenhalgh T., Wherton J., Papoutsi C., Lynch J., Hughes G., A'Court C., Hinder S., Fahy N., Procter R., Shaw S. (2017) Beyond adoption: A new framework for theorizing and evaluating nonadoption, abandonment, and challenges to the scale-up, spread, and sustainability of health and care technologies. *Journal of Medical Internet Research*, 19; 11: 25. Available at: https://doi.org/10.2196/jmir.8775

Grol R., Baker R., Moss F. (2002) Quality improvement research: Understanding the science of change in health care. *Quality and Safety in Health Care,* 11: 110–111. Available at: https://doi.org/10.1136/qhc.11.2.110

Grol R., Grimshaw J. (2003) From best evidence to best practice: Effective implementation of change in patients' care. *Lancet*, 362: 1225–1230. Available at: https://doi.org/10.1016/s0140-6736(03)14546-1

Harrison R., Fischer S., Walpola R. L., Chauhan A., Bablola T., Mears S., Le-Dao H. (2021) Where do models for change management, improvement and implementation meet?: A systematic review of the applications of change management models in Healthcare. *Journal of Healthcare Leadership*, 13: 85–108. Available at: https://doi.org/10.2147/jhl.s289176

Institute for Healthcare Improvement (2003) *The Breakthrough Series: IHI's Collaborative Model for Achieving Breakthrough Improvement.* IHI Innovation Series white paper. Boston, MA: Institute for Healthcare Improvement. Available at: https://www.ihi.org/resources/white-papers/breakthrough-series-ihis-collaborative-model-achieving-breakthrough [Accessed 22 April 2025]

Jackson G. L., Roumie C. L., Rakley S. M., Kravetz J. D., Kirshner M. A., Del Monte P. S., Bowen M. E., Oddone E. Z., Weiner B. J., Shaw R. J., Bosworth H. B. (2017) Linkage between theory-based measurement of organizational readiness for change and lessons learned conducting quality improvement–focused research. *Learning Health Systems,* 1; 2: e10013-n/a. Available at: https://doi.org/10.1002/lrh2.10013

Kilo C. M. (1998) A framework for collaborative improvement: Lessons from the Institute for Healthcare Improvement's Breakthrough Series. *Quality Management in Health Care,* 6; 4: 1–13. Available at: https://doi.org/10.1097/00019514-199806040-00001

Kotter J. P. (1995) Leading change. *Harvard Business Review,* 2; 1: 1–10.

Kotter J. P. (2012a) Accelerate!. *Harvard Business Review,* 90; 11: 44–54.

Kotter J. P. (2012b) *Leading Change.* Brighton, MA: Business Review Press.

Massoud M. R., Nielsen G. A., Nolan K., Nolan T., Schall M. W., Sevin C. (2006) *A Framework for Spread: From Local Improvements to System-Wide Change.* IHI Innovation Series white paper. Cambridge, MA: Institute for Healthcare Improvement. Available at: https://www.ihi.org/resources/white-papers/framework-spread-local-improvements-system-wide-change [Accessed 22 April 2025]

Matthews D. C., McNeil K., Brillant M., Tax C., Maillet P., McCulloch C. A., Glogauer M. (2016) Factors influencing adoption of new technologies into dental practice: A qualitative study. *JDR Clinical and Translational Research,* 1; 1: 77–85. Available at: https://doi.org/10.1177/2380084415627129

Maynard M. T., Kennedy D. M., Sommer S. A. (2015) Team adaptation: A fifteen-year synthesis (1998--2013) and framework for how this literature needs to "adapt" going forward. *European Journal of Work and Organizational Psychology,* 24; 5: 652–677. Available at: https://doi.org/10.1080/1359432X.2014.1001376

Nadeem E., Olin S. S., Hill L. C., Hoagwood K. E., Horwitz S. M. (2013) Understanding the components of quality improvement collaboratives: A systematic literature review. *The Millbank Quarterly,* 91; 2: 354–394. Available at: https://doi.org/10.1111/milq.12016

Ramoni R. B., Etolue J., Tokede O., McClellan L., Simmons K., Yansane A., White J. M., Walji M. F., Kalenderian E. (2017) Adoption of dental innovations: The case of a standardized dental diagnostic terminology. *The Journal of the American Dental Association,* 148; 5: 319–327. Available at: https://doi.org/10.1016/j.adaj.2017.01.024

Rogers E. M. (2003) *Diffusion of Innovations.* 5th Edition. New York, NY: Free Press. Scholar.

Schouten L. M. T., Hulscher M. E. J. L., van Everdingen J. J. E., Huijsman R., Grol R. P. T. M. (2008) Evidence for the impact of quality improvement collaboratives: Systematic review. *BMJ,* 336; 7659: 1491–1494. Available at: https://doi.org/10.1136/bmj.39570.749884.be

Song Y., MacEachern L., Doupe M. B., Ginsburg L., Chamberlain S. A., Cranley L., Easterbrook A., Hoben M., Knopp-Sihota J., Reid R. C., Wagg A., Estabrooks C. A., Keefe J. M., Rappon T., Berta W. B. (2022) Influences of post-implementation factors on the sustainability, sustainment, and intra-organizational spread of complex interventions. *BMC Health Services Research,* 22; 1. Available at: http://dx.doi.org.uhi.idm.oclc.org/10.1186/s12913-022-08026-x

van der Zande M. M., Gorter R. C., Wismeijer D. (2013) Dental practitioners and a digital future: An initial exploration of barriers and incentives to adopting digital technologies. *British Dental Journal,* 215; 11: E21–E21. Available at: https://doi.org/10.1038/sj.bdj.2013.1146

Weiner B. J. (2009) A theory of organizational readiness for change. *Implementation Science,* 4: 67. Available at: https://doi.org/10.1186/1748-5908-4-67

Weiner B. J., Amick H., Lee S.-Y. D. (2008) Conceptualization and measurement of organizational readiness for change: A review of the literature in health services research and other fields. *Medical Care Research and Review,* 65; 4: 379–436. Available at: https://doi.org/10.1177/1077558708317802

Wells S., Tamir O., Gray J., Naidoo D., Bekhit M., Goldmann D. (2018) Are quality improvement collaboratives effective? A systematic review. *BMJ Quality & Safety,* 27; 3: 226–240. Available at: https://doi.org/10.1136/bmjqs-2017-006926

Wilson T., Berwick D. M., Cleary P. D. (2003) What do collaborative improvement projects do? Experience from seven countries. *The Joint Commission Journal on Quality and Safety*, 29; 2: 85–93. Available at: https://doi.org/10.1016/s1549-3741(03)29011-0

Wutzke S., Benton M., Verma R. (2016) Towards the implementation of large scale innovations in complex health care systems: Views of managers and frontline personnel. *BMC Research Notes*, 9; 1: 327. Available at: https://doi.org/10.1186/s13104-016-2133-0

Zamboni K., Baker U., Tyagi M., Schellenberg J., Hill Z., Hanson C. (2020) How and under what circumstances do quality improvement collaboratives lead to better outcomes? A systematic review. *Implementation Science*, 15; 1: 27. Available at: https://doi.org/10.1186/s13012-020-0978-z

Chapter 10

Conclusions

Introduction

Quality is a primary consideration of dental treatment and oral health. Dental teams work in all settings, from publicly funded to private care, hospitals and clinics, affluent and low-income settings. No matter the setting and the context, dental services seek to deliver the best care they can with the resources they have available to them. As discussed in Chapter 1, quality is multi-dimensional. It can also be considered as hierarchical: most people would identify patient and staff safety as the foundation on which services should be built. Issues such as infection control and radiation safety are fundamental to the delivery of dental care. Staff wellbeing is similarly important. Exposure to environmental risks, verbal abuse and violence, exploitative work relationships and musculoskeletal problems all occur in many dental settings. Patients often take safety for granted, and staff should also be able to assume they will be safe at work. As all dental teams know, however, delivering patient and staff safety is not effortless.

Building on this, other aspects of dental care quality can be considered as layered on these prerequisites. Good technical care is essential, and this includes oral health and prevention advice. Most facets of dental care depend on individuals working with patients. This makes it understandable for the public to assume that quality is something delivered by individual clinicians to patients, and that it depends exclusively on their personal performance. Every dental team knows that there is more to it than that.

Even the smallest dental practice has staff with different functions who work together to deliver care. Hygientists, receptionists, cleaners, dental nurses, practice managers and dentists will be present in most settings. Specialist clinicians and nurses will feature in referral clinic services and hospitals. Their work is supported by dental technicians and internal or external laboratory services. Radiographic equipment is serviced and maintained by specialist staff or external companies, and dental chairs and other equipment such as autoclaves have a similar support network. Community pharmacies or specialist hospital pharmacies provide pharmaceutical supplies, and dental teams are dependent on access to other materials, again delivered by external companies.

Universities influence practice by what they prioritise and offer, usually based on requirements on them, but also on academic and professional interests. Research findings and local and national policies will affect what treatment can be delivered and in what manner. Specialist services set boundaries on who they will see and what treatment they will offer. Regulatory bodies make

 DOI: 10.4324/9781003493532-10

decisions on standards and on what requirements are placed on services and practitioners. Insurers and public funders decide what treatments will be funded, which impacts the quality of care that can be delivered.

This is a complex web of interactions that come together to influence the care that is delivered by individual clinicians. Training, experience, skill and personal qualities combine in a clinician to deliver care to patients, but the practitioner does not stand alone. Any clinician can make a mistake, and treatments have well-documented complications that can arise despite exemplary treatment. Other problems occur at least partly because the circumstances predispose to them. The time available for appointments; the complexity of the cases scheduled; the ability for patient and clinician to understand one another, for example because of limited access to translation services; the interventions for which funds are available; the availability and quality of materials; the familiarity and working relations of people in the clinical team; tiredness, illness and distraction, all combine to make problems more or less likely and a clinical interaction satisfactory or stressful for patient or clinician.

Quality and Safety

Quality is often thought of as a fixed characteristic. Some services are regarded as being of good quality, others of a lesser quality. This conceals the thousands of individual actions that take place in any service, and the constantly changing influences on how they happen. For services to deliver good quality care consistently, many things must go right. Any service that does not recognise risk in its own service does patients and staff a disservice. In these circumstances, if a service tries to maintain a view of itself as problem-free, blame for any reported incident is likely to fall on individual clinicians, which in turn will make reporting less likely.

As Chapter 2 discussed, patient safety theory is sometimes separated into Safety I and Safety II. Safety I is used as shorthand for learning from incidents and inquiries that are then turned into guidelines that learn from the problems, and which staff are expected to follow. The Safety II approach notes that, despite constant pressures, most services deliver safe care most of the time. Proponents of this model argue that work on safety should concentrate on understanding how services are able to cope with problems but still deliver safe care, and to maximise these processes and skills.

This is a largely theoretical divide. A proponent of learning from problems is likely to accept that clinicians constantly adapt to circumstances and avoid most potential hazards. An advocate for the Safety II perspective will similarly recognise that review of previous problems can tell services and clinicians much about the causes and influences on problems in care. For a dental service, learning from mistakes does not conflict with trying to build safer systems and supporting staff to act when they perceive a risk of a problem. Accepting that incidents occur and that it is important to identify, learn from and build safer, higher quality systems should not be a source of dissonance.

Audit and Quality Improvement

Like Safety I and Safety II, audit and quality improvement are related. Chapter 3 describes that audit is based around comparison to a standard. The standard will usually be from a national guideline, published research or compulsory requirement. While some audits are mandated, others are selected by a team, often based on their perception that a problem exists or that they may not be meeting the required standard. The method of comparison to a standard, analysis of the gap, and development and application of actions to close the gap between current and desired practice are not dissimilar from a PDSA cycle. Topics for some PDSA cycles are chosen because teams do not meet a desired standard. The expected standard may be self-generated in the planning phase of a PDSA cycle, but some services will use benchmarking or national or local data to identify the performance to which they aspire. These similarities go some way to explaining why, as reviewed in Chapter 2, published work suggests that teams may now be more likely to refer to quality improvement rather than audit. Many previous audits fit with activities in PDSA cycles.

Audit is a valuable and appropriate approach for many situations. The structure of the method, and the rigour that can be applied, discussed in Chapter 3, are often a comfortable fit for dental teams which are used to thinking in terms of meeting guidelines and funding and regulatory requirements. The rigour of the approach lends itself to careful and systematic application which again fits well with the way many dental professionals choose to work.

This same thoroughness can be carried through to less structured problems that may be tackled in a broader quality improvement project. The methods also overlap and the boundaries between what is an audit and what is a generic quality improvement project are permeable. Services can adapt methods to suit their own needs. What they have in common is that thoroughness of application brings dividends.

Influences on Quality Improvement

As with patient safety, quality improvement is not a value-free activity that exists in a vacuum. How an organisation supports its staff, what evidence there is of it placing an emphasis on quality, and what training and time it offers for quality improvement activities will all influence work on quality. Where an organisation or an individual employer demonstrates that they seek to deliver a good-quality service and are willing to take steps to do so, staff are more likely to follow.

Central to this is how the service treats its staff. If quality improvement is treated as entirely separate from business as usual, staff are quick to spot differences in perspective. Quality improvement work is underpinned by a willingness to talk about problems, share ideas and test out solutions. If the usual approach of a service or employer is to assume individual error and to attach blame, then bolting on quality improvement will be an uneasy fit.

As Chapter 4 notes, sharing leadership and supporting staff to take on roles in quality improvement is more likely to produce results. Quality improvement coaches can be invaluable, but the legacy of improvement support should be staff who feel knowledgeable and confident to participate in and lead quality improvement work. Creating an organisational atmosphere that permits staff to feel able to do this requires careful attention from managers and team leaders. Like dropping a ball of wool, a significant misstep in staff relationships can take a long time to rewind to the previous position. This does not mean that individuals are not accountable for errors, but it does require fairness when considering incidents and exploring causes of problems.

Timing and resources also play a part. There are unrelenting demands on staff time. For staff to feel able to take on quality improvement work, they must be supported to prioritise it. Staff are quick to detect a difference between rhetoric and reality. Expecting staff to undertake improvement work but offering immediate criticism when other work slows creates an obvious dissonance. The hard truth is that all work takes time, but if no improvement work is undertaken, nothing will change. Creating capacity and providing encouragement and active support to make changes is more likely to produce benefits than frequent remonstration.

Understanding Problems and Making Changes

Taking time to understand problems is time well spent. It is easy to assume that the causes are obvious, and this may be correct. Pausing and checking avoids the risk of pursuing a final cause while an underlying issue remains unaffected, resulting in ongoing problems. Teams do best when they combine their knowledge and experience. It is good to remember that seniority does not create familiarity with all parts of a process. In quality improvement work staff should treat one another with respect, but this is not synonymous with deference. The most influential insights may come from relatively junior staff who have the best view of a problem because they experience it every day. Senior staff can offer experience and organisational knowledge, but they should not assume that they have an automatic grasp of every problem.

Information review, process mapping and root cause analysis are best done as team processes. It is very helpful if a small team leads the work and takes responsibility for coordination, but involving as many staff as practical in exploring problems and deciding on tests of change contributes to engagement. When testing out changes, rigour is required. Thinking through what impact is expected and agreeing how to measure it are vital prerequisites. The change itself needs to be well described and understood. Scaling change works well and allows teams to learn the method in a safe manner. Some larger projects and linked pieces of work may need a different approach, but teams new to PDSA cycles can profitably benefit from measured changes that gradually increase in size and spread.

Conveying to teams that a change might not deliver the anticipated benefit is still valuable. Each test of change, if the work is clear, produces learning. The team may find that an instruction is less understandable than they thought; that a change works in some settings but not others, or that there is a complexity they had not appreciated. All these situations advance the project by delivering new information that can be incorporated into future change cycles. In some instances, the team will discover that their theory of the underlying problem was incorrect, and they must revisit their thinking. This is knowledge that would not have been gained without conducting the test of change, so even this situation advances the work by excluding an option and increasing the team's knowledge of the problem.

Embedding and Spreading Change

While it may not feel it, making a positive change is often the most straightforward part of the process. Maintaining changes over time is difficult. Habit is powerful. When teams come under pressure, it is easy to revert to old and internalised ways of working, even when they have not worked in the past. The monitoring phase of a new process makes a difference. Keeping track of what is happening and checking that new improved processes are adhered to helps to ensure that processes are embedded. If there are persistent problems, then the team may need to revisit the change to understand what circumstances are proving difficult. The same spirit of humble inquiry can be applied to understand what is causing difficulty, to learn from it, and if necessary, to test out solutions.

Spreading change to other teams or settings takes work. When a service has worked on a quality improvement project and is confident that it is effective, it can be bewildering to find that colleagues are slow to take it up or very resistant to even trying it out. Again, taking time to understand the issue helps. Where other teams have the same issue, giving them the opportunity to consider how the identified improvement can be applied in their area and then to test it out may be all that is required. In other situations, there may be cultural reasons why it is not supported related to organisational environment, professional preferences, or previous experience of change processes. Generally, senior support from managers and clinicians, engagement from at least one local leader and respectful listening and engagement will help to identify and resolve the problem. In some instances, there may prove to be an unanticipated circumstance that makes the identified solution inappropriate. In that instance, this is not a reason to abandon work, but rather for the other team or service to take the time to conduct their own PDSA cycles to identify how they can address the same issue in a way that works for their service.

When undertaking large-scale change across multiple settings, the Institute for Healthcare Improvement's Collaborative approach offers one tested method that can be applied. It is not the only possible approach, and organisations can think carefully about what method may work best for them, considering lessons from other large-scale quality improvement interventions. In very large-scale work, obtaining access to quality improvement coaching makes an important difference by providing advice on method, and a sounding board for problems. If coaches are engaged, or are available from elsewhere in the organisation, the aim should be to transfer as many skills to local staff as possible so that there is a legacy from the coaching expertise that is accessed.

Enhancing Quality Improvement in Dental Care

The graphs earlier in the book demonstrate the enormous increase in attention to audit and quality improvement from dental services. Inevitably, academic centres have been quicker to apply the methods and to publish results, but quality improvement provides a common grammar that can be used and understood across all types, locations and sizes of dental service. Regulating bodies and funders have often encouraged audit, but it is not always clear that complete audit cycles are conducted and that gains are achieved and maintained. Funders need to sustain interest and method over time to help embed quality improvement work in day-to-day practice.

Consistent teaching from universities can increase the familiarity of quality improvement with new graduates in dental professions. Services need to then let staff try out methods in practice and learn from working with established staff to maximise improvement gains in the services in which they come to work. All services have issues they would like to improve, but permission and an appropriate improvement environment are required for most staff to engage in quality improvement activities. Service heads, managers, clinical leads and trainers can all play a role in making this happen.

The speed of change related to artificial intelligence (AI) seems certain to be dizzying. Embedding decision support, electronic note-taking, diagnostic interpretation, treatment planning and even computer-aided surgery in routine practice is not going to be straightforward. AI will likely offer access to support on quality improvement methods. The application of quality improvement methods to AI in clinical services is likely to be at least as important. It can help services to develop and test new working methods that make use of these opportunities while continuing to deliver care to the highest possible standard given the resource available.

Quality and finance are not separate issues, but rather intertwined matters. No service can be successful if it is not financially viable, and quality allows services to survive and thrive. Future work in dental care will benefit from greater alignment of financial and quality issues, creating a virtuous interaction of financial and quality management. Several available methods seek to combine finance and quality in helpful ways, and further exploration of this in dental care will be a valuable development. Application of Lean methods, and methods associated with Lean accounting offer potential benefits to services.

Patient involvement has been limited in published dental quality improvement work. Dental services exist for patients, and in many systems, decision-making by patients decides whether services are clinically and financially successful. Establishing ways of more readily involving patients in quality improvement activity and learning from their experiences are also needed developments.

Conclusions

Quality is core to the delivery of dental services. Quality does not happen by accident, but rather by the organised efforts of the clinical team and the wider support system. Staff can feel helpless to influence quality, but experience in dental care and in wider health and social care contexts makes it clear that clinical teams can lead work on quality improvement. This can improve both patient experiences and the working experience of staff. Structured approaches grounded in improvement science fit well with dental training and give teams the tools with which to make changes.

This book has set out some of the background to quality improvement in dental care, building on the work of many dental pioneers, both in the UK and internationally. These pioneers, whose work has been cited throughout the book, have delivered a great benefit to dental care services by identifying relevant techniques and testing them out in dental care. Extending these techniques into routine dental practice and making quality improvement a core part of the work of all dental services will take time, but the benefits to patients, staff and services will be well worth the effort.

Glossary of Quality Improvement Terms

Active Error: An error, usually made by a clinician, that may result in an adverse event. The active error is usually the most visible cause of an adverse clinical event, but other system problems may have made the active error more likely. See also Latent Errors.

Affinity Diagram: A tool used to organise and categorise ideas or issues into groups based on their natural relationships, often used in brainstorming sessions. Affinity diagrams are very useful in helping teams to think through how they structure an issue, and to contribute to a shared understanding. See also Cause and Effect Diagrams.

Audit: Comparison of processes, systems, or outcomes to a set standard. The standard may be national, imposed by an external body, or agreed within a clinical service or team.

Audit Cycle: After a baseline audit, a team makes changes to the system to seek improvements and re-measures the effect.

Audit Spiral: Several audit cycles linked together to progressively improve a problem.

Balancing Measure: A measure selected to monitor a possible unintended consequence of the intervention.

Baseline Data / Baseline Audit: Initial data collected to understand the current state of a process or system, serving as a reference point for measuring improvements.

Benchmarking: Comparing processes, systems, or outcomes to national or local standards, or between organisations, to identify areas for improvement.

Change Readiness: Beliefs in an organisation, team or individual in the willingness and ability of the system to make quality improvement changes.

Clinical Governance: A framework used to maintain and improve the quality of clinical services. It is usually taken to include work on patient-centred care; clinical effectiveness; audit; patient safety and risk management; leadership and a governance structure; using information and information technology; training and education, and performance and monitoring.

Clinimetrics: The science of clinical measures, including rating scales and indices.

Collaboratives: A method developed by the Institute of Healthcare Improvement (IHI) in which multiple clinical teams work on similar problems at the same time and share learning from their work with the other teams.

Continuous Quality Improvement (CQI): A system of identifying and analysing quality in services, coupled with mechanisms to allow incremental improvements in processes or systems.

Crew Resource Management (CRM): An approach originally developed in aviation as Cockpit Resource Management but now extended to many settings where staff must make decisions under pressure. The approach aims to help teams combine the use of technology, the flow of information, and interpersonal activities such as problem solving and decision making to produce the best possible outcomes.

Dashboard: A visual display of key performance indicators (KPIs) and metrics, supporting monitoring and decision-making.

Driver Diagram: A diagram that shows a team's theory of why a problem occurs and what they might be able to do about it. The diagram includes primary and secondary drivers and change ideas to overcome the identified problems. It can be used in conjunction with a Measurement Plan.

Effectiveness: The degree to which a system or process produces desired outcomes or goals.

Efficiency: The ability to deliver the required quality with as few resources as practicable.

Fishbone Diagram: A visual tool used to show issues that may contribute to a problem, grouped by type. Useful to share knowledge across a team and to help identify areas to work on. Also known as an Ishikawa diagram after its originator, or a Cause-and-Effect Diagram.

Flowchart: A visual diagram showing the steps in a process.

High Reliability Organisation (HRO): An organisation that operates in complex, high-risk environments and delivers safe, effective care.

Histogram: A type of bar chart used to visualise the distribution of data.

Human Factors: Work on human factors looks at the behaviour of people and their interaction with other people and their environments. In Patient Safety, processes can be adapted to take account of how people work within a system, including how people respond to work when under pressure. See also Crew Resource Management.

Humble Inquiry: A technique described by Edward Schein, in which questions are used to draw out information from other people and to build a relationship with them based on interest and trust. The approach is also intended to reduce barriers to information sharing.

Improvement Science: The science of studying and applying methods to enhance the quality and safety of processes and systems.

Kaizen: A Japanese term referring to on-going improvement involving all staff members. Often used to refer to a process of improvement using small, incremental changes.

Key Performance Indicators (KPIs): Measurable values that assess process, system, or project success.

Knowledge transfer: The term generally refers to the transfer of academic knowledge, including clinical guidelines, into clinical practice.

Kotter's Change Model: One of the best-known change models, it includes eight stages believed to increase the likelihood of introducing and spreading a change successfully.

Latent Failure: A problem that, although distant from a clinical error, contributes to the occurrence of the error. This can include issues such as staffing problems; unclear or incorrect policies; pressures on staff; information system problems; scheduling issues, and training inadequacies. These problems can be linked to one or more potential active failures.

Lean: An approach to quality that focuses on maximising value to service users and reducing waste.

Likert Scale: A scale used to allow a range of responses rather than a yes/no response. Usually five or seven points, for example from 'very confident' to 'not at all confident', 'strongly agree' to 'strongly disagree', etc.

Logic Model: A framework used to outline the theory of how a program or initiative is intended to achieve its outcomes.

Measurement Plan: The plan for measurement in a quality improvement project. It lists the measures, including definition, collection method and the plan to present them.

Monitoring: The tracking of performance data to assess services against expected standards and previous performance.

Metrics: Numerical measures used to assess the performance of a system, process, or initiative.

Near Miss: An error or other problem that could have led to patient harm, but where the adverse event is avoided either by luck or because the error was identified and actively prevented from progressing to harm.

Process Improvement: Work to increase the efficiency, effectiveness, or appropriateness of a specific process.

Pareto Chart: A bar chart that shows categories arranged in numerical order from largest to smallest. A second axis shows the cumulative percentage in a line chart.

Pareto Principle: Also known as the 80/20 rule, it suggests that a small percentage of causes often accounts for most problems. A Pareto chart, which shows problems or issues ranked in frequency, together with cumulative percentage, is often used to illustrate it.

Plan Do Study Act (PDSA) Cycles: Small tests of change that plan a change based on available evidence; make the change; learn the impact of the change and revise further as necessary. Often linked together in a cycle of tests of change. Sometimes referred to as PDCA (Plan Do Check Act) cycles or Deming Cycles, after W. Edwards Deming, a quality improvement pioneer.

PDSA Ramping: Increasing the scale and reach of PDSA cycles. For example, the team may start with one patient and one staff member, and over successive PDSA cycles spread to more staff and different settings.

PREM: Patient-Rated Experience Measure. Patient completed ratings of the process of care.

Prioritisation Matrix: A diagram that teams use to help them prioritise improvement interventions. The diagram can be designed by the team, but it is common to use two axes, one showing the expected impact of addressing that issue, and a second showing how easy the improvement work is anticipated to be.

PROM: Patient Rated Outcome Measure. These are patient-completed ratings of the outcomes of treatment.

Psychological Safety: The conditions that allow staff to feel able to identify and share problems and to make suggestions for solutions. See also Safety Culture.

Qualitative Information: Non-numerical information used to understand performance and causes of problems. It can be used to obtain a nuanced view of staff experiences of change and improvement. Includes staff descriptions of issues in a process, and feedback from patients and sometimes carers.

Quality Assurance: The overall governance, service design, policies, training arrangements, procedures, measurements and quality improvement processes that give confidence in the quality of a service.

Quality Control: Systems to measure aspects of service quality and to identify variations that require a quality improvement response.

Quality Planning: The process to understand the needs of service users and to design high-quality services to meet these needs.

Quantitative Data: Numerical information used to measure and analyse performance or outcomes. Can include survey data, routinely collected information, or information collected specifically for an improvement project.

Reason's Swiss Cheese Model: A model used to conceptualise system failure, originally described by James Reason. It suggests that both Active Errors and Latent Errors can contribute to a failure in care when they align. It is also used to indicate that processes can be introduced or strengthened to prevent a mistake becoming an error in care.

Research: Work that is intended to produce generalisable knowledge. Most audit and quality improvement work is not research.

Root Cause Analysis (RCA): A method used to identify the underlying causes of a problem or defect. The method helps the team to look past the final cause of a problem to identify underlying causes.

Risk Assessment: A process for evaluating potential threats or vulnerabilities within a system or process.

Roger's Diffusion of Innovation Model: This model describes factors thought to be important in spreading new ideas and methods. It is not specific to healthcare, but has been widely applied, including in dental care.

Run Charts: Charts that show measurements over time. In Quality Improvement, a standard set of rules are used to interpret the charts.

Safety I: In Patient Safety, using information from the analysis of failures to identify preventable causes and introducing new or more rigorous measures to avoid repetition.

Safety II: A term used to describe work to identify what makes a system resilient and to understand how staff adapt to make services work despite barriers.

Safety Culture: The environment in an organisation that affects safety. It includes factors that influence behaviour, such as openness, blame, response to error, and the priority given to quality.

SBAR: A standard method used to hand over care. Stands for Situation – Background – Assessment – Recommendation. Sometimes given as ISBAR – Introduction – Situation – Background – Assessment – Recommendation.

Sentinel Events: These are patient safety incidents that produce significant harm, disability or death and which trigger immediate investigations into their cause and any preventable factors.

Six Sigma: A quality improvement method that uses statistical tools to support process improvement.

Statistical Process Control (SPC) Charts: SPC charts are similar to Run Charts with upper and lower control measures. They are used to identify variation. SPC charts allow a service to distinguish between variation related to the process or to other causes. These are known as common cause and special cause variation respectively. Having only common cause variation does not mean that a process is necessarily working as a team or service would wish.

Standard Work: A description of a work process agreed by the dental team. This includes who will undertake a task, how it will be conducted, and what equipment will be used. Like Standard Operating Procedures.

Sustainability: The ability to maintain improvements over time.

Theory of Change: PDSA cycles are tests based on the current understanding of a problem. A theory of change describes a team's view of the required conditions to make an improvement.

Triangulation: Combining different types of information to obtain a better understanding of a problem.

Value Stream Mapping: A method used to visualise the entire process leading to an outcome, for example from referral to assessment, to treatment, and finally to discharge.

Index

For Product Safety Concerns and Information please contact our
EU representative GPSR@taylorandfrancis.com Taylor & Francis
Verlag GmbH, Kaufingerstraße 24, 80331 München, Germany